KAMA SHILPA

A Study of Indian Sculptures Depicting Love in Action.

FRANCIS LEESON

' In the West Intellect is the source of life,
In the East Love is the basis of life.
Through Love Intellect gets acquainted with Reality,
And Intellect gives stability to the work of Love.
Arise and lay the foundations of a new world,
By wedding Intellect to Love.'

—IQBAL

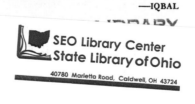
D. B. TARAPOREVALA SONS & CO. PRIVATE LIMITED
210 Dr. Dadabhai Naoroji Road, Bombay 1.

© 1962 by D. B. Taraporevala Sons & Co. Private Limited

Published by RUSSI JAL TARAPOREVALA
for D. B. Taraporevala Sons & Co. Private Limited, Bombay 1.

Printed by K. L. BHARGAVA
at K. L. Bhargava & Co., 89 Bhawani Shankar Road, Bombay 28.

PRINTED IN INDIA   (0-GSY)

For

KURT

PREFACE

" What did they mean to the men who are long since dust?
Whose fingers traced,
In this arid waste,
These rioting, twisting figures of love and lust?
Strange, weird things that no man may say,
Things humanity hides away—
Secretly done—
Catch the light of the living day,
Smile in the sun.
Cruel things that many may not name,
Naked here, without fear of shame,
Laugh in the carven stone."

—LAURENCE HOPE

Even in these enlightened times some authorities on Indian art still find it prudent to draw an academic veil over much that is important in the subject. Of the few writers who have so far sought to interpret the erotic aspect of Hindu, Jain and Buddhist sculpture, none has so far succeeded in presenting his arguments with full clarity or conviction. There is a notable tendency to " humbug " on the subject, and to produce long texts loaded with fine writing and abstract irrelevancies, accompanied sometimes by a few third-hand and vaguely identified illustrations.

A common misconception is that the erotic element in Hinduism is unique among the great religions of pre-Christian origin. That this is not so is confirmed by the comparisons drawn in my second chapter. These attempt to put the Aryan and Hindu elements into correct perspective with the ancient civilised cults of the West, and so reduce correspondingly their more sensational aspects.

Each authority seems tempted to propound a favourite theory to the exclusion of others, and that theory seems inevitably to be coloured by the mental attitude of its protagonist. In a subject with such strong sexual implications it is not surprising that the writer's personal moral philosophy is sometimes reflected in his opinions. In this treatise I offer no original explanations but instead attempt systematically to present the most common hypotheses with supporting quotations. It is for the student to judge from the text and the numerous accompanying photographs which interpretation is the most likely.

The plates have been selected by an eminent Indian scholar who has also written the legends to them.   He has moreover read the text and made various useful suggestions, some in the light of recent excavations.   I am grateful to him and to Mr. F. S. J. Richards for their co-operation.

F. B. L.

CONTENTS

2

I

ORIGINS AND COMPARISONS

The earliest extant piece of sculpture from the Indian subcontinent to which a possibly ithyphallic significance can be ascribed is the beautiful torso of a male dancer in action, only four inches high, and carved in greyish limestone, which is to be found in the Central Asian Antiquities Museum, New Delhi (Plate 2). Dating from the third millenium before Christ this fragment, together with another similar figure, was found at Harappa, in the Western Punjab.

There is nothing to compare with these sculptures in the perfection and sophistication of their modelling until we reach the classic period of Indian art nearly three thousand years later. They are even unique among other pieces found at Harappa and Mohenjodaro, and the limestone used for them is not to be found anywhere near the site of excavation. It is not surprising, therefore, that their association with the Harappa culture has been challenged.

Both figures have sockets for the attachment of head and arms, and, in the case of the one under study, for the genital organs. It is possible that originally there may have been more than one pair of arms, and following on this supposition, one authority has proposed that this is a prototype for the later Hindu conception of Shiva as Lord of the Dance:

> "Even in its present fragmentary state, the figure is imbued with a vital, dynamic quality and a suggestion of movement imparted by the violent axial dislocation of the head, thorax, and hips, exactly the same device employed to suggest the violence of Shiva's dance in the great Hindu bronzes of the Chola period." [1]

Another link with Shiva from the Indus Valley civilization is provided by the famous bull seals and figurines of Mohenjodaro, which indicate a possible cult of the bull as a fertility and lunar symbol, somewhat akin to its role in ancient Egypt and Babylon. Is it mere coincidence that Shiva's vehicle should be Nandi the bull? The figurine of a bull from Mohenjodaro in the Central Asian Antiquities Museum, New Delhi, has sockets for horns, ears, tail and sexual organs.

The bull as a non-Hindu symbol appears again two thousand years later on an Asokan pillar. Iconographically, the exact meaning of the bull as a symbol in Buddhism is not clear, but it is significant that the capital from Rampurva, Calcutta, is one of a pair, the companion being surmounted by a lion, a creature sacred to Durga, one of the forms of Shiva's consort.

From bulls as early symbols of fertility one may turn to the female figurines found in enormous quantities in all the sites inhabited by the Indus people. These "mother-goddess" images are of a type easily paralleled in Asia Minor and Mesopotamia, and have in common with present-day practice in the making of Sakti figures in the villages of north-eastern India the technique of pinching out the facial features in soft clay and adding breasts, eyes, nose, lips, head-dress and ornaments separately.

A further interesting link between these "madonnas" and the later sculptures of Hinduism is the appearance of a "harness" across the chest between the breasts on many of the Indus examples as well as on representations of the mother-goddess from Mesopotamia and Persia. This cross-harness is, in fact, referred to in the Atharva Vedas

[1] Dr. Benjamin Rowland: *The Art and Architecture of India*, p. 15.

12

(ca. 1200 B.C.) as a long-life charm, and appears as the *channavira* in carvings of the Yakshis, the pre-Aryan nature spirits associated with fertility.

No artistic remains survive from the Vedic period (1500-800 B.C.), probably because only perishable materials such as wood and ivory were used during this time. However, these centuries are of importance for during them the basic Hindu attitudes to life and death were developed—ideas which later were to find permanent expression in stone and eventually bronze. What we do know of these times is pieced together from the Vedic hymns of the Aryan invaders of the sub-continent.

The Vedas were composed when the Aryans were confined to north-western India. When they advanced into the plains they came upon the pre-Aryan inhabitants, the darker skinned aboriginals of India, who are described in the Vedas as dwelling in walled cities, to be black in colour, noseless, and practising phallic worship and other unfamiliar rites. A. K. Coomaraswamy, that eminent authority, has pointed out that the main elements in Hinduism are of pre-Aryan origin, in particular the worship of Shiva Mahadeva, Shivalinga, and Kali, the Hindu mother-goddess. In addition, it was the pre-Aryan cult of devotion, or *bhakti*, that encouraged the worship of images rather than abstract principles, and thus the first sculptural representations of specific deities came to be made, either in anthropomorphic or symbolic form.

Chief among these deities, and one who was and is worshipped in both forms, was Shiva, who symbolized the powers of destruction which are the bases of re-creation. Shiva in his procreative aspect was and is worshipped in the form of the *lingam* (Plate 36) which is both a phallic emblem and, by symbolic inference, the tree and axis of the universe itself. For the benefit of the uninitiated, it should be mentioned that a phallus (from the Greek φαλλός) is a conventionalised representation of an erect male organ, or penis, and that its use in religion was and is not confined to India.

13

8   9

Phallicism or Phallism is an anthropological term applied to that form of worship in which adoration is paid to the generative function of the male. Phallic emblems are found in many parts of the world, and there is a tendency to identify all obelisk-like stones and tree-trunks, together with rites like circumcision, as remains of phallic worship. The modern medical term "priapism" for a permanent and uncontrollable male erection comes from the name of the minor Greek god, Priapus, who was a god of fertility and the personification of the fruitfulness of nature.

Priapus was always represented as a man, usually grotesquely ugly, with an enormous and erect sexual organ. He was thought to be a son of Dionysus and Aphrodite, but as the phallus was a common luck-bringing object for the Greeks and Romans, he was worshipped by people in need of good fortune, such as hunters and fishermen, and also was frequently employed to ward off the evil eye.

Thus one can see that even beneath the apparently fine and restrained Nordic religion of the ancient Greeks, the land abounded with cults of a more ancient kind, having common origin with those of other parts of the world. For the sake of comparison, and to adjust the balance between East and West, it might be worth enlarging on these here. Pandit Nehru himself has written:

"Ancient India and ancient Greece were different from each other and yet they were akin, just as ancient India and ancient China had kinship in thought, in spite of great differences. . . . The Greeks chose Olympus as the abode of the gods, just as the Indians placed their gods and even their sages on the Himalayan heights. Both developed a mythology which was indivisibly mixed up with history, and it was not possible to separate fact from fiction. . . ." [2]

The cults of most interest to us in our study of the erotic aspects of Indian religion are those of Demeter and Dionysus. Demeter, in Greek mythology, was a mother-goddess, and, like Kali, her Indian counterpart, she was known in Arcadia, at least, as "the black one". At one of her festivals a sacrifice of the first-fruits of the harvest was

[2] *The Discovery of India*, Meridian Books (1956), pp. 141 & 142.

16

offered by a priestess, men being prohibited from undertaking the duty. An initiatory ceremony of women by a woman also took place, and was characterised by obscene jests and the use of phallic emblems.

Closely associated with Demeter was Dionysus, god of fruitfulness and vegetation—and hence of wine. His worship was essentially orgiastic, and in his ritual the phallus was prominent. There was also the savage rite of *omophagia* (eating of raw flesh) in which a victim, perhaps originally human in some cases, was torn to pieces and sacramentally eaten raw. In the springtime *orgia*, when the Delphian Thyiads—a troupe of women and girls specially selected (Plate 12) —climbed Mount Parnassus to the sacred Corycian Cave, they milked goats in the flowered meadows nearby and flirted with male participants with tied-on satyr-tails who carried skins of wine. No doubt exists that at this season there was sexual freedom, and the sanctified state of *ecstasis* left the Dionysians free to follow the instincts of nature.

The worship of Dionysus flourished in Asia Minor, particularly in Phrygia and Lydia. His cult was closely associated with that of numerous Asiatic deities, such as Sabazius of Phrygia, and, from the time of Alexander the Great, Dionysus even appears in Greek mythology as conqueror of India:

> " He . . . turned east and made for India. Coming to the Euphrates, he was opposed by the King of Damascus, whom he flayed alive, but built a bridge across the river with ivy and wine; after which a tiger, sent by his father Zeus, helped him across the River Tigris. He reached India, having met with much opposition by the way, and conquered the whole country, which he taught the art of viniculture, also giving it laws and founding great cities." [3]

This might be taken for a fanciful history of Alexander's own drunken progress to the Indus in 327 B.C. but, according to Graves, it is earlier in date and merely records the eastward spread of the vine.

[3] Robert Graves: *The Greek Myths*, I, pp. 104 & 109.

12

The Oriental Mysteries associated with Sabazius and Attis (Phrygia), Isis (Egypt) and Cybele (Asia Minor) which reached Greece and early Imperial Rome, were originally akin to the Mysteries of Demeter and Dionysus, containing, as has already been pointed out, many concepts in common with them. But their orgiastic ecstasies were more violent, and the psychical aberrations to which the devotees were prone through their passionate desire for divine communion were more dangerous. Emasculation was practised by the devotees of Attis, the high priest himself bearing the god's name. Communion with the deity was often attained by the simulation of a sacred marriage in which the initiate was corporeally united with the great god in a special bridal chamber.

In this rite there is more of a suggestion of the ritual wherein a Christian nun becomes the " Bride of Christ " at a church ceremony which she attends robed in white and at which she receives a " wedding " ring, than there is of any established rite in Hinduism.

The Great Mother of the Gods, or Cybele, as she was known in Greek and Latin literature, was sometimes identified with Demeter, the mother-goddess, but her worship was even more orgiastic in nature. Like Demeter, her sanctuaries were often on mountains and frequently in caves; like Durga, lions were her faithful companions. Her attendants, the Corybantes, were wild, half-demonic beings. Her priests, the Galli, were eunuchs attired in female garb, with long hair fragrant with ointment. Together with priestesses, they celebrated Cybele's rites with wild music and dancing until their frenzied excitement found its culmination in self-scourging, self-laceration, or exhaustion. As with Attis, self-emasculation sometimes accompanied this delirium of worship on the part of candidates for the priesthood.

The importance of Cybele in the history of religion is very great, for her cult, like the other mystic worships already described, at once formed a rival to Christianity and acted as a stepping-stone to it. Though their forms may appear strange and distorted, these cults have more in common with the subsequent religious phenomena of

Christendom, and, while they may have less in common with present-day Hindu practice, they may help us to understand better the significance attributed by some authorities to the erotic element in Indian sculpture.

II

THE EARLY CENTURIES

In the codes of later Hinduism, the Puranas, each god has assigned to him a Sakti, or female counterpart, who complements his power. Chief among these Saktis is Parvati, the consort of Shiva. Parvati is most widely worshipped in the form of Kali or Durga, in which roles she also plays the part of a mother-goddess. This " energy " partnership is paralleled in the case of Shivalinga by the *yoni*, which represents the female organ, or the creative force in its feminine aspect. The *lingam* often stands on its own, but the *yoni* is never seen symbolically without the *lingam*. When it appears, it is as the base for the *lingam*—the matrix, in fact. This *lingam-yoni* symbol is popularly known as the *kundi* (Plates 14 & 15), the union of the two representing the act of creation, that is to say, " genesis ".

> " But this twofold emblem would not take us to the very core of Indian thought if it did not also and above all express the resolving of the many into the one. By joining itself to the *yoni*, the *lingam*, the primordial axis, shows that the Absolute is deployed in multiple forms but is again resolved into oneness. Taken as one, the *lingam-yoni* expresses the antagonism of the male and female principles, and then in the triumph of singleness destroys that antagonism." [1]

[1] Max-Pol Fouchet: *The Erotic Sculpture of India*, p. 9.

23

This metaphor of sexual union, or *mithuna*, is, of course, expressed in other, more obvious ways, as we shall see, but there is one variation which sometimes tends to be overlooked, and that is the embrace of the Yakshi and the Tree. The Yakshi, and her male equivalent, the Yaksha, was a class of supernatural being, originally associated only with fertility cults, but later assimilated into the orthodox religions of Hinduism and Buddhism.

In the Yakshi and the Tree, a motif seen frequently, for instance, in the railing of the Buddhist stupa at Bharhut (185-72 B.C.), is a symbolism that goes back to a period in Indian history when trees were regarded as objects of worship, and which is associated with old fertility festivals when youths and maidens gathered the flowers of the *sal* tree. Although the exact original meaning of the motif is not known, there are many Indian legends relating the power of women and Yakshis to bring trees into immediate flowering by embracing the trunk or touching it with their feet (Plate 9), which may be interpreted as symbolical of the soul's union with the divinity.

In the portrayal of the Yakshis at Bharhut there is an emphasis on the attributes of fertility in the swelling breast and ample pelvis. In the Buddhacarita (IV, 35) Asvaghosa describes such women who

"leaned, holding a mango bough in full flower, displaying their bosoms like golden jars."

Another attribute of fertility, already recognised in the prehistoric figurines, is also present in the Yakshis in the shape of the cross-harness or *channavira*.

India's earliest history is veiled in obscurity. It is assumed, however, that the earliest buildings were of wood and did not survive in the climate. Evidence for this belief is to be found in the nature of the architecture of the famous rock-cut Buddhist temples, which reproduces the wooden pillars and beamed roof of a timber structure. Thus, the history and development of Indian sculpture as a tradition does not become clear to us until the second century before Christ, when the first great stone-built Buddhist stupas were erected.

24

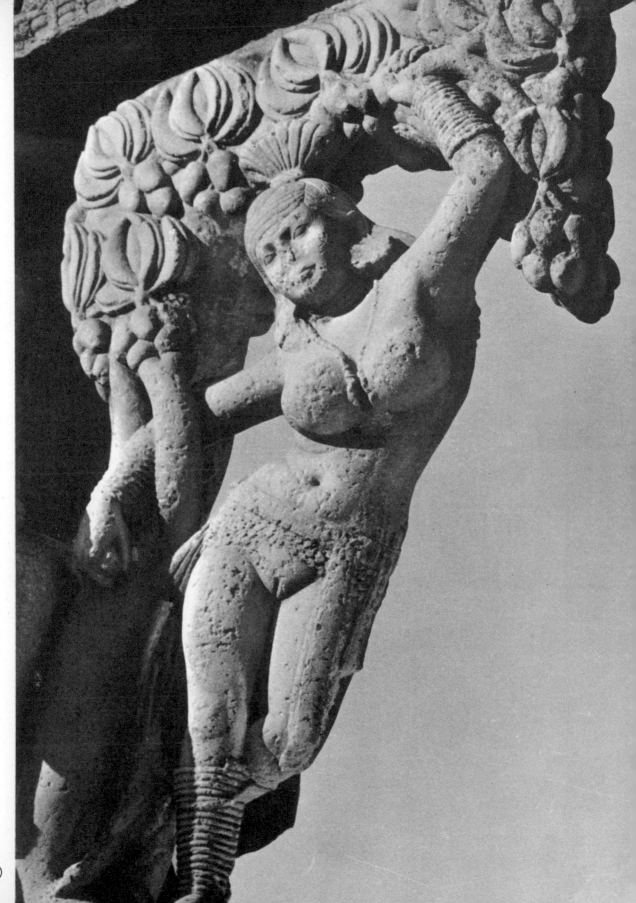

From the previous century, however, have survived at least the magnificent Asokan pillars and capitals, to which reference has already been made, and a few large human statues of rather uninspired aspect. In the second century, the great sculptural achievements were mainly Buddhist, and include the carved railings at Bharhut already referred to as well as the beautiful gateways at Sanchi. The latter may be dated in the first century before Christ, at least a hundred years later than Bharhut, and show a marked sculptural advance, the Yakshi figures in particular having aroused the admiration of connoisseurs. (Plate 16.)

One of these figures, carved in the round, is still in position as a spandrel on the North Gateway, and is a drastic and dramatically effective adaptation of the woman and tree motif:

> " It would be hard to imagine anything more simple, yet more dramatically effective both from the iconographical and aesthetic points of view, than this presentation of the tree-spirit. Her legs thrust with the force of a buttress against the trunk of the tree, and from this magic touch its encircling boughs flower and receive the caressing grasp of the Yakshi, so that she seems a living vine, part of the tree that she quickens. . . . A sense of vitality is communicated by the tense twisting of the torso on its axis. In the frankness of their erotic statement the Sanchi Yakshis are a perfect illustration of the union of spiritual and sensual metaphor that runs like a thread through all religious art in India." [2]

At Sanchi can also be seen, though on the second stupa, what may possibly be one of the earliest examples of mild *mithuna*. In the upper panel of the outer jamb of the eastern gateway are represented in low relief a man and woman who may perhaps be identified as donors, or as an early and tentative instance of the *mithuna*, the female figure merely affectionately clasping the arm of the male figure. A curious detail that supports the latter hypothesis is that the figures in this panel are represented as standing on pedestals, a convention normally associated with cult images or statues when carved fully in the round.

As one enters the equivalent of the Christian era in India, the

[2] Professor Benjamin Rowland: *The Art and Architecture of India*, pp. 57 & 58.

26

use of the *mithuna* motif in temple sculpture becomes more common and increasingly more complex. It is an aspect of Indian religious art which baffles most Westerners; yet, as we have already established, sexual rites in western worship, disguised as " Mysteries ", more often than not, were prevalent in ancient times, and continued, in a mainly negative aspect, into Christian times. Even the most casual research into the records of the Ecclesiastical Courts of medieval Europe will prove that such rites were by no means limited either to ancient Greek or Asiatic tradition.

The student seeking a single interpretation of the *mithuna* sculpture soon discovers that none exists. Each commentator is influenced by his education and upbringing. Those who justify the use of the images do so for widely differing reasons, and those who condemn them find they are not short of reasons for doing so. The practising Christian in particular finds it difficult to accept calmly these sculptures, because Christian theology contains the sexually negative tenets of ' immaculate conception ', ' virgin birth ', and in some instances celibacy of priests and nuns.

> " An ocean of carnality within us is continually lashing against the shores of our spiritual natures, the soul; and these mighty waves of Carnality and Sensuality drown the voices of the Divine within us. The deliverance of the Soul from the error of the senses—the lust of the flesh— is Salvation." [3]

It would be appropriate here to reproduce some judgments based on western standards. One of the earliest we have dates from 1794, and says:

> " We are totally unable, and equally unwilling to convey a full idea of these monstrous delineations; it must therefore suffice to say, that there is a great variety of not only human nudities in the most indecent, un- cleanly situations, but men and beasts, and beasts and women, exposed in the most shameful combinations that a brutal imagination could suggest, in all the filthy attitudes of unnatural depravity." [4]

[3] Sidney C. Tapp: *The Sexology of the Bible.*
[4] Captain Edward Moor, F.R.S.: *A Narrative of the Operations of Captain Little's Detachment.*

James Mill, in his *History of British India*, published in 1817, believed the sculptures encouraged the loosest morality:

> "A religion which subjects to the eyes of its votaries the grossest images of sensual pleasure, and renders even the emblems of generation objects of worship, which ascribes to the supreme God an immense train of obscene acts; which has them engraved on the sacred cars, portrayed in the temples and presented to the people as objects of adoration, which pays worship to the *Yoni*, and the *Lingam*, cannot be regarded as favourable to chastity."

One of the earliest Christian missionaries expressed himself rather more violently:

> "The Bible must supplant the narratives of their false divinities; their temples, covered now with sculptures and paintings which crimson the face of modesty even to glance at, must be demolished; the vile *lingam* must be levelled to the ground. . . ."[5]

It is little wonder that Pandit Nehru has commented:

> "To them (i.e. Englishmen), the Indian appears to be a special manifestation of original sin and all his works bear this mark."[6]

When Europeans began to study more fully and less bigotedly the religious background to the controversial sculptures, their judgments became less severe, and again it is Pandit Nehru who sums up the situation:

> "Indian art is so intimately associated with Indian religion and philosophy that it is difficult to appreciate it fully unless one has some knowledge of the ideals that governed the Indian mind. In art, as in music, there is a gulf which separates eastern from western conceptions."[7]

[5] Ferdinand de Wilton Ward: *India and the Hindoos* (1850).
[6] *The Discovery of India*, Meridian Books (1956), p. 205.
[7] Ibid., p. 203.

III

INTERPRETATIONS

At this point, with westerners beginning to think more logically about Indian temple sculpture, it may be appropriate to present the hypotheses, both European and Indian inspired, as to the origin and significance of its erotic aspects. Why, indeed, were these images of apparent human delight chosen to adorn the Houses of God?

Before discussing the various answers to this question in detail, it may be worthwhile to summarise them briefly as follows:

(1) The *mithunas* are symbols of *sakti*—both sexes in one God—representing the "oneness" of God, or the magic syllable "AUM".

(2) They are representations of supreme bliss—an attempt in earthly terms to convey the meaning of heavenly rapture.

(3) The *mithunas* are temptations to lewd thoughts, put there expressly to be overcome by the devout.

(4) They are just innocent depictions of a human activity in the same way as other sculptures show scenes of dancing, fighting, making music, praying, etc.

(5) The *mithunas* were intended as a protection against the "evil eye", lightning, etc.

(6) They attract grosser-minded people to "come to church", if only for the initial pleasure of examining them.

31

20

21

(7) The *mithunas* are there for the sexual education of the young and ignorant, as a sort of illustrated Kama Sutra.

(8) They are straightforward representations of ritualistic orgies or Yogic postures.

(1) Oneness

Dealing with these propositions one by one, and starting with the hypothesis of " Oneness in God ", we find the support of scripture:

> " The matrix of all forms born from all wombs is Nature Prakriti. I, the Father, giver of seed."
>
> (Bhagavadgita, XIV, 4.)

> " The *yoni* and the *linga* symbolise the creation of the world. Their union represents *Karma*."
>
> (Vatula Shuddha Agma)

> " The union of the sexes is equivalent to the mystic syllable AUM. When the two sexes come together, each fulfils the desire of the other."
>
> (Chhand. Up. I, 1, 6.)

Among those Europeans who see in the *mithunas* the symbolic union of the individual and the world soul is Mr. E. B. Havell, a former principal of the Government School of Art and Keeper of the Calcutta Art Gallery, who writes:

> " It would be wrong to infer that the obscenities which occasionally disfigure Hindu temples are necessarily indicative of moral depravity. In the matter of sexual relationship Indian civilization, in every stratum of society, holds up a standard of morality as high as Europe has ever done.
> " The ideas connected with sex symbolism in Hindu art and ritual are generally misinterpreted by those who take them out of the environment of Indian social life. In the Upanishads sexual relationship is described as one of the means of apprehending the divine nature, and throughout Oriental literature it is constantly used metaphorically to express the true relationship between the human soul and God." [1]

The conception of spiritual oneness has been elaborated by an

[1] *Ideals of Indian Art*, London, 1911.

34

Indian authority, A. K. Coomaraswamy, who writes:

> "The Indian sex-symbolism assumes two main forms, the recognition of which will assist the student of art: first, the desire and union of individuals, sacramental in its likeness to the union of the individual soul with God—this is the love of the herd-girls for Krishna; and second, the creation of the world manifestation, *lila*, as the fruit of the union of male and female cosmic principles—*purusa* and *sakti*." [2]

An American, Professor Benjamin Rowland, contributes:

> "Their embraces have been interpreted as typifying the idea of *moksha* or union with the divine, the achievement of that primordial unity broken at the time Purusa divided himself to create the world. Numerous quotations from the texts support such an interpretation. . . ." [3]

In the oneness hypothesis, the *mithuna* is often bracketed with the *lingam-yoni*:

> ". . . the union of the two gives a direct representation of the creation of the world. Uncompromising in their grandeur, they symbolise Genesis itself. But this twofold emblem would not take us to the very core of Indian thought if it did not also and above all express the resolving of the many into the one. By joining itself to the *yoni*, the *lingam*, the primordial axis, shows that the Absolute is deployed in multiple forms but is again resolved into oneness. . . . Need we repeat that representations of amorous embraces signify the union of separate principles, and are to be regarded as symbolic of oneness with the Divine?" [4]

Finally, Mulk Raj Anand traces the origins of the conception of oneness in his *Kama Kala* when he refers to the philosophies embodied in the aphorisms of the sages whose thoughts later become collected into the Brahmanas and the Upanishads:

> "The essence of these speculations was the inauguration of a supra-sensual kingdom of belief in the One Absolute God, Brahman, who splits himself through desire into the Many and into whom the Unit, or One God, all multiple elements wish to return. . . . The parallelism of human impulse to procreate offers a clue to this creation of the cosmos:
>
>> ' He desired
>> I am One
>> Let me be many that creation may be.' " [5]

[2] *Arts and Crafts of India and Ceylon,* London, 1913.
[3] *Art and Architecture of India,* p. 162.
[4] *The Erotic Sculpture of India,* Max-Pol Fouchet, pp. 9 and 75.
[5] *Kama Kala,* Geneva, (1958), p. 9.

23

(2) BLISS

" In the embrace of his beloved a man forgets the whole world—
everything both within and without; in the very same way, he who embraces
the Self knows neither within nor without."

(Brihad Aranyaka Upanishad)

Nothing can give us an adequate idea of Eternal Bliss, but the theory is that in Indian art the keenest of human pleasures is taken as its symbol. The act of love is chosen to represent that ultimate state where the individual and the Universal are no longer separate. It represents more directly the moment when the self *(atman)* becomes merged through Release with the supreme impersonal Spirit. In a word: copulation figures Bliss. Mulk Raj Anand again analyses this proposition more deeply:

"As against His Joy, the condition of human existence is merely a lack of Joy, a form of suffering, which will last as long as men and women do not struggle to emancipate themselves from birth and rebirth, through worship and dedication and merge with the Supreme God or Bliss. Our human happiness gives but a glimpse of the boundless Joy in store for us, insofar as we recognise our true self for the briefest moment. For this reason, the sacred act of procreation is to be valued, as it affords the intensest moments of Joy we can experience while we strive for the ultimate and complete absorption into the Deity.

"With that characteristic genius for elaborating the highest sanctions, the ancient Hindus, therefore, accepted an anthropomorphic view of God, in which not only is human sexual pleasure exalted as the Joy nearest to God in realisation, but everything in life becomes divine, every action becomes, when properly understood, the concrete expression of some universal law, the shimmering surface of the deeper connection, the image of a less or more intimate approach to the Supreme Bliss, the starting point for the attempt to pierce the dreamy veil to the shadows which are more consecrated, and beyond whose dazzle of muslin lies the superabundant Joy. . . ." [6]

And so on.

[6] *Kama Kala*, p. 18.

(3) Temptation

The hypothesis of temptation is closely related to the theory of "cleansing", both being based on the fact that the *mithunas* are generally only to be found on the outsides of temples. In his famous *Bengal Lancer*, Francis Yeats Brown puts the theory of cleansing into the mouth of the Temple Superintendent at Puri, who says:

> "The approach to the shrine of Jaganath is by avenues corresponding to man's life in the exterior and interior worlds. First there are the snares of the senses, portrayed by paintings and sculptures which your missionaries described as of 'appalling indecency'. Is Freud indecent? Can truth be indecent? . . . If the worshipper be blinded by his carnal appetites in these outer courts, he must return and compose his mind, for he is not worthy of the god." [7]

Other writers have explained that the worshipper should be able to give free vent to his imagination outside the shrine and cast away all lascivious thoughts before entering it. P. Thomas comments:

> "This is a modern interpretation inspired by the western notion of the indecency of sex, and it is doubtful if this was the real intention of the builders of the temple." [8]

Alain Daniélou considers the erotic sculptures to be the touch-stones by which the man of renunciation can test whether his will to chastity is genuine, and he quotes a commentary on the Kama Sutra itself in support:

> "The seekers of Liberation achieve their aim through the detachment which can only come after attachment. For the minds of beings are by their nature inclined towards the objects of the senses."

Finally, Fouchet quotes the instance of Tibetan Buddhists with a Tantric bias who apply certain tests in the course of initiation to discover whether the novice is virtuous:

> "The lama-to-be is asked to look at paintings of a suggestive nature. If his serenity of mind remains undisturbed he is entitled to feel that he

---

[7] *Bengal Lancer*, London (1930).
[8] *Kama Kalpa*, Bombay (1959), p. 139.

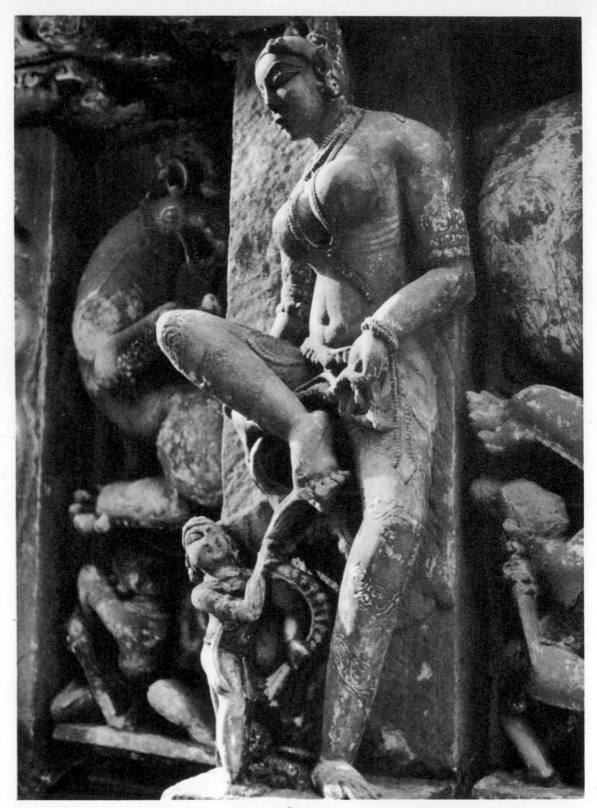

is on the true path. Sometimes the test is more realistic: the devotee is shut in a room to see women perform lewd dances, or couples miming lechery. Meanwhile a monk observes the patient. If he shows no flutter of desire, he is considered worthy to approach the truth and profess it." [9]

(4) INNOCENCE

While considering the motives behind the *mithunas* one should not overlook the possibility that there were no motives at all. This idea has occurred to others, notably to Pandit Nehru, who writes:

" In India we find during every period when her civilization bloomed an intense joy in life and nature, a pleasure in the act of living, the development of art and music, and literature and song and dancing and painting and the theatre, and even a highly sophisticated inquiry into sex relations." [10]

And Coomaraswamy writes:

" Popular explanations of such figures are scarcely less absurd than the strictures of those who condemn them from the standpoint of modern conventional propriety. They appear in Indian temple sculpture, now rarely, now frequently, simply because voluptuous ecstasy has also its due place in life; and those who interpreted life were artists. To them such figures appeared appropriate equally for the happiness they represented and for their deeper symbolism." [11]

(5) PROTECTION

Among some of the more naive theories advanced to account for the presence of the *mithunas* is one that they were meant to resist the evil effect of the jealous gaze of observers, to ward off evil spirits that might have desired to possess the building, and to protect the structure against lightning, cyclones, or other such visitations of nature.

[9] *The Erotic Sculpture of India*, pp. 77-78.
[10] *The Discovery of India*, p. 71.
[11] *Arts and Crafts of India and Ceylon.*

On this subject, an American, Wilber Theodore Elmore, has written:

"The Dravidian idea of the evil eye is that there are innumerable evil spirits waiting at all times to do harm. These spirits appear to be very much dependent on human suggestion and initiative. If special attention is directed to any object or person, and especially if something complimentary is said about it, some listening spirit will take notice, and thinking the object is desirable for itself, or out of jealousy and evil-mindedness, will bring about some evil. . . .

"With the idea of making the spirits think an article is worthless some flaw is left in everything. No house is ever completed. The weaver leaves a flaw in his cloth. . . . The placing of obscene figures and carvings on idol cars and temples is often explained in the same way." [12]

In the same year Mr. E. B. Havell confirmed this quaint piece of folklore:

"A Vishnu temple was a symbol of the active or dynamic principle of nature, and most of the external sculpture was popular art interpreting vulgar notions of the philosophic concept, but not necessarily implying any moral depravity. The indecency was generally introduced on account of the popular belief that it was a protection against the evil eye. There was never any obscenity in the sculpture of the sacred images worshipped within the sanctum and elsewhere." [13]

But a modern French authority is sceptical of this idea:

"Popular tradition in Orissa makes another such attempt to justify the existence of erotic friezes on the temples of Konarak. They are said to protect the buildings from storms and scare lightning away. Far from attracting, they repel. A very simple and pious explanation! But it entirely ignores the look of contentment on the faces of the 'sinners'. We must face the fact that the attitude of the artist in these representations of eternal bliss is *indulgent*." [14]

[12] *Dravidian Gods in Modern Hinduism*, 1915.
[13] *The Ancient and Medieval Architecture of India*, 1915.
[14] Max-Pol Fouchet: *The Erotic Sculpture of India*, p. 11.

44

(6) Attraction

Another simple explanation for the *mithunas*, though the converse of the above, is that they were there because they were particularly amusing to the people and attracted them to the temples. Alain Daniélou gives this theory serious consideration and describes how, according to their stage of development, there are three main ways of attracting people's attention towards a sanctuary:

> " The first approach suited for men of developed intellect is through abstract interest in a symbol; the second, meant for those more interested in forms than in philosophy, is through appreciation of artistic merit; the third for those more deeply immersed in worldly interests, and the only remaining way to attract them, is purely sensuous. The spiritual man is in no way affected by erotic pictures or descriptions . . . but the common man fears pain and is attracted by suggestions of sensuous pleasure. To discover images of this kind in a temple he has to wander into its dark corners and examine it from plinth to architrave. He will walk round the pillars, round the inner shrine. But in doing so, smelling the flowers and the incense, seeing the sacred lights, hearing the bells of worship, he will come under the influence of the sacred place. . . ." [15]

(7) Education

The idea that the *mithunas* were a form of sexual education—a sort of sculptural Kama Sutra—is a popular one and has many supporters. Lawrence E. Gichner, describing how the temple was used both as a place of worship and a centre of social contact, says:

> " Here the latest news was exchanged and discussed, and they could and did see and examine the numerous sculptures which were their books, source of knowledge and model for their own behaviour. . . . The lesson which these sculptures taught the Hindu was toward the enjoyment of the senses, rather than the denial of them. Hindu thought has always insisted upon the importance of sex and its physical manifestations. Thus, the temple decorations contain many carvings which demonstrate the various positions of the marital embrace." [16]

[15] *Marg Magazine*, Bombay (1948), p. 89.
[16] *Erotic Aspects of Hindu Sculpture*, U.S.A. (1949), p. 13.

45

28

Alain Daniélou is more precise in his reference to this explanation for the *mithunas*:

"Sexual curiosity is one of the chief causes of perversion of the mind. If spiritual progress is to be made 'complexes' must be resolved and the mind made healthy. Sexual education through images, of every possible form of sexual enjoyment, is a useful means of mental clarification. It is a duty of the teacher to see that no latent longing remains in the mind of his pupil that may later prove a hindrance to spiritual progress or even cause a dangerous fall." [17]

This is confirmed by Mulk Raj Anand, who adds:

"The hypothesis seems to be that since sexual curiosity is, apart from the awakening of sensibility towards Reality, also one of the main causes of the perversion of the mind, it must be satisfactorily explained and analysed, so that education can lead not only to healthy enjoyment of the variegated pleasures of the body but also clarify the mind of all filth attached to the secret act." [18]

(8) YOGA AND TANTRA

It is widely suggested by some authorities that the eighty-four postures of *yoga*, which help to change the subtle centres of the body and so attain harmony, find their equivalent in the *mithunas*, on the erotic plane. Dr. Benjamin Rowland says that the practice of sexual intercourse with a "*sakti*" is permitted certain classes of adepts in *yoga*. Mr. Georges Guette adds that one would have to become a *yogi* before attempting some of the contortions figured in stone.

The erotic postures of *yoga* are sometimes described as "Tantric Yoga" and this description leads logically to the final major explanation for the *mithunas*, that is to say, that they are of Tantra, or Kaula, significance. Tantra is a word popularly used to describe those sacred scriptures which lay down rules for the worship of *Sakti*, the female aspect of the godhead, through *Panchatatva*. The burden of the Tantras is to make worship attractive to men:

[17] *Marg Magazine,* Bombay (1948), p. 89.
[18] *Kama Kala,* p. 26.

48

"Where there is worldly enjoyment there is no liberation; where there is liberation there is no worldly enjoyment. But in the case of the excellent devotees of Sri Sundari both liberation and enjoyment are in the hollow of their hands."

The rules of *Panchatatva* are commonly known as "The Five Ms", and these are *Madya* (liquor), *Mansa* (meat), *Matsya* (fish), *Mudra* (corn), and *Mithuna* (coition). P. Thomas has described the most important and significant ritual of the *Panchatatva* in detail in his *Kama Kalpa* :

"The rite is usually performed at night in the house of a wealthy *Sakta* where secrecy can be ensured, or in the inner shrine of some temple inaccessible to the public. The room where the rite takes place is cleaned and consecrated for the worship, and a circle of prescribed radius is drawn. At the centre of the circle is drawn a *Yantra* (mystic diagram) in which sits the host and his *Sakti*. Around them sit the guests, each beside his (own) *Sakti*.

"The *Saktis*, represented of course by living women, are said to be of three kinds: *Sviya*, or one's own wife, *Parakiya* or another man's wife, and *Saddharani* or common woman. Some texts ordain that *mithuna* is permissible only with the *Sviya*, while others hold that there is no harm in *mithuna* with any woman, as every woman is in effect the living embodiment of *Sakti*."

After describing the opening phases of the ritual, Mr. Thomas goes on :

"Drinking may now start. With the first cup the devotees eat meat, with the second fish, with the third gram, with the fourth all these and with the fifth anything he desires. The Mahanirvana Tantra ordains that no more than five cups of wine must be drunk during the worship after which sexual union must take place. . . .

"One of the objects of Tantric rites is said to be the raising of the devotee above all sense of right and wrong, an ideal often emphasized in Hindu mysticism; and we know for certain that the Tantric rites of Mahayana Buddhists were attended by much debauchery and exhortation to actions which Society considers evil or sinful." [19]

Mulk Raj Anand is less condemnatory in tone when he describes the Tantric (or Kaula) ritual, and ends somewhat cynically :

[19] *Kama Kalpa*, pp. 122-123.

㉚

" The so called vulgarity which later Hindus have come to see in the eroticism implicit in the Kaula cult is probably derived from the western Christian approach which considers the very central Hindu doctrine of the procreation of the Universe through the union of male and female as sin." [20]

Anand describes another, more secret cult, less rational and more instinctive than Kaula, which flourished about the same time. These were the Kapalikas, who associated human sacrifice with their ritual and laid greater emphasis on the erotic impulse. They located the soul in the *yoni* and believed in *Moksha* through the complete enjoyment of woman. (Plate 44.)

*　　　　*　　　　*　　　　*

These then are the eight hypotheses of the *mithuna*. None of the protagonists quoted can be said to have proved his pet theory or theories, and the sculptures themselves give no definite clues. Which conjectures come nearest the truth? Perhaps the reader will be able to form an opinion for himself when he has read the next chapter and compared text and illustrations.

[20] *Kama Kala*, p. 35.

IV

THE CLASSICAL PERIOD AND
LATER CENTURIES

After Sanchi the erotic motif as such is not found persistently for another thousand years. During this period, which included the Golden Age of Indian sculpture—the Gupta period—the extreme *mithuna* was a rarity, though voluptuous *Saktis* and *Apsarases* (celestial dancers) were commonplace. The lingering predominance of Buddhism may have had some influence in effecting this restraint, but gradually the Shaivite cult of Hinduism gained the ascendant, and the image of Shivalinga began to appear more frequently.

One of the few surviving gems of Hindu architecture of the Gupta period is the Temple of Vishnu at Deogarh. This fragmentary building, probably dating from the fifth century after Christ, is one of the most ornate and beautifully composed examples of Gupta art. Within the framework of the main doorway are enclosed narrow vertical bands of decoration with representations of amorous couples. (Plate 42). Thus the non-sectarian provenance of erotic sculpture was established early on, in the same way as Indian art in general. The early convention, initiated by Fergusson, of classifying Indian art and

53

34

architecture by religion has often proved misleading. Buddhists, Jains, and Hindus of every sect alike have drawn upon, and in turn contributed to, a tradition of art common to India as a whole.

However, as has been said, Shaivism predominated towards the end of, and after, the Gupta period. The seventh century cave temple on Elephanta Island, near Bombay, is well known for its *lingam* shrine. Shiva also appears at Elephanta in his androgynous, or half-female, form, Ardhanari. At Ellora (8th Century) Shiva appears as Bhairava, a fearsome aspect, dancing the wild *tandava* (Plate 33). He also appears with his consort in a scene popularly known as " Shiva's Marriage ". With one of his four hands he holds one of Uma's, and with another his own *kamarband* (Plate 34). This representation of Shiva's wedding, like that at Elephanta, has been described as

> " A timeless scene of bliss wherein the fire of life, the energy of the creator, is quick with the ardour of its eternal source and at the same time throbbing with the pulse of time." [1]

Above the happy couple hover airborne *devas*, come to praise the climax of the god's union with his Himalayan bride, a wedding that

> " typifies the world and all its myriads proceeding from the reunion of the One who was never divided." [2]

*   *   *   *

At Mamallapuram, on the Coromandel Coast, the waves dash today against a sea-wall built to protect the Seven Pagodas from the rough swell of the Bay of Bengal. On the wall stands a square-cut phallic-tipped lamp-post (Plate 35), and in line with it, back in a small dark sanctuary facing out to the waves, is a shattered sixteen-sided black basalt *lingam*. Ptolemy the Greek mentioned Mamallapuram in the second century after Christ as a seaport, and Hiuen Tsang of China confirmed this in the seventh, when the Seven Pagodas were built and carved from the living rock by the Pallavas.

The dynasties that succeeded to the power of the Gupta Empire

[1] Zimmer: *Philosophies of India*, New York (1951), p. 199.
[2] Benjamin Rowland: *The Art and Architecture of India*, p. 178.

56

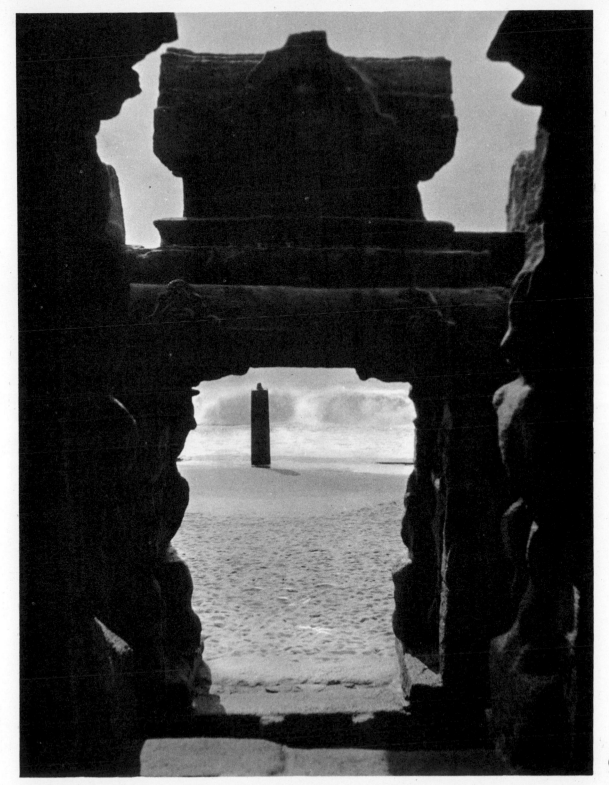

35

in central and northern India introduced a new style of architecture known as the *nagara* or Indo-Aryan, and one of the earliest examples of this style, the chief feature of which was the curvilinear spire (*sikhara*) over the shrine, is to be found at Bhubaneshwar in Orissa. The earliest temple, the Parashurameshwar, dates from A.D. 750, and the latest, the Lingaraja, from about A.D. 1000. During the intervening period both the architectural style and the quality of the statuary improved, developing from a naive simplicity to a sophisticated self-confidence.

The more advanced type of *mithuna* is much in evidence at Bhubaneshwar (Plates 44-51) and even more so at the twelfth century temple of Jagannatha, Lord of the Universe, at Puri (Plate 52) and to the famous Surya Temple at Konarak, dating from the thirteenth century (Plate 53). The Konarak Temple, known also as the " Black Pagoda ", is perhaps the finest example of the Orissan style. Its composition and outline represent a classical feeling which underlies the whole tradition of art in Medieval India :

> " Like a lighthouse echoing to the hammers of the sea, like a dark pyramid on a waste shore, or some caravan forgotten by wandering gods and turned to stone—such is Konarak, Temple of the Sun, fallen fragment maybe of that star, with a coating of erotic imagery; caressing, copulation, orgasm and desire." [3]

A unique feature of this temple is the twenty-four great stone wheels (Plate 54) on either side of the base, making the structure into a giant " juggernaut " car, or chariot of the sun. Round the base run two friezes of sculpture of a highly erotic nature, including animal as well as human couples (Plates 55-59). Professor Benjamin Rowland propounds a special theory that at Konarak the function of these endlessly repeated pairs in dalliance must have had something to do with actual orgiastic rites conducted in association with a cult of the sun as a universal fructifying force. He quotes a suggestion that an esoteric Magian phase of sun worship, perhaps originating in the famous temple at Multan, was followed at Konarak.

[3] Max-Pol Fouchet: *The Erotic Sculpture of India*, p. 51.

During the period of development of the Orissan temples great and terrible things were happening on the other side of India. In A.D. 986-988, Sabuktigin, the ruler of the little mountain kingdom of Ghazni, in what is now Afghanistan, invaded the Punjab and captured Peshawar. Using this foothold, his successor, Mahmud of Ghazni, made annual raids into India. The most famous of Mahmud's exploits was his raid, across trackless desert sands, on the great temple of Shiva at Somnathpur, or Somnatha-Patan, in the Kathiawar Peninsula, in A.D. 1025.

At that time, Somnath was one of the Sacred Cities of India, and the temple, with its tens of thousands of priests, was a town in itself, surrounded by a series of massive fortifications. Supported by 56 wooden pillars coated with silver, the innermost shrine sheltered a giant stone *lingam* encrusted with jewels, which was washed every day with water from the Ganges and garlanded with flowers from Kashmir. The Muslims fought their way to this sanctuary, sacking the temple and putting 50,000 *brahmins* to the sword. Mahmud refused the fabulous sums offered in ransom for the great *lingam* by the surviving priests, and ordered it to be smashed into fragments and carried back to Ghazni. There the pieces were buried under the threshold of the Great Mosque and are trampled on to this day by True Believers as they enter and leave the mosque.

The first invasions of north-western India made with any lasting effect were those of Mohammed of Ghor, who had himself overthrown the rulers of Ghazni. Like Mahmud, however, he had one eye on this world and one on the next. He too combined the breaking of idols with the collecting of diamonds totalling nearly half-a-ton in weight during the course of his nine raids.

In 1202 the army of Qutb-ud-din, the Viceroy of Mohammed of Ghor, penetrated to the Bundelkhand in north-central India. where it reduced and plundered the fort Kalangar and its temple, not far from Khajuraho, the capital of the Rajput Chandella kings, who had risen to power in the first half of the tenth century after Christ. Some of the temples at Khajuraho were built in the reign of King Dhanga

59

36

(*ca.* A.D. 950-1002).   Prithviraj, the last great Hindu ruler of northern India, devastated and occupied the territories of the last of the Chandella Kings in A.D. 1182-83, and a few years later the Muslim hordes swept over the country, looting, plundering and destroying in the name of their religion.

Only twenty of the original eighty-five temples of Khajuraho are now standing.   The way in which they fill a now desert area covering only a square mile seems to imply some special object, such as an organisation of religious orders not unlike that planned by the Oratorians in Italy in the sixteenth century.   Mulk Raj Anand suggests that two of these cults were the Kaulas and Kapalikas (see pp. 49, 52), as there are references to them in the play " Prabodha Chandrodaya ", which was itself performed in the presence of the Chandella King Kirtivarman in *ca.* 1051-1098.

Percy Brown, an acknowledged authority on Indian architecture, comments :

> " As at Konarak, it is proved by the carvings on these temples that the same sinister ritual which degraded that monumental conception also prevailed at Khajuraho, and it is possible that the religious community concerned suffered the same fate.   Such may be one of the explanations for the almost complete absence of life within the precincts of these beautiful buildings, and their disuse over such a long period of time." [4]

Whatever the ideals were, they stimulated the building art to a remarkable degree, as these temples, rising like small mountains of buff masonry above the dusty scrub, amply testify.   Although the surviving shrines are dedicated to Shiva, Vishnu and the Jain saints, there is, as expected, no essential difference in their architectural character, although this is itself quite different from that in any other part of the country.

Each shrine stands on a high masonry terrace, without any enclosure wall.   The vertical is emphasized throughout, from the high base, through the successive walls and roofs, to the ultimate range of lesser peaks that constitute the main spire.   This stressed verticality,

[4] *Indian Architecture*, Vol. I, p. 133.

according to Professor Benjamin Rowland, was intended to lead the gaze of the worshipper upward to the point of magic union with the divine and, in like manner, the sculptural decoration also led the way to that desired union. This decoration takes the form of two, and sometimes, three, parallel friezes, peopled with groups of half-lifesize statuary carved in high relief, representing a moving pageant and never-ending procession of life-like forms — 650 on one temple alone — shapely in appearance, exquisite in workmanship and of inexhaustible interest.

The erotic carvings show a particular refinement when compared with those from other parts and periods. The figures are predominantly female, and they participate in tableaux of a complicated orgiastic nature. (See Plates 29, 62, 63, 64, 65.) All possible variations on the main theme of physical love are illustrated, with every stage demonstrated, from preliminary caresses, through passionate kissing, to acrobatic consummation. In one particularly arresting group a girl participant, apparently overcome with coyness, turns away and holds a hand to a shyly smiling mouth. (Plate 26.)

In contrast to the relatively refined artistic treatment of the tableaux on the temples proper, one side of the terrace of the Matangeswara and Lakshmana Temples bears a reduced-scale frieze in which the sculpture is naive and earthy. (Plate 65.) This band is nothing less than a film of carnal delights — a mirror of frenzied fornication, in which numerous couples participate at the same time. It is a matter for speculation as to just how these particular scenes fit into the established hypotheses for erotic sculpture.

In this connection, Professor Douglas Barrett, Deputy Keeper of Oriental Antiquities at the British Museum, in conversation with the author, compares Khajuraho with Konarak, pointing out that both the Kings of Orissa and the Chandella Kings of Bundelkhand were "*junglis*", that is to say, both dynasties were of barbarian origin. Only rulers who maintained large *harems*, as "*junglis*" did, could enjoy the company of so many lovely girls in their sexual orgies, and it is only in Bundelkhand and Orissa that one will normally see any-

38

39

thing more than *couples* in *mithuna*.   His theory is that the tableaux
illustrated the privileges of these kings for the visual pleasure of the
commoner, the purpose being to convey to the ordinary man a conception of heavenly bliss—i.e. unlimited women for an unbridled lust.
[See Chapter III(2).]

*   *   *   *

Something similar to the frieze on the temple base at Khajuraho,
both in size and plastic treatment, may be seen a thousand miles away
in distance and some two hundred years in time, at Somnathpura in
Mysore.   There, in the Hoysala period temple of Prasanna Channa
Kesava built in A.D. 1270, are a dozen little love scenes, each occupying a six-inch high recess in a frieze running round the outer base of
the temple.   (Plates 76 & 77.)

Elsewhere in south-central and southern India, the erotic motif is
to be seen only sporadically in the temple decoration of the succeeding
centuries.   (See Plates 78, 79, 81, 82.)   One of the most curious
instances is at Kanchipuram, on a pillar of the Vedanta Desika shrine
in the sixteenth century Varadaraja Perumal Temple (Plate 80).
A trio of worshippers, manhoods erect, face a line of tiny *kundis* and
appear to worship a naked goddess, probably Parvati, above them.
She holds a parrot, the pet of Kama, god of Love.   Further up the
column a lady is being taken in an acrobatic pose by a fellow who
is not to be deterred from blowing a trumpet at the same time.

After the Vijayanagar period (1370-1565), the *mithuna* almost dis-
appears as a feature in Indian sculpture, and in any case is to be found,
not on the base, walls, or pillars of the temples, but tucked away among
the myriad figures on *gopuram* or *vimana*.   Among the temples of the
south, where, following the Muslim conquest of most of the rest of the
country, Hindu temple architecture enjoyed its final classical phase
under the Nyaks in the seventeenth century, mention may be made
of the Temple of Tiruvatakudi, near Karikal, where, on the *gopuram*,
one man may be seen enjoying, ingeniously and simultaneously, no

66

less than six women—recalling the Kama Sutra's " Congress of a Herd of Cows ".

*   *   *   *

With the decline of indigenous architecture which coincided with the spread of European influence in India in the eighteenth and nineteenth centuries, temple sculpture deteriorated in originality and style and the erotic motif itself gradually disappeared. Far to the north, however, and inaccessible until recent times to western ideas, lay Nepal, where temple art continued to flourish under the Newars, and later, even under the Gurkhas. In fact, in 1905, one traveller went so far as to say: " Nepal is still an authentic replica of an India that has disappeared." [5]

Nepal shared the common Buddhist origin of Indian temple art, and there is a direct link with Sanchi, across nearly two thousand years, in the Yakshi figures that support the sideways-projecting lintels of Nepalese temple doorways in the same way that they support the outer ends of the cross-bars of the Sanchi gateways (Plate 16).

The Newar inhabitants of Nepal, who probably originally came from the north, possessed an artistic sensibility of a particularly exuberant nature. The pagoda-like structure of their wood-and-brick shrines lent itself in general to elaborate treatment, and a particular feature of interest to us in our specialised study is the carved wooden struts which support the overhanging roofs. These usually consist of a many-armed godhead acting as a sort of diagonal caryatid and standing on a pedestal. This pedestal, or *predella,* is carved in deep relief and often brightly coloured and depicts what Perceval Landon describes as

" An allegorical scene, recognised as religious at once by the Nepalese, but often disconcerting in its realism to a visitor fresh from Europe." [6]

In other words, an erotic scene. (See Plates 83-94.) Percy Brown, an authority on both Indian and Nepalese architecture,

[5] Sylvain Levi: *Le Nepal,* Paris (1905-08).
[6] *Nepal,* London (1928), Vol. I, p. 184.

67

41

attributes these scenes to the Tantric element in Nepalese Buddhism, and I have not seen this assignation denied anywhere. Some of the scenes, however, have a vulgar humour which seems to belie a spiritual intention. Take, for instance, the bracket on the Shiva Temple in Kathmandu (Plate 86) where a porter, with a child in his head-slung basket, has intercourse with a woman who still has a baby at her breast, or another motif, often repeated (Plate 84), where a girl is taken, apparently by surprise, from the rear as she works at a churn.

More solemnity is accorded to another erotic aspect of Nepalese (and Tibetan) Buddhism, and this is the striking conception of " AUM ", or the Oneness of God [see Chapter III(1)] as visually represented by the " Adi-Buddha ". This manifestation is composed of two figures clasped in *mithuna*. The twelve-armed, four-headed deity—the Yi-dam Samvara or Hevajra of Nepal, the Yi-dam Sang-dui of Tibet—tramples on Time as his single-headed, normal-handed Sakti clings round his waist and embraces him passionately.

Buddhism and Hinduism are inextricably mixed in Nepal, and religion itself is closely interwoven with everyday life. Erotic motifs appear not only on temples but on secular buildings such as public shelters (Plate 95) and even military barracks (Plate 96), while sometimes, in remote parts, boundary-markers are adapted to serve as *lingams*. Finally, in jungle clearings the traveller may stumble on small groups of phallic-shaped stones placed significantly.

Thus is emphasized something of the philosophy of life in the Indian sub-continent: that religion and life and sexuality are one, and not three separate entities kept rigidly apart and secluded in privacy as they have been for centuries in the West:

> " No couples are seen in the shrines of the Christian Occident. They only appear under the baleful signs of malediction and exorcism. The first couple are driven out of Eden; they are symbols of banishment and fear, and proclaim the chastisement of the flesh. But India's civilisation, being both spiritual and sensual, irradiates the union of man and woman with bliss." [7]

[7] Max-Pol Fouchet: *The Erotic Sculpture of India*, p. 95.

49

54

61

66

67

69

70

71

(72)

73

74

75

78

79

90

89

88

87

96

NOTES TO PLATES

1. COURTESAN. (KHAJURAHO). 11TH CENTURY.

The bejewelled Apsara wearing a flowing scarf and *sari* stands in a bewitching posture. She stretches her right arm behind her head and places her left hand suggestively on a breast.

2. MALE DANCER. (HARAPPA, WESTERN PAKISTAN). *c.* 2400-2000 B.C.

The head, arms, breast, nipples and the genitals (all now missing) of this grey limestone statuette were cut separately and socketed into the torso. Originally, perhaps, this figure was ithyphallic and bore some relationship to the Rudra-Shiva cult of the Indus Valley peoples.

3. BULL SEAL. (MOHENJODARO). *c.* 3RD MILLENIUM B.C.

Many steatite seals have been found on the sites of the Indus Valley Civilization, almost all with characters in a script not yet deciphered.

4, 5. FRONT AND BACK VIEWS OF MALE LIMESTONE TORSO. (HARAPPA). *c.* 3RD MILLENIUM B.C.

6, 7. FRONT AND BACK VIEWS, BRONZE DANCING DOLL. (MOHENJODARO). *c.* 3RD MILLENIUM B.C.

8. SUDARSANA YAKSHI. (BHARHUT). 2ND CENTURY B.C.

An ancient Indian fertility cult connected with Yakshas and Yakshis was very popular. It is significant, however, that as depicted in ancient art Yakshas and Yakshis, though closely connected with sex and eroticism, hardly give an impression of frank eroticism. Sudarsana or the 'Beautiful' Yakshi standing on the *Makara*, a fertility symbol, is very decorously dressed. Her left hand below her navel may, however, express her erotic nature.

9. YAKSHI CHULAKOKA. (BHARHUT). 2ND CENTURY B.C.

The heavily bejewelled Yakshi stands under an Asoka tree in full blossom. Her left arm and leg entwine the tree and with her right hand she holds one of the branches. The elephant below is her emblem.

10. YAKSHI CARRYING A BIRD-CAGE. RAILING PILLAR (MATHURA). KUSHANA, 2ND CENTURY.

The Yakshi standing on a dwarf is the prototype of a contemporary courtesan. She wears ornaments and a thin transparent *sari* held to the waist with an elaborate girdle, which reveals her sex. She holds a bird-cage in her right hand; the bird, which may well be a fighting-cock, is perched on her left shoulder. At the top, a courtesan grasping a mirror with an attendant holding a toilet-box is engaged in her toilet.

11. YAKSHI. (DIDARGANJ, PATNA). 2ND CENTURY B.C.

Her body is beautifully modelled, giving the feel of the flesh, and follows closely the ideal of female beauty enjoined in Sanskrit poetry. The ornaments are simple but effective and the folds of the *sari* and *uttariya* are neatly done. The *chauri* in her right hand may be her symbol.

12. VILLA OF THE MYSTERIES. (POMPEII, ITALY). 1ST CENTURY B.C.

This painting, one of 29 scenes in fresco, illustrates the initiation of young girls into the mysteries of the Dionysiac festival. The girl on the right whirls in a dionysiac dance, as the girl on the left is beaten symbolically with a stick by a priestess (Flagellation).

13. NAGRAJA WITH HIS WOMEN. (AJANTA, CAVE 19). 6TH CENTURY.

Within the lotus roundel is depicted a seat with footrests. The Nagraja is depicted in *lalitasana*, with his queen reclining on him and an attendant on either side.

14. SHIVALINGA. DARBAR SQUARE (BHATGAON, CENTRAL NEPAL). 17TH CENTURY.

This is the usual form of the *lingam* in both India and Nepal. The *Kundi* combines both the upright phallus and the *yoni* representing the female organ serving as the matrix. The square recessed base with the lotiform pedestal represents a *Yantra*, an important article in the *Sakta* cult. The *yoni*, or *Arghya*, takes the overflow of libations poured over the *lingam*.

15. LINGA-WORSHIP. KANDARIYA MAHADEVA TEMPLE (KHAJURAHO). 11TH CENTURY.

The *lingam* is in the centre with four devotees on either side, who may well be the Pasupatas. They are offering garlands, playing musical instruments and saluting the god.

16. YAKSHI BRACKET. (SANCHI, NOW IN THE BRITISH MUSEUM). 1ST CENTURY B.C.

The Yakshi, her transparent *sari* revealing her sex, stands with legs crossed under a mango tree symbolising love and spring.

17. MITHUNA. CHAITYA CAVE (KARLE, NEAR POONA). 1ST CENTURY B.C.

The couple have plump but lithesome figures. On the left stands a bejewelled girl with legs crossed. Her crooked right arm is taken back playfully while her left hand is on the shoulder of her partner who stands gracefully.

18. MITHUNA IN A DANCING POSE. CHAITYA CAVE (KARLE, NEAR POONA). 1ST CENTURY B.C.

The bejewelled female dancer wearing a thin transparent *sari* which reveals her sex is dancing with her legs flexed and her hands overhead in the attitude of adoration. The turbaned and bejewelled male has one hand on the breast of the female partner and the other on his waist. The careful modelling has caught well the rhythm of the dance.

114

19. CELESTIAL COUPLE. PILLAR MEDALLION. (BADAMI, CAVE IV). *c.* 7TH CENTURY.

The couple are in a close embrace. The woman touches the cheek of her beloved, who holds her by the wrist. A female attendant stands to the right.

20. VISHNU WITH HIS CONSORT LAKSHMI. PARSVANATHA TEMPLE (KHAJURAHO). 11TH CENTURY.

The ancient Vedic god Vishnu in course of time became associated with the goddess Sri Lakshmi, symbolising fertility, abundance, beauty and good fortune. According to Puranic conception, Vishnu and Lakshmi stand for the ideal human relationship of a man and his wife. The bejewelled figure of the four-handed Vishnu stands in a slightly flexed position embracing Lakshmi, who is looking lovingly towards her divine spouse.

21. SEXUAL CONGRESS. PARSVANATHA TEMPLE (KHAJURAHO). 11TH CENTURY.

The male partner seated on a chair has crooked his right leg to support his disrobed partner, who is astride him. She is clutching a lock of his hair with her right hand. The emotional intensity of the act is well marked on their faces.

22. AN AMOROUS COUPLE. DEVI JAGADAMBA TEMPLE (KHAJURAHO). 11TH CENTURY.

This close-up view of the couple in love-making shows the vigorous movement of the female partner. Her left arm holds her partner's neck tightly and her right hand clutches a lock of his hair. Clutching the hair in sexual congress to enhance the emotional intensity of the act is enjoined in the Kama Sutra.

23. TENDER LOVE. DEVI JAGADAMBA TEMPLE (KHAJURAHO). 11TH CENTURY.

This relief is quite different from the usual run of erotic sculptures at Khajuraho and shows a tender moment in the meeting of lovers. The male with rather a feigned smile is holding the arm of his beloved, who, apparently displeased by his vagaries, is, with a finger on her lips, begging him to cease the profession of his love. In the language of *Nayikabheda* literature the sculpture depicts *Manini Nayika*.

24. PREPARING FOR THE DANCE. PARSVANATHA TEMPLE (KHAJURAHO). 11TH CENTURY.

The dance in ancient India required careful training and preparation. The *Bharata Natyasastra*, the most important text on dancing, gives directions on the preparation to be made before the actual commencement of the performance. Here the danseuse, after putting on her ornaments, the breast-band, and a slick patterned *sari*, is tying the tinklers (*ghunghrus*) to her raised right foot. An attendant in the foreground holds up an anklet of tinklers for her mistress's use.

115

25. AN INTIMATE KISS. KANDARIYA MAHADEVA TEMPLE (KHAJURAHO). 11TH CENTURY.

The couple hold each other in a close sexual embrace. Their mouths are in close proximity and the tenseness of their faces shows the union as an act of dedication.

26. THE FOND EMBRACE. VISVANATHA TEMPLE (KHAJURAHO). 11TH CENTURY.

The female partner, partly disrobed, is clinging fast to her lover who has crooked one of his legs to support her. The woman attendant on the right, apparently not used to such scenes, is hiding her face.

27. THE EMBRACE. (KHAJURAHO). 11TH CENTURY.

The male figure has caught the female from behind. She is touching her lover's head and he in his turn is fondling her breasts. Their closed eyes and tense faces show the intensity of love-desire.

28. AMOROUS COUPLE. (KHAJURAHO). 11TH CENTURY.

The male partner stands in a slanting position with a smile playing on his lips. The female is astride him from the front, the deep curvature of her posterior catching the rhythm of the act.

29. AN ACROBATIC SEXUAL POSTURE. KANDARIYA MAHADEVA TEMPLE. (KHAJU RAHO). 11TH CENTURY.

The man stands on his head with his interlocked legs supporting his squatting female partner. Female attendants on either side participate in the act by supporting the couple.

30. BACCHANALIAN SCENE. (MATHURA). KUSHANA, 2ND CENTURY.

A courtesan in the last stages of drunkenness is kneeling on the ground in almost complete nudity. She is being supported by her lover on the left and a girl cup-bearer on the right. The old bawd on the same side stands in disgust. The scene represents a *goshthi*.

31. MITHUNA FIGURES. (DEOGARH, U.P.) EARLY 6TH CENTURY.

The *mithuna* figures in the Gupta sculpture lose their earlier lascivious character and gain a new sobriety in which the emphasis is on spiritual love. In the panels depicted in the plate the couple are either conversing intimately or the *nayika* is showing her feigned resentment towards her lover—two outstanding motifs in the poetry of the Gupta period.

32. KING WITH HIS RANIS. (AJANTA, CAVE 19). 6TH CENTURY.

Within a lotus roundel is shown a bed on which is seated the king with queens on either side whom he is caressing.

116

33. THE DANCE OF SHIVA. (ELLORA, CAVE 14). 8TH CENTURY.

This relief represents the Tandava dance of Shiva, 'under whose violent thumping of feet the mountains crumbled and the entire world including the seas were agitated'. The eight-handed Shiva holding various symbols is dancing with great fervour on a bare rock. There are drummers and a piper on the left and Parvati with Kartikeya and Ganesa on the right. The gods in the sky are witnessing the dance.

34. SHIVA'S MARRIAGE. DHUMAR LENA (ELLORA). 8TH CENTURY.

In Shaivite mythology the marriage of Shiva with Uma signifies the union of male and female principles to ensure the continuity of creation. In the sculptural representations, however, the incident gains in tenderness as it represents the Hindu marriage which, in the presence of the gods, unites two souls till death parts them. Shiva's marriage is here represented on a grand scale. In the centre stands Shiva holding the right hand of Parvati. Brahma is himself acting as chief priest. To the left stand the parents of Parvati. A congregation of gods and goddesses floating in the sky is witnessing the solemnisation of the marriage.

35. SEVEN PAGODAS. SHORE TEMPLE (MAMALLAPURAM). 7TH CENTURY.

The waves of the ancient Mahodadhi (Bay of Bengal) wash the base of phallic-tipped lamp-post to warn the unwary navigators against the dangers of the sea.

36. LINGODBHAVA MURTI. TRIMURTI SHRINE (MAMALLAPURAM). PALLAVA, 7TH CENTURY.

In the foreground is the *lingam* from which emanates the visual form of the four-handed Shiva, symbolising the creative energy of the male.

37. A CELESTIAL COUPLE. TREE BRACKET OF A CAPITAL (BADAMI, CAVE III). A.D. 578.

The bejewelled couple stands under a stylised tree. The male, in resplendent finery, embraces his beloved, who shows a coy grace. The lover holds her hand, but she has averted her face in shyness, though a gentle smile reveals her consent to his advances.

38. CELESTIAL COUPLE. TREE BRACKET OF A CAPITAL (BADAMI, CAVE III). A D. 578.

The couple standing under a tree betray an attenuated modelling and smooth grace closely akin to the Pallava tradition. While both the male and female are profusely ornamented, their garments are reduced to the minimum. The male holds a garland-like object touched by his partner. An attendant stands in the foreground.

117

39. CELESTIAL COUPLE. TREE BRACKET OF A CAPITAL (BADAMI, CAVE III). A.D. 578.

The couple stand under a mango tree, which symbolises love and spring in Indian poetry. The male stands rigidly, holding the extended left leg of his beloved in his right hand while her left hand touches his head-dress.

40. LOVE SCENE. (HUCHCHIPANA MATH, MYSORE). 8TH CENTURY.

The male standing to the right wears, besides jewellery, a sacred thread. His left hand holds the plaited braid of his beloved's hair and his right hand supports her raised leg. She in turn is gripping his head with both hands. An attendant is in the foreground.

41. MITHUNA COUPLE. (HUCHCHIPANA MATH, MYSORE). 8TH CENTURY.

The couple, bejewelled and wearing only loin-cloths, stand in a decorous mood, gently caressing each other. Their heavy faces are lit with broad smiles.

42. MITHUNA FIGURES. A PART OF THE DOOR FRAME (DEOGARH, U.P.) EARLY 6TH CENTURY.

In the top, bottom and middle panels frolicsome dwarfs are depicted. In the second panel the *nayika* in a dejected mood is being flattered by her lover. In the fourth panel the couple is shown in lively conversation.

43. GENERAL VIEW. LINGARAJA TEMPLE (BHUBANESHWAR). *c.* A.D. 1000.

The Lingaraja or Great Temple occupies the centre of a quadrangular enclosure, 520 feet by 405 feet. The most impressive feature is the great tower of the Sri Mandir. The outer walls are covered with a profusion of figure compositions of an absorbing nature, *mithuna* figures being greatly in evidence.

44. RELIGIOUS ORGY. PERHAPS FROM THE MUKTESVARA TEMPLE (BHUBANESHWAR). *c.* A.D. 950.

The scene represents the ritualistic orgy of the Kaula-Kapalikas. Starting from the left a Kapalika embracing the Kapalavanita; sexual congress; Kapalika tilting the chin of a woman; coitus invertus. The entire composition represents *Bhairavichakra* or unbridled sexual orgy, an act of faith with the Kapalikas.

45. SHIVA-PARVATI. PARASHURAMESHWAR TEMPLE (BHUBANESHWAR). *c.* A.D. 750.

Shiva is seated in *maharajalilasana* with a lotus of dalliance in his right hand, holding Parvati tightly in embrace. His erect phallus indicates his *Lakulisa* form. The bull and the lion, respective vehicles of Shiva and Parvati, are in the foreground; a shy female attendant is to the right.

46. MITHUNA. RAJA RANI TEMPLE (BHUBANESHWAR). *c.* A.D. 1150.

The couple is associated with a tree. The lover with a meaningful smile is untying the knot of the *sari* of his beloved who is responding to his movements in perfect accord. Untying the *sari* knot of the beloved is a common motif in Sanskrit poetry.

47. DISCREET LOVE. LINGARAJA TEMPLE (BHUBANESHWAR). *c.* A.D. 1000.

The lover, wearing elaborate ornaments, with a gentle smile on his face has drawn his beloved towards him. Her shy response is indicated by a smile revealing confidence in her lover. The theme may represent a motif in *Nayikabheda* in which the heroine receives her husband returning after a long sojourn in a distant land.

48. AMOROUS COUPLE. RAJA RANI TEMPLE (BHUBANESHWAR). *c.* A.D. 1150.

The female partner has stepped forward to meet her lover, whose left hand is round her shoulders while with his right hand he unties her *sari* knot. She is coyly dissuading him. The soft modelling and graceful smiles of the figures stand in contrast to the grim emotional intensity of most Khajuraho *mithunas*.

49. AMOROUS COUPLE. RAJA RANI TEMPLE (BHUBANESHWAR). *c.* A.D. 1150.

This seems to be a representation of *Mugdha Nayika*. The hero clad in a simple *dhoti* is embracing his beloved who is offering a feeble resistance. Note their meaningful smiles and the graceful plasticity of the sculpture.

50. SEXUAL UNION. RAJA RANI TEMPLE (BHUBANESHWAR). *c.* A.D. 1150.

The bearded male is kissing his female partner whom he has stepped forward to embrace. Note the graceful modelling of the figures, almost lyrical in its undulations.

51. MITHUNA. BRAHMESHWAR TEMPLE (BHUBANESHWAR). 10TH CENTURY.

The woman wearing the minimum of dress and ornaments stands smiling and embracing her male partner. Not a shred of clothing or ornament decorate his person. Possibly he is a Kaula teacher whose cult encouraged sexual union as one of the means of emancipation.

52. AMOROUS COUPLE. (PURI). 17TH CENTURY (INDIAN MUSEUM, CALCUTTA).

The couple fondling each other stand under a tree, the right hand of the woman holding a branch. The smiling faces and wide open eyes of the couple add charm to the composition. The *tilak* on the forehead and the shaved pate of the male indicate that he is a votary of Jagannatha enjoying the company of one of the temple dancing-girls.

53. GENERAL VIEW OF THE JAGAMOHANA. SURYA TEMPLE (KONARAK, ORISSA). 13TH CENTURY.

The Sun (Surya) Temple of Konarak, known as the Black Pagoda to the European navigators of the 17th century, is a mightily conceived example of Orissan temple architecture almost in its last phase. A distinguishing feature of the sculptured reliefs of Konarak is their frank eroticism in which the artists do not hesitate to represent even erotic postures (*bandhas*) impossible to execute in life.

119

54. THE CHARIOT WHEEL. SURYA TEMPLE (KONARAK, ORISSA). 13TH CENTURY.

The mighty temple at Konarak was conceived in the form of the Chariot of the Sun. The hub, the spokes and the rim of each wheel are richly carved with animal and floral designs and the figures of Hindu gods and goddesses.

55. LOVE-MAKING. SURYA TEMPLE (KONARAK, ORISSA). 13TH CENTURY.

The male, affecting rich ornaments and a bun-shaped hair style, is holding his female partner in a close embrace. Note the tautness in modelling expressive of the force of sexual desire. With his left hand the man tilts the face of his partner while she lovingly enfolds him.

56. MITHUNA PAIR. SURYA TEMPLE (KONARAK, ORISSA). 13TH CENTURY.

The pair is shown standing under a tree on a lotus pedestal. The male, who sports a moustache and a conical cap fringed with beads, is kissing his female partner, who clings round his neck. Her feet are being supported on his palms.

57. EROTIC SCENE. SURYA TEMPLE (KONARAK, ORISSA). 13TH CENTURY.

The male partner stands against a stylised tree with his left leg bent inward. He has an angular face. His buxom female partner grasps his neck with both hands and lifts her right leg up to his waist.

58. MITHUNA COUPLE. SURYA TEMPLE (KONARAK, ORISSA). 13TH CENTURY.

The male figure stands to the right facing his partner. Note the conical cap fringed with beads and *patra-kundala*. His heavy face is lit up with a smile and his left hand is playing with the breasts of his partner, whose right hand is toying with his genitals.

59. EROTIC SCENES. SURYA TEMPLE (KONARAK, ORISSA). 13TH CENTURY.

The four erotic reliefs on the base mouldings represent different stages in love-making. Significantly, all four *mithunas* are associated with trees, reminiscent of the ancient Woman and Tree motif which had a close connection with fertility cults. From the artistic viewpoint, the reliefs lack the dynamic sex-urge, and their lack of movement shows that they were intended mainly to illustrate the sexual postures enjoined by mediaeval works on the erotic art.

60. CLOSE-UP OF A FEMALE MUSICIAN. SURYA TEMPLE (KONARAK, ORISSA). 13TH CENTURY.

In the general estimation of art historians, the fame of Konarak rests mainly on its erotic sculptures. To accept this view implicitly however would be doing an injustice to the builders of Konarak who were very much alive to the physical beauty of the human figure. The female musicians represented at Konarak combine all the physical graces enjoined by Sanskrit literature yet hardly evoke carnal desire.

120

61. JAIN TEMPLE (KHAJURAHO).

The Shikhara and the upper part of the façade are here shown. The latter is covered with sculptural panels, some depicting *mithuna* figures.

62. DETAILS OF SCULPTURES ON NORTH FACADE. KANDARIYA MAHADEVA TEMPLE (KHAJURAHO). 11TH CENTURY A.D.

The façade is literally covered with the figures of gods and goddesses, women at toilet, and erotic scenes depicting women astride their male partners supported by male and female attendants.

63. DETAILS OF SCULPTURES ON THE SOUTH FACADE. KANDARIYA MAHADEVA TEMPLE (KHAJURAHO). 11TH CENTURY.

The south façade of the temple is covered with the figures of gods and goddesses, women at toilet and erotic scenes—a man fondling a woman helped by an attendant; a woman astride her male partner; and a man standing on his head with a woman astride him supported by two women.

64. EROTIC SCENE. VISVANATHA TEMPLE (KHAJURAHO). 11TH CENTURY.

An acrobatic sexual posture in which three women and a man are participating. A large number of such postures have been described in the Kama Sutra and similar texts, but it is doubtful whether they were ever practised.

65. RITUALISTIC ORGY. MATANGESWARA-LAKSHMANA TEMPLE TERRACE (KHAJURAHO). 10TH CENTURY.

In the liturgy of the Kaula-Kapalikas wine and women were supposed to act as a means of liberation, and this resulted in grossest kind of sexual excesses in the name of religion and yoga. The scene represents *Bhairavichakra* in which all decencies are thrown to the wind. The unadorned persons of the male participants, their hairdressing and beards and the ritualistic objects they carry leave little doubt of their identification. The scenes represented are, from left to right: exotic love-play; *amrachushaka* or *fellatio;* the 'mare-and-horse' posture and bottom *kakali* posture.

66. MITHUNA FIGURE. DEVI JAGADAMBA TEMPLE (KHAJURAHO). 11TH CENTURY.

The couple is engaged in a very close embrace with their animated faces in close proximity. In order to emphasize their firm and lithesome limbs, the clothes and ornaments have been reduced to a minimum by the sculptor.

67. MITHUNA. DEVI JAGADAMBA TEMPLE (KHAJURAHO). 11TH CENTURY.

In a close sexual embrace the female partner grips the top knot of her lover, the act being reciprocated by him. The rhythmic flow of their bodies and the movement of the hands are emphasized, while the minimum of clothing and ornaments shows the firm flesh of their bodies.

121

68. MITHUNA. (KHAJURAHO). 12TH CENTURY.

The dresses and ornaments of the couple except for elaborate head-crowns are reduced to the minimum, the main emphasis being on the preliminaries of love-making. The proximity of their faces, their bodies in delicate embrace, the female partner in the act of disrobing her lover, are expressive of a deep and understanding love.

69. DANCERS. LAKSHMANA TEMPLE (KHAJURAHO). 10TH CENTURY.

The ecstatic dance in which men and women equally took part was a distinguishing feature of the Kaula ritual. The male partner, his face calm and ecstatic and his legs crossed, is playing castanets while his smiling female partner is playing the cymbals.

70. MITHUNA. (KHAJURAHO). 11TH CENTURY.

The intricate hair-dresses and details of simple costumes and ornaments are effectively represented. The outstanding point of the sculpture is the tension of passion resulting in taut muscles, firmly closed lips and half-closed rolling eyes.

71. DANCE POSE. PARSVANATHA TEMPLE (KHAJURAHO). 11TH CENTURY.

A moment of gay abandon in the dance is caught and rendered with subtlety. The right hand delicately poised over the head, the left hand holding the necklace, the crossed legs, the flowing *dupatta*, and, above all, the face absorbed in the rhythmic movement of the dance, express the technical achievements of the sculptor.

72. LOVERS. (KHAJURAHO). 11TH CENTURY.

The effect of frank sensuality of the couple is toned down by the heaviness of modelling and rather awkward hand postures.

73. AN AMOROUS COUPLE. VISHVANATHA TEMPLE (KHAJURAHO). 11TH CENTURY.

The ancient Indian erotic texts advise love-play to be accompanied by music as depicted here in the form of the flautist.

74. STANDING LOVERS. PARSVANATHA TEMPLE (KHAJURAHO). 11TH CENTURY.

A mild form of *mithuna*, but the expression on the faces of the couples speaks eloquently of growing love.

75. DALLIANCE. KEDARESVARA TEMPLE (HALEBID). 13TH CENTURY.

Within a pillared and fringed room furnished with a bed, the couple is shown in the act of love-making. Similar scenes are found in the contemporary Orissan temple sculpture.

76. LOVE-SCENES. PRASANNA CHANNA KESAVA TEMPLE (SOMNATHPURA, MYSORE). HOYSALA, A.D. 1270.

These scenes appear as a part of a frieze surrounding the outer base of the temple. On the left is a bed provided with mattress and a pillow on which the male is making love in a reclining posture with his partner. On the right the female is clinging to her male partner. Her right arm is round her lover's neck while the left hand is pulling his hair-lock.

77. LOVE-MAKING. PRASANNA CHANNA KESAVA TEMPLE (SOMNATHPURA, MYSORE). HOYSALA, A.D. 1270.

This love-scene occurs on a frieze round the base of the temple. On the left a couple stand quite decorously; on the right is depicted a chamber provided with decorative hangings and a bed. The couple are engaged in love-making in a way described in the Kama Sutra as the *Kakali* posture.

78. SHIVA-PARVATI. KALYANA MANDAPAM (VELLORE). VIJAYANAGAR STYLE. 16TH CENTURY.

The four-handed standing Shiva is profusely ornamented. His natural right hand cups the chin of Parvati and his left hand goes around her shoulders. She stands in a rigid posture reminiscent of contemporary bronzes.

79. MITHUNA. KALYANA MANDAPAM (VELLORE). VIJAYANAGAR STYLE. 16TH CENTURY.

The male, wearing a tall head-dress and an embroidered garment, has raised his right hand while his left passes round his female partner, who clings closely to him. The composition shows that even in the latter days of Indian classical sculpture, a lyrical feeling, reminiscent of earlier works, persisted.

80. EROTIC SCENE. VARADARAJA PERUMAL TEMPLE (KANCHIPURAM). 16TH CENTURY.

In the Vedanta-desika shrine appears on a pillar an almost life-size bas-relief of Parvati holding a parrot and worshipped by three Saivite devotees with erect organs. On a pedestal a Pasupata devotee blowing a horn, an important musical instrument in Saivite rites, enjoys his acrobatic partner.

81. COITUS INVERTUS. RANGANATHASWAMI TEMPLE (SRIRANGAM). 17TH CENTURY.

This temple is one of the holiest shrines of Vishnu in India. The appearance of erotic scenes on the drum of one of the pillars in the celebrated Horse Court proves that erotic sculptures were not confined to Saivite temples only. To the left is shown a woman performing acrobatics with a couple below engaged in love-making; on the right, within an arched room, another couple is engaged in coitus invertus.

82. AMOROUS COUPLE. VARADARAJA PERUMAL TEMPLE (KANCHIPURAM). 16TH CENTURY.

This scene occurs in the Kalyana Mandapam of the temple. The male, his head quite out of proportion to his body, affects an elaborate hair style and sports a Vaishnavite *tilaka* on his forehead. His hands are caressing his female partner, who stands on her toes to meet the embrace of her lover, whose cheeks she holds with her hands.

83, 84. EROTIC SCENES ON THE BASES OF ROOF STRUTS. SHIVA TEMPLE (KATHMANDU). 19TH CENTURY.

Erotic scenes, both in wood and metal, are common in Brahmanic and Mantrayana Buddhist sculptures in Nepal. Such erotica, however, are not of great artistic merit, though they show the continuity of an ancient tradition. The postures represented here are coitus (left) and 'horse and mare' motif (right).

85, 86. EROTICA ON THE BASES OF ROOF STRUTS. SHIVA TEMPLE (KATHMANDU). 19TH CENTURY.

The left-hand pair imitate a horse and a mare, while in the right-hand scene a lusty porter with a child in his head-slung basket, dallies with a woman who still has an infant at her breast.

87, 88. EROTICA ON THE BASES OF ROOF STRUTS. SHIVA TEMPLE (KATHMANDU). 19TH CENTURY.

The scene on the left represents lesbian love and the one on the right coitus invertus.

89, 90. EROTICA ON THE BASES OF ROOF STRUTS. SHIVA TEMPLE (KATHMANDU). 19TH CENTURY.

The scene on the left depicts sexual aberration and that on the right represents an amorous couple at play.

91, 92. EROTICA ON THE BASES OF ROOF STRUTS. SHIVA TEMPLE (KATHMANDU). 19TH CENTURY.

A bedroom scene, with an attendant, appears on the left while that on the right represents coitus invertus.

93, 94. EROTICA ON THE BASES OF ROOF STRUTS. SHIVA TEMPLE (KATHMANDU).

On the left coitus invertus; on the right, a 'mare-and-horse' posture sanctioned in *ars amoris*.

95. PUBLIC SHELTER. CHITLONG (CENTRAL NEPAL). 18TH CENTURY. (?)

Miniature carvings depicting *mithunas* can be seen above the wooden pillars.

96. BARRACKS. DHANKUTA (EASTERN NEPAL). 19TH CENTURY. (?)

A terra-cotta *mithuna* is built into the brick walls enclosing this ramshackle barracks outside a Nepalese provincial capital.

GLOSSARY

Adi-Buddha:	The primal Buddha, identical with the Supreme Being of Hinduism.
Amrachushaka:	A sexual posture known to the West as *fellatio*.
Aphrodite:	Greek Goddess of Love and Beauty, counterpart of the Roman Venus.
Apsaras:	A heavenly nymph, a courtesan of Indra's heaven.
Ardhanari:	The androgynous, or half-female, form of Shiva, personifying the bi-sexual conception of God.
Arghya:	Yoni (q.v.).
Atman:	The soul, or self.
Attis:	The lover of Agdistis, Phrygian Mother of the Gods. Sometimes identified with Adonis, Pan and Sabazius.
Aum:	The mystic mono-syllable symbolising the Oneness of God.
Bacchanale:	Festival of Bacchus, the Roman God of Wine.
Bandha:	A posture of the body, sometimes of an erotic nature.
Bhagavadgita:	The Song Celestial. A poem of 700 verses found in the Mahabharata containing the cream of Hindu philosophy.
Bhairava:	The fearsome aspect of Shiva, also known as Khandehrao.
Bhairavichakra:	A sexual orgy in Sakti-worship.
Bhakti:	The cult of devotion to a deity.
Bharata Natya-sastra:	The most important text on Indian dancing.
Brahma:	The Creator, the first manifestation of the Absolute in Hindu philosophy. First person of the Hindu trinity.
Channavira:	The harness of crossed scarves worn by fertility goddesses.
Chauri:	Fly-whisk symbol of royalty.
Corybantes:	The male companions of Cybele (q.v.).
Cybele:	Great Mother of the Gods of the Greeks.
Devas:	The thirty-three Vedic deities.
Durga:	Shiva's consort in mother-goddess form.
Galli:	The priests of Cybele (q.v.).
Gopuram:	Monumental gateway of an Indian temple.
Goshthi:	The Indian equivalent of a Bacchanale (q.v.), a drunken revel.
Hevajra:	The Yi-Dam Samvara (q.v.).
Isis:	Sister-wife of the ancient Egyptian god Osiris, and mother of Horus.
Jagannatha:	A form of Vishnu (q.v.), as Lord of the Universe.
Kakali:	A sexual posture, a form of reciprocal *fellatio*.
Kali:	'The Black', a terrible form of Shiva's consort.
Kama:	Hindu God of Love and the pursuit of pleasure.
Kama Sutra:	The earliest and most authoritative work on the art of love, written by Vatsyayana, probably in the Gupta era.
Kapalavanita:	A Tantric 'consort'.
Kapalikas:	An extreme Tantric cult.

125

Karma:	The idea of retribution in the life cycle.
Kaulas:	A Tantric cult.
Krishna:	A reincarnation of Vishnu.
Kundi:	The *lingam* and *yoni* represented together.
Lakshmi:	The consort of Vishnu, Goddess of Fortune, Beauty and Happiness.
Lakulisa:	Shiva in a rampant aspect.
Lalitasana:	A Yogic posture.
Latabandha:	An erotic posture simulating the embrace of a creeper and a tree.
Lesbianism:	Female homosexuality.
Lingam:	The phallic emblem of Shiva.
Lila:	The supernatural world.
Maharajalilasana:	A Yogic posture.
Makara:	A crocodile-shaped creature, emblem of water and fertility. Also used to describe the five elements of Panchatatva (q.v.).
Manini Nayika:	A " courting " phase of love-making.
Mantrayana:	Incantational symbolism.
Mithuna:	Sexual union. An erotically inclined couple.
Moksha:	Union with the divine. Release from worldly existence.
Mugdha Nayika:	A flirtatious pose.
Mysteries:	Rites secret from all save the initiated.
Nagraja:	King of the serpents or water-spirits.
Nandi:	Shiva's bull charger and chief of the *ganas* (demi-gods).
Nayika:	An emotional state.
Nayikabheda:	Romantic emotion.
Omophagia:	The eating of raw flesh.
Oratorians:	A Christian religious order consisting of a number of independent houses first organised in 1575 by a Florentine priest, Philip Neri.
Panchatatva:	The five *makaras*, or elements of fundamental principles: *Madya* (liquor), *Mansa* (meat), *Matsya* (fish), *Mudra* (corn), *Mithuna* (intercourse).
Parvati:	The consort of Shiva, daughter of the Himalayas.
Pasupatas:	The sect of the uninitiated.
Phallus:	The male organ of generation.
Priapus:	A Greek god of fertility.
Puranas:	The 18 sacred books of Hindu mythology and epic, including the Ramayana and the Mahabharata.
Purusa:	The male cosmic principle.
Rudra-Shiva:	The god of the Vedas from whom Shiva was derived.
Sabazius:	A Phrygian or Thracian deity frequently identified with Dionysus and sometimes Zeus.
Saktas:	Those Hindus who consider the godhead to be essentially feminine.
Sakti:	The consort or female energy of a deity. The active power of a god as his feminine complement. The creative force in its female aspect.
Shiva:	The Destroyer and Reproducer, third person of the Hindu trinity.
Shivalinga:	Shiva in his phallic form, the *lingam* (q.v.).
Surya:	The sun god of the Vedic pantheon.

126

Tandava:	Shiva's dance in the cemeteries and burning-grounds, symbolic of his cosmic function of creation and destruction.
Tantra:	The 22 volumes of mystic treatises of the Tantra system, which, with its emphasis on *sakti* (q.v.) worship first influenced Buddhism in N. India towards the end of the 6th Century A.D., later also influencing Hinduism.
Trimurti:	The triad or trinity of Hinduism: Brahma, Vishnu and Shiva, symbolised by a three-faced figure.
Uma:	A name of the consort of Shiva in her mild form.
Upanishads:	The mystical doctrines attached to the Vedas (q.v.).
Vedas:	The four books containing the sacred knowledge for the peformance of Brahmanic priestly ritual. The most famous is the Rig Veda, composed in the 1st Millenium B.C.
Vimana:	Towered sanctuary of a temple containing the cell in which the deity is enshrined.
Vishnu:	The Preserver, and Second Person of the Hindu Trinity.
Yaksha:	One of a class of supernatural beings perhaps originally associated only with fertility cults and later assimilated into the orthodox religions.
Yakshi:	A female *Yaksha* (q.v.).
Yantra:	A mystic diagram of the Sakti cult sometimes worn in the form of a charm, or drawn, painted or carved in association with mystic letters.
Yi-Dam Samvara:	The twelve-armed, four-headed Nepalese manifestation of the oneness of the Godhead.
Yi-Dam Sang-Dui:	The Tibetan equivalent of the Yi-Dam Samvara (q.v.).
Yoga:	Communion with the Universal Spirit by the practice of ecstatic meditation. Introduced into Hinduism by Patanjali in the 2nd Century B.C.
Yoni:	The female sexual organ.

BIBLIOGRAPHY

(Acknowledgment is here made to the authors and publishers of the works marked with an asterisk, from which quotations have been made, and separately acknowledged, in the text of this book.)

ANAND, Mulk Raj: *Kama Kala*, Nagel Publishers, Geneva, 1958.   *

BROWN, Percy: *Indian Architecture*. Taraporevala, Bombay.

CODRINGTON, K. de B.: *The Art of India and Pakistan* (Essay on Sculpture), Faber and Faber, London, 1950.

COOMARASWAMY, A. K.: *Arts and Crafts of India & Ceylon*, London, 1919. *

DANIELOU, Alain: *An Approach to Hindu Erotic Sculpture*, Marg Magazine, Bombay, 1949.

ELMORE, W. T.: *Dravidian Gods in Modern Hinduism*, 1915.

FOUCHET, Max-Pol: *The Erotic Sculpture of India*, Allen & Unwin, London, *
    1959.

GICHNER, Lawrence E.: *Erotic Aspects of Hindu Sculpture*, 1949.   *

GRAVES, Robert: *The Greek Myths*, Penguin Books, 1959.   *

HAVELL, E. B.: *The Ancient & Medieval Architecture of India*, 1915.   *
              : *Ideals of Indian Art*, London, 1911.   *

IRWIN, John: *Indian Art* (Essay on Sculpture), Faber & Faber, London,   *
    1947.

KRAMRISCH, Stella: *The Hindu Temple*, Calcutta, 1946.

LANDON, Perceval: *Nepal*, London, Constable, 1928.   *

LEVI, Sylvain: *Le Nepal*, Paris, 1905-08.

MOOR, Captain Edward: *A Narrative of the Operation of Captain Little's   *
    Detachment*, 1794.

NEHRU, Jawaharlal: *The Discovery of India*, Meridian Books, London,   *
    1956.

ROWLAND, Benjamin: *The Art and Architecture of India*, Penguin Books,   *
    1953.

SELTMAN, Charles: *The Twelve Olympians*, Pan Books, 1952.

TAPP, Sidney C.: *The Sexology of the Bible*.   *

THOMAS, P.: *Kama Kalpa*, Taraporevala, Bombay, 1959.   *

WARD, F. de W.: *India and the Hindoos*, 1850.   *

YEATS BROWN, F.: *Bengal Lancer*, London, 1930.   *

ZIMMER: *Philosophies of India*, New York, 1951.   *

INDEX

(Figures shown in italics refer to notes to the plates.)

131

132

ACKNOWLEDGEMENTS

Following list shows sources from which photographs were gathered.

PLATES 3, 6, 7, 8, 9, 10, 11, 15, 16, 19, 21, 22, 30, 31, 33, 40, 41, 42, 46, 47, 48, 49, 50, 51, 52, 53, 55, 56, 57, 58, 60, 62, 63, 64, 65, 66, 67, 73, 74, 75 } Copyright reserved by Department of Archaeology, Government of India.

2, 12, 14, 34, 35, 36, 76, 77, 80-96 ... F. Leeson

1, 61, 72 ... Darshan Lall

13, 32 ... O. P. Sehgal

17, 54 ... Raj Bedi (Fotoflash)

20, 23, 24, 25, 26, 27, 29, 69, 71 ... Shama Kilanjar

28 ... Amiya Banerji

37, 38, 39 ... A. L. Syed

44, 45 ... C. J. Bhatt

59 ... R. J. Chinwalla

68, 70 ... Moti Ram Jain

78, 79 ... E. S. Mahalingam

CONTENTS

121

Ernesto Galarza

124

Severo Ochoa

127

José Limón

130

Luis Álvarez

134

The Braceros and the Mojados

139

The American G.I. Forum

142

Desi Arnaz

145

Antonia Pantoja

148

Tito Puente

151

Celia Cruz

154

César Chávez

159

Lauro Fred Cavazos

161

Ruben Salazar

165

Pancho Gonzales

169

Rolando Hinojosa-Smith

172

Jaime Escalante

175

Marisol

178

Roberto Goizueta

★ PREFACE

Hispanic Americans have played a vital role in the history and development of the United States. Their influence is felt throughout the American culture. The purpose of this collection of biographies is to provide a broad view of that influence and to look at Hispanic people who have made their mark in the social, political, and scientific life of the United States.

But what exactly do we mean by the word *Hispanic*? And why use this term, as opposed to Spanish American or Latino or any of the possible subdivisions such as Cuban American or Mexican American? To me, Hispanic is the most encompassing term of all. The way I understand the term, a Hispanic person is one with a Hispanic culture—a culture derived from the countries and regions that were once part of the vast Spanish colonial empire.

Due to the historical circumstances that led to the formation and development of the Spanish colonial empire, we can find all kinds of races and their combinations within the definition of Hispanic. A Hispanic can be white, black, Native American (related to the peoples that inhabited North and South America prior to the Spanish conquest), Asian, and so on. The Spanish people who conquered the American continents were mostly from southern Spain, which had been ruled by Muslims for about eight hundred years. These people proceeded to mix with the native people; then the African diaspora played a part in the creation of the American plantation system and the use of slaves. Later on, with the abolition of slavery, indebted laborers were imported from Asia, mostly from China. Other migratory movements have further contributed to this huge

Crowds at the Puerto Rican Day Parade in New York City

Hispanic diversity, including the migration of Japanese to Peru. Under this enormous palette of skin color lies one of the most varied and encompassing cultures of all.

When the Hispanic culture comes in contact with the U.S. culture, it does exactly what it has been doing for many centuries. First, it assimilates the culture, meaning it understands and comprehends it. Then it transforms the culture, meaning it makes changes to it. Finally, it makes the culture its own through a renewal process. There are multiple examples of this phenomenon in action, but if we just look at the music industry, we can see clear-cut examples of such a process. One of them would be the use of the Spanish language in many pop songs—ranging from Ricky Martin's "Livin' la Vida Loca" to a variety of songs by Jennifer Lopez. Hispanic artists have assimilated, transformed, and renewed their own music with the influence of pop music.

Language is another identifying feature of the Hispanic culture. For Hispanics, their culture and the Spanish language are very much connected. The language is a sort of glue that connects all the cultural diversity and gives it common ground.

There has been a Hispanic presence in the United States since before its creation as a republic. Portions of California, Oregon, Louisiana, Mississippi, Texas, Florida, and southern Alabama were a part of the Spanish colonial empire before their annexation by the United States. This means that these regions were influenced by the Hispanic culture before the United States came into being. Additionally, there have been a variety of migratory waves from Spanish-speaking countries to the United States for a variety of reasons. Some Hispanics came to the United States because of economic hardship; others were escaping dictatorships in their homeland. Regardless of when they came, why they came, or how they came, they brought along their culture, which had been tested through the years, ever since the first conquistador set foot in the New World.

The Hispanic culture in the United States today is a product of many years of renewing itself and adopting new, compatible forms. Hispanic Americans are growing, celebrating their heritage, and becoming part of a melting pot, or, rather, a soup, and enriching its flavor forever—in spite of many obstacles.

Hispanic Americans have long been plagued by negative stereotypes. These stereotypes hinder the cultural prestige of the Hispanic people. Some of our best actors are Hispanic, some of our best musicians are Hispanic, some of our best composers are Hispanic, some of our best minds (creative or analytic) are Hispanic—and yet many struggle for the recognition they deserve. The aim of this book is to highlight extraordinary Hispanic Americans, people who have excelled in their respective fields. Due to editorial constraints, we are not able to include a complete, exhaustive list but, rather, a sample, which provides a view of the Hispanic culture that differs from the stereotypes—a view of a Hispanic culture that is growing, transforming, and renewing itself, even as we read.

EXPLORING THE NEW WORLD

11

★ THE CONQUISTADORS

Christopher Columbus's voyage of 1492, and three more he made afterward, gave Spain new lands that became the heart of a vast overseas empire. This growth was of special interest to Spain's soldiers. Many were knights from Castile, a major region of Spain with a tradition of warfare. These deeply religious and patriotic men wanted to extend Spain's power among the native people of the Americas, win converts to their Catholic faith, and seek riches for themselves. These Spanish soldiers were soon known as conquistadors, meaning "conquerors."

The conquistadors were well trained, well armed, and notorious for their brutality. Soon after Columbus's voyages, the conquistadors began raising armies and sailing for the New World. They seemed fearless as they marched into unknown jungles, mountains, and prairies. In their own eyes, they were doing vitally important work. But to the people they fought, they were unwanted invaders and enslavers. The Spanish called these native tribes Indians, thinking Columbus had sailed to the East Indies.

On their missions for Spain, the conquistadors faced intense tropical heat and bitter mountain cold, as well as peoples desperate to protect their homeland. Yet the Spanish troops overran the local populations with dizzying speed, and in fifty years they had taken much of South and Central America. Some of the modern nations in this region include Cuba, the Dominican Republic, Panama, Venezuela, Honduras, Peru, Colombia, Ecuador, Paraguay, and Chile.

Spanish conquistador Hernán Cortés

What drove the conquistadors? Serving their king and the Catholic Church was truly important to some. Others merely longed for adventure and were unfazed by the risks and dangers. Still others faced legal problems at home and saw the conquest of new lands as one way to escape. All hoped to find the wealth and power they knew they could never have in Spain, where a small number of elites controlled all parts of society.

Many conquistadors were also lured by the exotic nature of lands that Europeans had never seen before. In the jungles were colorful birds that the natives could teach to talk; crickets that chirped through the night; and handsome people covered with gold jewelry. Because they could see such wonders up close, some conquistadors also believed in mythical lands that existed only in dreams and fantasies. A fountain of youth or cities filled with gold did not seem impossible in the wondrous New World.

As the conquistadors poured into the Americas in the years after Columbus's voyages, the successes of a few became well known. Hernán Cortés and Francisco Pizarro, to name two of them, had taken Mexico and Peru, respectively. They returned to Spain wealthy and powerful men.

These early successes, however, were hard to repeat. The swift and total victory that the Spaniards enjoyed in South and Central America did not come as easily once the soldiers moved farther north. In Mexico and Peru, the native people had fought bravely, but they were slaughtered by soldiers who wore metal armor, fought with steel weapons, and rode horses—animals that had become extinct in the New World thousands of years before.

North of Mexico, however, the native people were not as easily defeated. The Spaniards' heavy armor and weapons weighed them down. As soldiers stopped to take aim, skilled Indian archers dashed from tree to tree. These hit-and-run attacks slowed the conquistadors' advances, though they still inflicted horrible damage in parts of what is now the southern United States. Still, Spanish officials did not think that fighting the tribes there was worth the effort, since the region did not have the great natural resources of Mexico or Peru.

JUAN PONCE DE LEÓN

EXPLORER

1460?–1521

Juan Ponce de León came from a poor, noble family. Seeking fame and fortune, the restless soldier volunteered to accompany the great explorer Christopher Columbus on his second voyage to the New World. By the time he died in 1521, Ponce de León had made his own historic discoveries, becoming the first European to land in what is now Florida. Stories of his life also include tales of a mythical fountain of youth, which supposedly inspired his explorations.

On his trip with Columbus in 1493, Ponce de León landed on the islands of Boriquen (Puerto Rico) and Hispaniola before returning to Spain. Within a decade, he set out again for

Painting depicting Pónce de Leon in Florida in 1513

Hispaniola, where he served briefly as a local official and amassed a great fortune as the island became a source of sugarcane for European markets. In 1508, Ponce de León led his own expedition, sailing east from Hispaniola to Puerto Rico. Stories of gold may have lured him to the island, where he founded the first Spanish settlement at Caparra, near present-day San Juan.

In 1508, the Spanish Crown named Ponce de León governor of Puerto Rico. He was considered an able ruler, though he was known for his cruelty to the Taíno Indians, who lived on the island. Ponce de León enslaved them, and it was said he grew rich on "the labors, blood and sufferings of his subjects." Three years later, the king of Spain replaced Ponce de León as governor with Diego Columbus, the oldest son of Christopher Columbus. A disappointed Ponce de

León then asked the king to let him explore and settle new lands to the north of Cuba. The king agreed, and in 1513 Ponce de León left on his journey.

At the time, tales swirled around the region about a spring with magical waters. Drinking from the spring, it was said, would keep a person young forever. There is no proof that Ponce de León set out to find this "fountain of youth." Still, the stories about it may have influenced the route he took. And the gold he thought he would find was enough reason to set off in unknown waters.

For his expedition, Ponce de León commanded three small ships. Sailing in March, they soon passed the Bahamas and spotted the mainland of Florida on Easter Sunday. A week later, on April 3, 1513, they came ashore near present-day Cape Canaveral. The strange new land was flat and full of groves, and the sailors breathed in the sweet scent of the abundant flowers. Ponce de León thought it right to name this new land *Florida*, Spanish for "full of flowers," both to honor its flowery aroma and for the Spanish Feast of Flowers associated with Easter.

The explorers next headed south along the shore, passed through the Florida Keys, and then sailed northward along the west coast of Florida. They reached perhaps as far north as Pensacola Bay. At various stops, Ponce de León met up with native tribes, especially the Calusa. The Indians and Spaniards fought several battles before the Calusa, filling eighty war canoes, finally drove off the fleet.

Back in Spain, Ponce de León was greeted as a hero because he had claimed new lands for the Spanish Crown. In 1521, he sailed again for Florida, hoping to establish a permanent colony. On this expedition, Ponce de León traveled with two hundred colonists. They landed on the west coast and built temporary shelters, but the local Calusa Indians saw them as unwanted invaders. In a battle with the tribe, Ponce de León was hit in the leg with a poison dart or arrow. His men took their wounded leader to Cuba for medical help, but Ponce de León died in Havana in July 1521.

HERNANDO DE SOTO
CONQUISTADOR
1500?–1542

Working with several great explorers and conquistadors, Hernando de Soto learned the ways of conquest and plunder. Tales of the great riches waiting in North America led de Soto to head his own expedition. The conquistador did not find the riches he sought, but he and his men took part in a number of historic firsts. Among these were being the first Europeans to cross the Appalachian Mountains and to see the Mississippi River.

As a young man, de Soto served with Vasco Nuñez de Balboa in Panama. Balboa explored present-day Colombia before embarking on a trek that made him the first European to see the Pacific Ocean. In Panama, de Soto worked for Balboa, capturing Indians and forcing them into slavery. In 1524, de Soto joined a military mission to conquer what is now Nicaragua. He became one of the most important residents of that new Spanish colony. As a soldier, he was famous for his riding skills and his bravery.

De Soto was not satisfied with his prominent position in Nicaragua, so he joined Francisco Pizarro for the conquest of Peru. South America, the Spanish had learned, was filled with riches, and the conquistadors loaded their ships with as much gold and jewels as they could find. In the process, they killed hundreds of Indians and destroyed many temples. When his service ended in Peru in 1536, de Soto returned to Spain a rich man.

De Soto soon heard the tale of the failed Narváez mission and Álvar Núñez Cabeza de Vaca. Although the mission had not founded a new colony, the story suggested that North America might hold great riches. De Soto decided he could gain new wealth and glory in lands bordering the Gulf of Mexico. He imagined that Florida could become a seat of power such as Peru or Mexico. When the ambitious conquistador told King Charles of his plans for the western gulf, he was granted the right to settle there.

The eager conquistador bought ten ships with his own money and chose the best crew he could find. He also asked Cabeza de Vaca to go as a guide, but he declined. Perhaps he was tired of expeditions to North America after the long years he had spent trudging through the Southwest. Or perhaps Cabeza de Vaca sensed that de Soto would run into trouble as he had made few plans for keeping his settlement alive. De Soto's main goal was riches, not building a colony.

De Soto's expedition left Spain in April 1538. After stopping in Cuba to take on supplies, the ships reached western Florida in May 1539, somewhere between modern-day Fort Meyers and Port Charlotte. De Soto came ashore with some 600 soldiers, 250 horses, pack animals, and fierce dogs specially trained to attack humans. The captain wasted no time applying the lessons he had learned in Panama and Peru. He enslaved the Indians and stole their food.

Cabeza de Vaca crossing North America from Texas to Mexico in the early 1500s

Some Timucuas Indians fought back, but the Spaniards kept marching inland, determined to find riches. Scouts relayed the message from captured Indians that an "abundance of gold, silver, and many pearls" lay ahead.

The expedition turned northwest, toward modern-day Tallahassee, Florida. The cruelty to the local Indians continued along the way, and some tribes became smarter in how they dealt with de Soto. They began to tell him what he wanted to hear, that great riches waited for him—far away from where he was. So the Spaniards headed north to what is now Augusta, Georgia. They then traveled west into the Blue Ridge Mountains and south again to Mobile Bay, marking the first European crossing of the Appalachians. De Soto and his men spent the winter of 1540–1541 in Chickasaw Indian territory, in what is now Mississippi.

In the spring, the Spaniards went north and then west. Just below the site of Memphis, Tennessee, they came upon the mighty waters of the Mississippi River. De Soto had his men build four barges, and in May 1541, about 250 men and 20 horses crossed the river. The next few months were spent moving slowly among the Indian villages in northern Arkansas. The expedition found good supplies of corn, beans, and dried fruits, but nothing that could be called a treasure.

By the end of the winter of 1542, de Soto decided to retreat to the Gulf of Mexico. Near the site of Natchez, Mississippi, a rare spring snowstorm stopped the party's progress. De Soto became very sick with a fever and died on May 21, 1542. His body was weighted with sand and dropped into the Mississippi River.

With a new commander in place, the expedition moved west hoping to reach New Spain (Mexico) by land. They crossed Louisiana and passed into Texas. After four months of traveling, they gave up this route and headed back toward the Mississippi. Now the commander decided to sail down the great river and reach New Spain by boat. The men built seven boats and set sail in July 1543. The sorry survivors of the de Soto expedition finally reached Mexico a few months later. They did not arrive on ships loaded with jewels and precious metals, as de Soto had hoped. Instead, they were starved and dressed in rags.

The de Soto expedition was a tragedy, for both the Spaniards and the Indians they treated so cruelly. But de Soto's men gave Europeans their first glimpse of the land and inhabitants of the southeastern portion of North America. And de Soto's experience shaped how future Spaniards would act when they came to North America. They would come with both weapons of war and the tools needed to found lasting colonies.

FRANCISCO VÁSQUEZ DE CORONADO

EXPLORER

1510–1554

As governor of New Galicia in the Spanish colony of New Spain (Mexico), Francisco Vásquez de Coronado had wealth and power. But he left his comfortable position to lead an expedition into unknown lands to the north. On his journey, he became the first European to explore large parts of what is now the southwestern United States, reaching as far north as Kansas.

In 1540, the viceroy of Mexico chose Coronado to lead an expedition into the "Northern Kingdom" beyond New Spain. The accounts of two earlier travelers, Álvar Núñez Cabeza de Vaca and Fray Marcos de Niza, had given Spain new hope that great riches lay in that region. De Niza had heard tales about the seven cities of Cíbola, fabled places filled with gold. And he himself had seen the Indians of the north with gold, turquoise, and fine leather goods. The Spanish assumed they would easily subdue the Indians with their well-armed forces, then help themselves to the riches of Cíbola.

For his journey, Coronado assembled a massive expedition, with about six hundred soldiers, both Spaniards and Indians, one thousand Indian and African slaves, and hundreds of mules and horses. Fray Marcos joined the expedition to serve as the guide. He led the group north from the Pacific coast

Coronado begins his expedition in 1540

town of Compostela, through what he'd earlier described as "green valleys [and] passable trails" and then "over the one small hill."

The expedition left Compostela on February 23, 1540, with a confident General Coronado in the lead. With his helmet and full suit of armor, he looked every inch the conquistador. Before long, however, the "green valleys and passable trails" became dangerously steep and rocky paths; the "one small hill" became the Sierra Madre Occidental, a towering mountain range. Several horses died of exhaustion as they carried men up and down the trails. As Coronado later wrote, the Spaniards "felt disturbed" that so much of what Fray Marcos had told them "should be found so very different." Spirits were low as the men turned east from the Gulf of California and headed for the border between Mexico and Arizona.

Soon Coronado sent a scouting party ahead to look for Cíbola. They returned with bad news: All they could spot was a simple village, not a city filled with gold. Still, Coronado kept moving, and in July he and his men reached the

Zuni Indian village of Hawikuh. (Today, the Zuni and other tribes of northern New Mexico and Arizona are called Pueblo Indians, a reference to the stone and adobe-mud villages they built in the mountains. *Pueblo* is the Spanish word for "village.") Since his men needed food, Coronado approached the pueblo.

Fearful of the Spaniards and their horses, the Zuni launched a hail of arrows. Coronado ordered an attack. The Spaniards and their Mexican Indian allies stormed the pueblo, firing guns and arrows. The Zuni fought back with arrows, and twice Coronado was knocked to the ground "by countless great stones which they threw down from above." Finally, Coronado's forces subdued the Zuni, and the general set up his headquarters within the village.

Hawikuh, Coronado soon learned, was one of seven small villages that together were called Cíbola. And not a single house in any of the villages had the gold or other riches Fray Marcos had described. Realizing this, Coronado sent Fray Marcos back to Mexico, where he was nicknamed "the lying monk."

From Cíbola, Coronado sent out scouting parties. They came back with reports of more cities to the north, which were the home of Hopi Indians. To the west were a great river, now called the Colorado, and an immense canyon. The scouts were the first Europeans to see the Grand Canyon. Scouts who traveled east from Cíbola saw another large river, the Rio Grande, lined with villages. The Indians there were friendly and generous, the scouts said, so Coronado decided to move his troops to the east for the winter, near the site of modern-day Albuquerque, New Mexico.

At the winter camp, Coronado spoke with a Pawnee Indian whom the Spanish nicknamed "the Turk." He was a slave for the local Indians and had originally lived to the north, on the Great Plains. Hoping the Spanish would help win his freedom, the Turk talked about the riches found in his homeland, which he called Quivira. He insisted that gold bells hung from trees, and their ringing lulled his tribe's leader to sleep. When spring came, Coronado headed for Quivira, with the Turk as his guide.

The expedition headed south and then east, reaching northwest Texas. The Spaniards were impressed by the wild bison they saw roaming the grassy plains. Coronado, however, began to think the Turk was lying about where he was taking them. Finally, the Turk admitted he was lying about how to reach Quivira, and Coronado had him killed. For the rest of 1541, Coronado and his men headed north and east, following directions they received from some local Indians. By this time, Coronado was traveling with a small party, having sent most of the men back to winter camp along the Rio Grande.

Coronado's quest took him into Kansas, where he met some Wichita Indians. They took him to a village that seemed to be the Quivira that the Turk had described. Once again, the general was disappointed to see only simple huts, not a city filled with gold. He decided to return to his winter camp and then head back to Mexico.

Just after Christmas that year, along the Rio Grande, Coronado and two of his officers were exercising their horses. They broke into a race, the story goes, and the general quickly took the lead. Suddenly, the cinch on his horse's saddle broke, and Coronado fell to the ground. One of the other horses then accidentally kicked him in the head.

After his fall, the general never recovered. His spirits were broken by both his injury and the failed expedition to the Northern Kingdom. "He is not the same man he was when your majesty appointed him to that governorship," wrote one official to Spain's King Philip II. Francisco Vásquez de Coronado lived out his days as an invalid and died in Mexico City on September 1554. Despite his own feelings about his expedition, Coronado and his men had made history, becoming the first Europeans to venture far into the interior of North America.

★ PEDRO MENÉNDEZ DE AVILÉS
NAVAL OFFICER, FOUNDER OF
ST. AUGUSTINE, FLORIDA
1519–1574

A military mission to Florida gave Captain Pedro Menéndez de Avilés the distinction in 1565 of founding the first permanent European settlement in North America. That settlement was St. Augustine, a military fort that he used as a base to thwart French attempts to build a colony in Florida. Menéndez then expanded the town and built missions before further exploring the region.

In the sixteenth century, Spain saw Florida as a key part of its vast overseas empire. Not only was it full of sweet-smelling, brilliantly colored flowers and trees, but its location was of vital strategic significance. All shipping from the West Indies, Peru, and New Spain (Mexico) had to enter the Straits of Florida from the west and sail to Cape Canaveral before riding the Gulf Stream east to Europe. Ever since Juan Ponce de León landed on the peninsula in 1513, the Spanish believed Florida was rightfully theirs. So when King Philip II learned in 1565 that a group of French Protestants, called Huguenots, were building a fort on the Atlantic coast, he was very concerned.

The king promptly chose Pedro Menéndez de Avilés to speed across the Atlantic to stop them—even though the captain was in prison at the time. He had been caught smuggling, but Philip decided that Menéndez's military skills outweighed his crime. With a contract he signed in March 1565, Menéndez became *adelantado* (a term that means "governor" or "commissioner") of Florida. He was ordered to drive out, however he could, any settlers not controlled by the Spanish. The mission also gave Menéndez a chance to carry out an idea he had suggested a decade before: building a permanent guard station in Florida to keep away hostile French and English ships.

Captain Menéndez left Cádiz, Spain, in June. His expedition included eleven ships and two thousand men. By late August, his fleet arrived on the Florida coast and spotted Timucuas Indians onshore. Menéndez landed with eight hundred men and peacefully took over the village. The Spanish built defensive walls around it and called the settlement St. Augustine.

By this time, Menéndez and his men had already had a brief fight with the Huguenots, who were led by Jean Ribault. The French decided to end the Spanish threat by attacking St. Augustine. In mid-September, they sailed from their base at Fort Caroline, near present-day Jacksonville and about 30 miles (48 kilometers) north of the Spanish camp. A violent storm, however, drove the French past St. Augustine, and Menéndez decided to attack the undefended Fort Caroline. The Spaniards struck brutally, killing nearly all the fort's occupants, including women and children.

Menéndez's fleet then returned to St. Augustine. The Spaniards soon learned that members of Ribault's hurricane-battered fleet were stranded in an inlet on the coast. They set out toward the French sailors, who surrendered when they learned Fort Caroline had fallen. Instead of taking the French prisoner, however, Menéndez killed them at a spot that was later called Matanzas—the Spanish word for "slaughters." A few days later, the Spanish came upon another group of French survivors from the shipwreck, including Ribault. The French commander offered money for their safe treatment, but Menéndez was driven by his faith and his distrust of the French Protestants. "I am very sorry," he said, "if I should lose such rich spoils and ransom, since I have full need of this help to aid in the conquest and population of this territory; it is my duty to plant the Holy Gospel in it, in the name of my King." Once again, Menéndez had the captured French killed.

Despite a long, distinguished career in service to Spain, Pedro Menéndez de Avilés is probably best remembered for this brutal treatment of the French Huguenots. In Europe, the French protested to King Philip that Ribault's men should have been taken prisoner and returned to France. Philip, however, never disputed that Menéndez was carrying out the Crown's wishes.

With the French settlers out of the way, Menéndez worked to firmly establish Spain's control of Florida. He rebuilt Fort Caroline, renaming it San Mateo, and began a new fort in what is now South Carolina. Menéndez also traveled to Florida's west coast and started a small colony at Tampa Bay. But the new colony had problems. For several years, Menéndez struggled to convince Spanish officials in the Caribbean to send aid to the settlements in Florida. The men who served under him were not as able as he was. They argued among themselves and treated the Indians cruelly. As the Spanish should have learned from previous tries at settlement in America, the cooperation of the local Indian tribes was vital.

Despite an enthusiastic (if violent) start, Spanish forts and settlements in Florida never prospered. By 1572, when King Philip called Menéndez back to Spain for other duties, there were only seven families living in St. Augustine and none in the forts farther south.

The Spanish settlement of St. Augustine

Menéndez returned to Spain and spoke with King Philip about an effort to colonize Florida. The captain wanted permission to wage war against the Indians and then bring in hundreds of Spanish families to set up households. The king was interested in the idea, but first he assigned Menéndez to draw up plans for a naval invasion of England. The captain, however, never sailed with what would become the Spanish Armada, which was defeated by England in 1588. He was killed in 1574 while serving the king.

St. Augustine experienced some rocky years after Menéndez left. In 1586, it was attacked and burned by England's Sir Francis Drake. The Spanish rebuilt the town, and the development of missions in the region helped it grow. When St. Augustine came under English control in 1763, about three thousand people lived there.

JUAN DE OÑATE
EXPLORER AND COLONIST
1550?–1626?

Thanks to a family fortune founded on silver mines in Mexico, Juan de Oñate sponsored and led the first successful Spanish colonizing effort in New Mexico. Oñate conquered the Pueblo Indians and became the first governor of the colony he founded. He also explored the Southwest, reaching the mouth of the Colorado River and going as far north as present-day Kansas.

Despite the efforts of Coronado and other earlier explorers, New Mexico in 1595 was still largely unsettled and, to Spanish eyes, "uncivilized." Spanish officials in New Spain (Mexico) were reluctant to send new expeditions into the northern lands. Despite rumors of huge stores of gold and silver, all who had traveled into what is now New Mexico and Arizona had returned empty-handed—if they returned at all.

In 1595, however, Juan de Oñate volunteered to pay for a new expedition into what the Spanish called the Northern Kingdom. He wanted to both start a colony and convert the Indians to Christianity. Oñate also seemed intrigued by the stories of the mythical land of Quivira that Coronado had sought. After receiving permission for his trip from both the viceroy of New Spain and King Philip II of Spain, Oñate began recruiting colonists, ranging from children to elderly soldiers.

Finally, in January 1598, Oñate led 400 soldiers out of New Spain. About 130 of the men brought their wives and children, and the expedition also included Roman Catholic missionaries and Indians who carried supplies. Oñate brought eight hundred head of livestock—horses, cattle, oxen, sheep, and goats—four bells for a church, and many personal belongings. Slowly, this long train of people, animals, and goods moved north along the Rio Grande, through heavy rains and desert heat.

By April, they were within 25 miles (40 km) of present-day El Paso, Texas. Oñate ordered a church built, and on April 30, 1598, the colonists held what some historians call the first Thanksgiving feast celebrated in what would become the United States. The Spaniards held a religious service, staged a play, and shared a meal with the local Indians. All of this took place more than twenty years before the more famous Pilgrim Thanksgiving celebration in Plymouth, Massachusetts.

From there, Oñate and an advance group of settlers visited several Pueblo Indian villages near present-day Santa Fe. They claimed one for themselves as the capital of their new colony, and Oñate called it San Juan de los Caballeros. It was the first permanent Spanish settlement in New Mexico and the first European town west of the Mississippi River.

Although seeking to start a colony, Oñate also wanted gold, and he sent workers out to look for the precious metal. The Spaniards spent more time searching for gold than working the land, and they forced the Pueblo Indians

The pueblo of Acoma

to give them food. The settlers began to grumble about their new life, and a few deserted the colony. Two of them were tracked down and killed. As for the Indians, they disliked the Spanish intrusion on their lands and being forced to work for the demanding strangers. They also resented the new religion, which the missionaries tried to force on them with a heavy hand.

The tensions between the Spaniards and the various Pueblo tribes finally erupted into violence near Acoma. The pueblo there sat high on a desert mesa, and the Acoma called their village Aku (meaning "sky city"). Oñate visited the pueblo in October 1598 and was warmly received. But a few weeks later, his nephew Juan de Zaldivar stopped by, demanding food from the Indians. Uninvited, Zaldivar and his men climbed the steep walls protecting Acoma and entered the village's streets. Accounts differ on who attacked first, but fighting broke out, and Zaldivar and several other Spaniards were killed.

Oñate was angered by the Acoma attack, and he ordered his soldiers to strike back. After several days of fierce fighting, about seventy well-armed Spaniards had killed nearly eight hundred Indians. Hundreds, mostly women and children, were taken prisoner and forced into slavery. The adult men were also ordered to have one foot cut off, though there is no proof this punishment was carried out.

Even with peace, however, the colonists were not happy. Some disliked the intense heat and cold of the high desert. Others struggled to find food and feared future Indian attacks. Life was not any easier after Oñate moved the capital to the other side of the Rio Grande and founded the village of San Gabriel. Finally, late in 1600, more colonists and supplies arrived from New Spain, and Oñate turned his attention from the settlement to exploring the nearby territory.

In June 1601, he and about eighty soldiers headed north and east, reaching present-day Kansas. On a later expedition in 1605, he went west and came upon the mouth of the Colorado River, then reached the Gulf of California. A Spanish monk later reported that the governor entered the water there wearing his armor, "slashing the water with his sword and declaring, 'I take possession of this sea and harbor in the name of the king of Spain.'" Oñate also sent back wild reports about "extraordinary riches and monstrosities never heard of before." Spanish officials doubted these reports, and the viceroy of New Spain also heard from unhappy settlers about their difficult life in San Gabriel. In 1608, Oñate was relieved of his command as *adelantado* of New Mexico. He returned to Mexico City in disgrace, and a few years later, a new capital for the colony was founded at Santa Fe.

Just like Coronado before him, Oñate spent his entire fortune trying to find riches in the province of New Mexico. And like the earlier explorer, he never recovered from his failure. But Oñate took the first successful step in giving Spain a permanent presence in the western half of what would become the United States.

GASPAR PÉREZ DE VILLAGRÁ
COLONIST, POET
c. 1555–1620

In 1598, Gaspar Pérez de Villagrá was a well-educated soldier traveling with Juan de Oñate on his expedition from New Spain (Mexico) to the so-called Northern Kingdom. Captain Pérez de Villagrá had a passion for poetry and a flair for history. Sensing that he was part of a historic mission, he kept notes about Oñate's explorations and the settlement he founded, which became New Mexico. Some twenty years later, Pérez de Villagrá published his *Historia de la Nuevo Mexico* (*History of New Mexico*), the first written epic poem about America.

Pérez de Villagrá was born in Spain and studied at the University of Salamanca. For seven years, he served as an adviser to King Philip II in Madrid. But like many other young Spaniards of the day, he was hungry for adventure. He returned to New Spain and eagerly joined Oñate's effort to colonize New Mexico.

Pérez de Villagrá's *Historia de la Nuevo Mexico* helped Spaniards understand the difficulties faced by the colonists. The land, they learned from his epic, was desolate, and the Indians were hostile. In an early passage, Pérez de Villagrá describes the hardships the colonists faced on their journey out of New Spain:

> And now the horses, being blind,
> Did give themselves most cruel blows
> And bumps against the unseen trees,
> and we, as tired as they,
> Exhaling living fire and spitting forth
> saliva more viscous than pitch,
> Our hope given up, entirely lost,
> Were almost all wishing death.

Historia de la Nuevo Mexico blends a journalist's flair for details with a poet's fancy images and words. In some ways, Pérez de Villagrá copied the style of *The Odyssey*, the great epic written by Homer, an ancient Greek poet. Modern historians have also called *Historia de la Nuevo Mexico* one of the first published travel journals about the New World.

In his work, Pérez de Villagrá is one of the main characters, and he describes one harrowing adventure near the Acoma pueblo. Alone and facing starvation, he strikes his beloved dog, planning to kill it for meat that will help him survive. In the end, however, he cannot eat his pet, after watching it "in pain and wounded sore / . . . lick[ing] my hands, till they / were stained and well-bathed with his blood." Luckily, soldiers from the expedition found Pérez de Villagrá before he starved.

Historia de la Nuevo Mexico also provides details about the relationship between the Spanish colonists and the Pueblo Indians they met and conquered. The chronicle ends with the Spaniards' destruction of the Acoma pueblo and the Indians killing one another rather than be taken prisoner.

Pérez de Villagrá went back to New Spain to recruit more colonists for New Mexico, then decided to return to his homeland. In about 1609, he went to Spain and wrote his epic poem. He died in 1620, on his way to taking a government position in Guatemala. His words, however, live on, giving modern readers a feel for Spanish colonial life in North America.

THE MISSIONS OF NEW MEXICO AND THE PUEBLO REVOLT OF 1680

Juan de Oñate's mission to start a colony in New Mexico ended in failure. In 1608, he was called back to New Spain (Mexico), and his king, Philip III, considered abandoning the struggling colony to the north. But then news reached him that the missionaries who had followed Oñate had achieved great success. These monks, who belonged to a religious order called the Franciscans, had converted some seven thousand Indians to the Roman Catholic faith. Although few Spaniards were in New Mexico, Philip, as a devoted Catholic king, could not abandon the new converts. In 1609, Philip made New Mexico a royal colony, which placed it directly under his control.

The new royal governor promptly moved the colony's capital from San Gabriel to a new village called Santa Fe. The Spanish monks then began to increase their efforts to convert the Pueblo Indians of the region. They did not merely try to change the Indians' religious beliefs; they also hoped to turn them into proper Spaniards. Over time, the project created resentment among the native peoples and led to conflict.

Daily contact between the Indians and their Spanish rulers came at the missions. These communities of Indians were led by one or more priests. The Spanish built mission churches as close to the center of existing Indian pueblos as possible. The church was always the highest, most imposing building,

The ruins of the Spanish mission at Pecos Pueblo, New Mexico, seat of the Pueblo Revolt

commanding the attention of everyone in the village. The priests expected the respect and obedience of the mission's residents. If the Indians decided to resist the church's authority, they faced the wrath of the Spanish soldiers stationed at every mission.

What the Spanish ignored was that the Indians already had their own culture and religion, and these meant as much to them as Christianity did to the Spanish. The Franciscan friars expected the Indians to live, work, and even dress like Spaniards. They outlawed all Indian songs, dances, and religious symbols. After a time, the Spaniards convinced themselves the converted Indians had accepted this new lifestyle and forgotten their own religion. In reality, the Indians had only hidden their old beliefs and practices from their conquerors.

Starting around the 1640s, the Indians faced epidemics of smallpox and measles. A decade later, a severe drought hit the region, leading to starvation. Adding to their woes, unconverted Apache Indians, who lived as nomads, sometimes attacked and killed converted Pueblo Indians.

Some Pueblos were convinced that their troubles stemmed from abandoning their old ways. If their spiritual leaders , or shamans, could perform the traditional rain dances, the crops would grow again. And the shamans could fight disease just as well as the Spanish doctors. More priests came out of hiding and began to challenge Spanish rule. The Spanish responded by arresting shamans who practiced the old ways. A few were killed; most were whipped.

One of the Indian priests who felt the Spanish lash was named Popé. A Tewa Pueblo Indian, he fled Santa Fe for the more remote pueblo of Taos. There, in 1680, he and other resisters planned a revolt against the Spanish. They worked in secret, so Indians loyal to the Spanish would not reveal their plan. Popé and his assistants picked August 11 as the day for their attack. Runners carried knotted cords made of yucca plants from one village to another. One knot was untied each day, and the number of knots left told the villagers how many days remained until the revolt would begin.

On August 9, two runners were captured by the Spanish. Fearing that their plan was discovered, Popé and the others decided to attack the next day. The revolt was swift and brutal. Years of anger at their treatment by the Spaniards poured out, and the Pueblo Indians attacked every Spanish village they saw. On August 21, after the death of more than four hundred settlers, the governor fled Santa Fe. The stunned colonists left their homes and began the long march south. The Indians let the Spaniards go. They did not need to kill any more because they had achieved their goal of driving the dreaded Spanish priests and soldiers from their homeland.

The Spanish resettled in El Paso, knowing that someday they would attempt to recapture New Mexico. That day would come just a little more than a decade later, when Spanish troops marched north and recaptured Santa Fe. But the Spanish still felt some shame for being the only Europeans ousted from a New World colony by Indians.

FATHER JUNÍPERO SERRA
FOUNDER OF THE CALIFORNIA MISSIONS
1713–1784

Miguel José Serra dedicated his life to serving the Roman Catholic Church. As a Franciscan monk named Father Junípero Serra, he founded the first Spanish mission in California in 1769. In the years that followed, he started eight more missions along the California coast, converting the local Indian tribes and paving the way for Spanish settlement in California.

Serra was born in Majorca, a sunny Mediterranean island off the east coast of Spain. As a teen, he studied at the university in Palma, Majorca's capital city. The school was run by the Franciscans, a religious order founded by Saint Francis of Assisi, who devoted himself to helping the poor. At age sixteen, Serra decided to join the Franciscans. Known for his intelligence and speaking skills, he became a college professor at age twenty-four. By 1749, he was eager for a new challenge and decided to become a missionary in New Spain (Mexico).

The long boat trip from Spain took more than three months, and food and water were in short supply. Finally, the ship landed at Veracruz, and Serra and two other priests headed to the College of San Fernando in Mexico City. They walked for more than 200 miles (322 km) over rough, rocky terrain to get there. One night, an insect bit Serra in the leg while he slept. The bite became infected and never healed properly, causing Serra pain for the rest of his life. The priest, however, became famous for his energy, refusing to let anything slow him down.

Once in Mexico City, Serra began his work among the Indians of Mexico and Baja (Lower) California. He crisscrossed the region on foot, visiting the missions and teaching the Indians about Christianity. At times, he also taught and preached in Mexico City. In 1768, the Spanish government decided to put the Franciscan order in charge of all its colonial missions. Serra was then given the job of running the missions in Baja California.

The next year, Spanish officials decided to build new missions in Alta (Upper) California—today's state of California. At the time, Russian explorers and traders based in Alaska seemed ready to move down into California. Spain wanted to establish a permanent presence in Alta California to keep the Russians away. Serra was chosen to start the new California missions.

Along with Gaspar de Portolá, the governor of Baja California, Serra prepared for the expedition. The plan was to travel by both land and sea. The Spanish had never traveled by land into Alta California, but their ships had explored its coast for more than 150 years. The Spanish knew that Monterey and San Diego offered excellent harbors. Portolá and Serra decided to locate a mission at each of these spots, and a third somewhere in between.

Serra was in the last of the two land groups, which left for Alta California in May 1769. The priest's bad leg and overall weak health made it hard for him to mount his mule; two soldiers had to help him into the saddle. At one point, Portolá told the suffering priest to turn back, but he refused. As Serra wrote in his diary, "I trust that God will give me the strength to reach San Diego, as He has given me the strength to come so far. . . . Even though I should die on the way, I shall not turn back."

The expedition was overjoyed when, on July 1, they all stood on top of a hill and saw San Diego Bay below them. Already anchored there were the expedition's two ships, the *San Antonio* and the *San Carlos*. Their joy turned to sadness, however, when they learned that many of the ships' sailors had died from disease. Governor Portolá sent the *San Antonio* back to Baja California for medicine, supplies, and a new crew. In the meantime, he decided to begin the overland expedition to Monterey Bay, some 450 miles (724 km) to the north.

Father Serra was too weak to go with Portolá on the long trip to Monterey. He remained behind to care for the sick and to find a spot to build the first Spanish mission in Alta California, which he named San Diego de Alcala. On July 16, 1769, a cross was raised at the site and a chapel was built from tree branches.

About six months later, Portolá and his men returned from the north. The overland expedition had failed to find Monterey Bay, although some scouts had spotted a huge arm of the ocean, which they named San Francisco, after Saint Francis. By now, Portolá was discouraged by the expedition's progress. His men continued to die from disease, and armed Indians, most likely members of the Ipai and Tipai tribes, were all around. Moreover, the *San Antonio* still had not returned with supplies. The governor prepared to return to Baja California.

Serra, however, wanted to carry out his missionary work. He convinced Portolá to wait a few more weeks, until after the feast of Saint Joseph on March 19. When that morning came and the ship still hadn't arrived, Portolá ordered the men to prepare to leave. But that evening, as thick fog lifted over the harbor, Serra saw the sails of the *San Antonio*. Portolá immediately called off the return trip and prepared for a second expedition to find Monterey Bay.

Serra joined this trip onboard the *San Antonio*, which shadowed the overland explorers as they went up the coast. Within two months, the Spaniards had found Monterey Bay, and Serra went ashore to found his second mission. Soon after, Portolá returned to New Spain (Mexico)—his work in California was done. But Father Serra, though almost sixty years old, was just beginning his mission. He and his fellow Franciscans soon founded a third mission, in a beautiful valley just east of Monterey at the mouth of the Carmel River. Serra loved the site so much that he made it his permanent home.

By 1782, Father Serra and the Franciscans had founded six more missions, with San Francisco the farthest north. His missions, however, led to hardships for the Indians. The priests converted some five thousand Indians to the Catholic faith, often using Spanish soldiers to force them into the missions. Serra and the other missionaries taught the converts skills, such as weaving and wine making. But they also forced the Indians to use their labors for the mission's benefit, as the food and goods they produced were traded to New Spain (Mexico). In the years after Serra's death in 1784, other missionaries noted that the California Indians were often treated badly—some say they were subjected to the most cruel treatment in history.

Today, Serra is praised by some for his deep faith and tireless efforts to spread it. The Roman Catholic Church is in the process of naming him a saint. Some Indians, however, condemn him for the harsh life the Indians endured at the missions. But no one denies the major role he played in settling California for Spain and spreading its culture there.

★ JACOB RODRÍGUEZ RIVERA
1719–1789

AND
AARON LÓPEZ
1731–1782

COLONIAL MERCHANTS

The year Christopher Columbus sailed across the Atlantic was a bleak one for the Jews of Spain. For centuries, they had faced discrimination, but many had thrived by converting to Christianity. Others, however, refused to convert, and some who did convert continued to practice their Jewish faith in secret. In 1492, Queen Isabella and King Ferdinand ordered all Spanish Jews to become Catholic or leave the country. Those who still practiced Judaism in secret would be hunted down and arrested. Several years later, the Spanish monarchs pressured neighboring Portugal to follow suit.

The hundreds of thousands of Jews who left Spain and Portugal—called Sephardim—included the ancestors of the Rivera and López families. By the mid-eighteenth century, these two families were related and living in Newport, Rhode Island. There they became successful merchants and contributed to one of America's first major Jewish communities.

Jacob Rodríguez Rivera lived for a time in Spain as a Marrano—a converted Jew who still secretly practiced Judaism. In 1748, Rivera came from the Dutch island of Curaçao to Newport, Rhode Island. He took with him his business, which made candles from spermaceti, a waxy substance that comes from whale oil. Rhode Island, unlike most British colonies in North America, had been founded on the principle of religious tolerance. Newport already had a small Jewish community, and Rivera quickly became one of its leaders.

Aaron López, a cousin of Rivera's, was living in Portugal as a Christian when he, his wife, and their baby daughter headed for New York City. López's brother already lived there, and the family knew that they could openly practice their faith in this city.

In 1752, López agreed to become Rivera's business partner, and he moved to Newport. He began work as a shopkeeper and quickly became involved with every aspect of international trade. He not only shipped Rivera's whale-oil products but began bringing in loads of rum, sugar, chocolate, and molasses from Europe, the West Indies, and Africa. Within a decade of his arrival in Newport, López was one of the wealthiest men in Rhode Island. Rivera was not far behind.

In 1759, the Sephardic families of Newport bought land to build a temple where they could worship. Then, with generous contributions from Jewish friends in New York, they hired Peter Harrison, a well-known architect, to design the building. The Touro Synagogue, as it was later named, opened in 1763, making it the first synagogue in America. It was and still is considered a place of quiet rest and beauty. Both López and Rodriguez played active roles in founding and running the synagogue.

As the 1770s began, Aaron López and Jacob Rodríguez Rivera were major shipowners, and their business interests were wide-ranging. Those interests included the transporting of slaves, which made many New England merchants wealthy. In this tragic business, the two men sent ships carrying rum to the west coast of Africa. The rum was traded for slaves, who were then taken to the West Indies, where they were traded for sugar. The sugar then went on the López and Rivera ships to Newport. For these and other prosperous merchants, slave trade, unfortunately, was just another business.

The coming of the American Revolution, however, ended business as usual in Newport. Merchants could no longer trade freely, as the British set up blockades around several American ports. In 1778, with the British occupying Newport, López and Rivera fled with their families to Leicester, Massachusetts. By now, López was Rivera's son-in-law, having married his daughter after the death of his first wife. His family included seventeen children. López became active in his new community, and he provided supplies to American troops for the remainder of the Revolution.

In May 1782, on his way to Newport to visit friends, López fell into a pond and drowned. His funeral was held at Touro Synagogue and was attended by the leading dignitaries of the day. The eulogy was given by the Reverend Ezra Stiles, the president of Yale College. López was praised for his honesty and generosity. Stiles later wrote in his diary that López "did business with the greatest ease and clearness—always carried about with him a sweetness of behavior . . . and unaffected politeness of manners. Without a single enemy and the most universally beloved by an extensive acquaintance of any man I ever knew."

Newport's leading shipping merchant was buried in the Jewish cemetery there, not far from the famous synagogue he helped found. Jacob Rodríguez Rivera, who died in 1789, lies nearby.

ANDRÉS ALMONESTER Y ROJAS
1725–1798

AND
THE BARONESS DE PONTALBA
1795–1874

BENEFACTORS OF NEW ORLEANS

In 1762, France secretly handed New Orleans and the rest of the Louisiana Territory over to Spain, giving the Spanish the sea outlet for half a continent. Despite the city's key location, few Spaniards wanted to move to New Orleans, a town of dirty, dusty streets and shabby wooden buildings surrounded by bug-infested swamps. But one Spaniard, Andrés Almonester y Rojas, had the vision to see what New

Orleans could become. He used his own fortune to turn the town into one of the most elegant cities in North America. Decades later, his daughter Micaela, the Baroness de Pontalba, sponsored her own construction project, adding to the city's charm.

Almonester was a successful shipper and business owner who made it clear to Spanish officials that he was willing to invest in New Orleans. In 1777, Spanish officials let him buy public land in the city, where he built commercial buildings that he rented to others. That venture increased his wealth, and soon he was using some of his fortune for public buildings. In 1779, a hurricane tore through the city, destroying the Charity Hospital, which had been built in 1736. Almonester spent his own money to replace the damaged hospital with a far greater structure.

Then on March, 21 1788—Good Friday that year—a candle in a private home tipped over and started a huge fire. The winds were high, and within five hours, more than eight hundred buildings were destroyed. The loss was devastating, and to make matters worse, local officials had no money to rebuild the hospitals, churches, and government buildings that had burned. Almonester once again came forward to help.

First, he replaced the St. Louis Cathedral with a far lovelier building. The new cathedral, facing the Place d'Armes—later called Jackson Square— became New Orleans's most imposing landmark. In addition, he provided for a new municipal building, which became known as the Cabildo, the name of the governing body it housed. Almonester also used his influence to rebuild private buildings at a low price.

New Orleans officials tried to prevent future devastating fires, but they were not successful. In December 1794, another terrible fire destroyed more than two hundred buildings in the city's shopping district. One more time, Almonester stepped forward, this time building a new customs house. And like the St. Louis Cathedral, the new building was grander than the original one.

Gradually, through years of fires and rebuilding, the makeshift wooden structures of the old French City were replaced by the stone, brick, and stucco ones favored by the Spanish. New Orleans began to take on a distinctive Spanish look with its ornate iron balconies, shuttered windows, and central courtyards. This style suited the hot, humid climate of the Mississippi Delta.

During the 1850s, long after Almonester's death in 1798, his daughter Micaela, the Baroness de Pontalba, undertook her own project. Although raised in New Orleans, she spent most of her adult life in France. After she returned to her hometown, she completed New Orleans's most elegant collection of townhouse apartments on land near Jackson Square that she inherited from her father. She designed the brick structures, called the Pontalba buildings, and personally supervised their construction. In the wrought-iron railings on the balconies, she placed her initials—A for Almonester and P for Pontalba—and the railings are still there today.

In 2005, Katrina, one of the most destructive hurricanes ever, struck New Orleans. The French Quarter, home of the Baroness de Pontalba's buildings as well as her father's St. Louis Cathedral, escaped without heavy damage. These structures still stand, reminding visitors of the influence of New Orleans's Spanish benefactors.

★ JOSÉ CAMPECHE
PAINTER

1752–1809?

During the eighteenth century, the age of empire was still thriving in Spain. Wealthy and well-educated Spaniards thought not much of value came from the New World colonies except sugar, coffee, and other natural resources. But in Puerto Rico, an extraordinarily talented man named José Campeche y Jordán proved that "backward" colonists could match the Old Masters of Europe for artistic skill. Working as a painter, sculptor, and architect, Campeche was the first renowned artist from his home island and one of the greatest eighteenth-century painters in the Americas.

Campeche was born on January 6, 1752, in San Juan, Puerto Rico. His mother, María Jordán y Marqués, was a Spaniard from the Canary Islands. His father, Tomás de Rivafrecha y Campeche, was a freed black slave. The elder Campeche was a prosperous painter, decorator, and gilder (someone who covers works of art with thin layers of gold). At an early age, Campeche began working with his father, often creating religious images based on existing prints. Religion was central to José's life, and he joined the Dominican order as a tertiary— that is, he followed the order's rules and pursued its holy mission without actually becoming a monk or priest.

In late 1775, the Spanish painter Luís Paret y Alcazar (1746–1799) arrived in Puerto Rico. Although a highly skilled artist, Paret had a falling out with King Carlos III of Spain, who exiled him to the island colony for three years. In Puerto

Rico, Paret showed Campeche the finer points of painting as taught in Europe at the time. The Spaniard helped the slightly younger Campeche perfect his talent for painting portraits and possibly showed him the technique of painting on mahogany panels. Paret also helped Campeche make connections at the royal court in Madrid. Throughout his career, however, Campeche never ventured beyond Puerto Rico, despite his growing reputation.

La Natividad *(The Nativity), an oil painting by Campeche*

Campeche's greatest burst of artistic activity came between 1785 and 1801. He often reflected his strong faith through his religious works depicting Mary, the mother of Jesus, as well as saints and other biblical figures. The artist also painted the people and scenes of his homeland. In his well-known portraits of Puerto Rico's political and social leaders, Campeche captured military events and costumes, interior settings, and tantalizing glimpses of the old city of San Juan. In his portrait *Don Miguel Antonio de Ustáriz*, Campeche shows the governor of Puerto Rico standing in front of an open window. If viewers tired of the governor's face, they could gaze through the window and see what Campeche saw beyond his main subject—the paving of San Juan's streets. Other Campeche paintings depict historical events, such as an unsuccessful British invasion of Puerto Rico in 1797. Campeche was also a skilled designer and carver of wooden altars. He built the altar for St. Anne's Church in San Juan as well as altars for other churches in the capital city.

Although Campeche never married, he was the principal provider for his large extended family and the manager of the family's painting studio workshop. He died in his hometown around 1809 after completing more than four hundred paintings. Many of these works are still on display in museums across Puerto Rico.

FATHER ANTONIO JOSÉ MARTÍNEZ

PRIEST, EDUCATOR

1793–1867

New Mexico passed from Spanish to Mexican control in 1821, and in the years to come, schools there were woefully short of money. Father Antonio José Martínez decided to step in to help. His work to improve education was one of many examples of his dedication to the poor and needy of New Mexico. Martínez also fought to protect the rights of Indians and Mexicans when New Mexico came under U.S. rule.

Padre Martínez, as he was generally called, was a native New Mexican, born in Abiquiu in 1793. His family moved to Taos several years later. As a young man, Martínez married and had a child, but after both his wife and daughter died, he went to Durango, Mexico, to study for the priesthood. Along with learning more about his Roman Catholic faith, Martínez developed a strong streak of Mexican nationalism. He and other nationalists believed that Mexicans should be proud of their culture and their land and not look to Europe or the United States for ideas.

In 1822, Martínez was ordained a priest, and a few years later he returned to Taos. In the years to come, Martínez studied law and entered politics, serving in the local assembly between 1830 and 1836. During those years, he founded a seminary so local boys could study to become priests. He also opened the first primary school in Taos, which both boys and girls attended, and the priest taught all of the classes. Building on his interest in law, Martínez also opened a law school. Taos became a center for education, and a whole generation of New Mexicans studied with Martínez.

In 1835, Martínez's love of learning led him to buy the first printing press used west of the Mississippi River, originally brought to Santa Fe, the capital of New Mexico. Martínez hauled the press through the mountains to Taos, where he printed a newspaper and textbooks for his school. He also wrote and published works on historical events.

Although a scholar, Martínez was also a man of action, as his political work showed. Twice when trouble broke out in northern New Mexico, the priest sided with the residents who felt their rights and freedoms were at risk. In 1837, to protest new taxes, rebels took over Santa Fe and killed the governor. Martínez supported the aims of the rebels, if not their use of violence.

Almost a decade later, U.S. troops came to Taos, as part of the Mexican-American War (1846–1848). Some Americans had already settled in Taos, which was an important trading center at the time. In January 1847, local Mexicans and Pueblo Indians killed the U.S. governor, hoping to drive the Americans out of the region. For years, some Americans believed that Martínez was actively involved in the violence that time, but historians now doubt this. Instead, he tried to hold back the rebels, knowing they had little chance to defeat the better-armed U.S. force in their midst. And Martínez protected some of the people slated to be killed during the revolt, offering them safety in his home.

Realizing that New Mexico was destined to become part of the United States, Martínez decided to work with U.S. officials. In 1851, he served as president of the New Mexico assembly, the lawmaking body for what was now a U.S. territory. Martínez, however, was not willing to accept all the changes that came with the loss of independence. That same year, the Roman Catholic Church sent Archbishop Jean-Baptiste Lamy to New Mexico. Lamy was a Frenchman who had served in the United States for a number of years. He looked down on the Mexican Americans and their priests, such as Martínez. Lamy believed that few Mexicans would be able to follow modern progress. That attitude, and the changes Lamy made in the New Mexican churches, set up a clash between the new bishop and Martínez.

Lamy disliked the Hispanic approach to the Catholic faith, which included entering political discussions on behalf of the poor. Lamy was devout and disciplined, and he wanted to reshape the local church in the French image, which meant strictly following church rules. He also wanted to replace traditional Spanish churches with French architecture. Most upsetting to Martínez and the young, local priests he had trained were Lamy's financial policies. The bishop continued the practice of expecting the poor to pay fees to receive certain church rites.

In the 1850s, after Martínez protested Lamy's policies, the bishop had him excommunicated, or thrown out of the church. Although no longer officially a priest, Martínez continued to perform church services in Taos until his death in 1867. Years later, U.S. author Willa Cather wrote a novel about Lamy and his battles with Martínez. In *Death Comes for the Archbishop*, a character based on Lamy is the hero, while Cather casts Martínez as a villain. But to the people of northern New Mexico, Martínez was the true hero. After his death, a New Mexican newspaper said he "was universally loved by all who knew him," and in 2006, a bronze statue of Martínez was unveiled in Taos.

★ DAVID (JAMES) GLASGOW FARRAGUT

U.S. ADMIRAL, CIVIL WAR HERO

1801–1870

When the Civil War began in 1861, David Farragut faced a decision many Southern military officers pondered: Should he fight for the new Confederate States of America, or remain loyal to the Union forces of the United States? Farragut decided to move from Virginia to New York, then waited see what role Secretary of the Navy Gideon Welles wanted him to play in the Union navy. In December of that year, Welles gave Farragut an important command, and Farragut responded with several key victories in the South. As a result, Farragut became one of the greatest U.S. naval heroes of all time and the first given the rank of admiral.

David Farragut had been in the U.S. Navy since 1810, when he entered it at the astonishing age of nine. David followed a family tradition by going to sea. His father, Jorge (George) Anthony Farragut, was from the Spanish island of Minorca. As a young man, George Farragut set sail from his homeland to fight against the British in the American Revolution. By the war's end in 1783, the elder Farragut was a decorated U.S. Navy officer. He then retired to Tennessee, married a woman from North Carolina, and began raising a family. On July 5, 1801, his second son, James Glasgow Farragut, was born near Knoxville. Although a proud American, Farragut taught his son Spanish, and the future admiral spoke it throughout his life.

In 1807, the Farraguts left Tennessee and moved to New Orleans. The next year, Mrs. Farragut died of yellow fever, leaving a shattered husband and five children. Around the same time, an odd string of events set young James off on his naval career. David Porter, an elderly man, was fishing on a boat in New Orleans. The old man became ill, and George Farragut found him and took him to the Farragut home to try to help him recover. Despite this kindness, Porter died. His son, also named David Porter, wanted to repay Farragut for his efforts and ease some of the pain of his wife's recent death. Porter, a high-ranking naval officer, offered to train James as a sailor. James jumped at the chance, and he later changed his first name to David in honor of his "adoptive" father.

Using his influence with the secretary of the navy, Porter was able to have the young Farragut made a midshipman. Boys of nine or ten often served on ships at that time, helping sailors and learning the ways of the sea. When the War of 1812 broke out, David Farragut went to the Pacific with Commodore Porter onboard the *Essex*. Farragut served during and after the war, and in 1823 he commanded a naval mission to search for pirates in the West Indies. For most of his naval career, however, the United States was at peace, and Farragut saw no action. He performed his duties well but often took time off to care for his ailing wife, Susan, who died in 1840. He married again a few years later, and during the 1850s he settled his family in the navy town of Norfolk, Virginia.

A Union Navy fleet captures New Orleans, Louisiana, in 1862

By this time, the United States was deeply divided over slavery. The North had already abolished it, but Southern states relied on slaves to keep their economies rolling, and they knew that the U.S. Constitution—as it stood at the time—allowed slavery. Abraham Lincoln's election in 1860 upset many Southerners, who feared Lincoln would try to end slavery across the country. Starting in December 1860, Southern states began to secede from the Union, and they formed the Confederacy. Virginia did not immediately leave the Union, but when it finally did, in April 1861, Farragut, now a commander, moved his family to New York.

Now almost sixty years old, Farragut waited for his orders. Finally, he was called to Washington, D.C., where he was asked to lead the Union's naval expedition against the city of New Orleans. His orders told him to "proceed up the Mississippi River and reduce the defenses which guard the approaches of New Orleans, when you will appear off that city and take possession of it under the guns of your squadron."

Farragut's assignment was a reward for his loyalty to the Union and his many years as a skilled officer. Now he would be able to show his true talents in the heat of battle, at a time when his country needed him most. He began preparing for this dangerous mission with amazing thoroughness. Finally, on February 2, 1862, Commander Farragut was ready and headed for New Orleans in his flagship, the *Hartford*. In March, the other ships of his squadron began meeting up with the *Hartford*.

The battle began on April 18. Union gunboats bombarded Fort Jackson on the west side of the Mississippi River, just south of New Orleans. The bombing lasted several days, with both sides suffering heavy losses. Finally, Farragut decided to move his fleet upriver, past the Confederate forts that protected New Orleans. To protect his ships from Southern guns, he had his men string iron chains over the wooden hulls, then put mud over the ships to make them harder to see.

Before dawn on April 24, seventeen Union ships and a number of smaller boats steamed past the forts. What followed, Farragut later wrote, was like "all the earthquakes in the world and all the thunder and lightning . . . going off at once." The fighting was fierce, but by noon the next day Farragut managed to push into New Orleans, which he then easily captured. The taking of New Orleans was a great Union victory, as the South lost control of the lower Mississippi and its largest port. The successful battle also highlighted the courage and energy of David Farragut. Soon he was a national hero, and President Lincoln named him one of nine rear admirals, the highest rank in the U.S. Navy at that time.

After capturing New Orleans, Farragut wanted to move on to Mobile Bay, Alabama, but he received orders to sail northward to Vicksburg, Mississippi. Located high on a bluff, Vicksburg was well defended, and Farragut's forces failed to capture it. Meanwhile, other U.S. naval forces had better luck taking the city of Memphis, Tennessee. A few months later, a second attack in Vicksburg also failed.

A year later, Farragut was still on the *Hartford* in New Orleans, having gone more than a year without a day off. But one more great naval victory still awaited him. By 1864, the Union navy controlled all of the Mississippi and most of the major ports on the Gulf of Mexico. The one holdout was Mobile Bay. In August, Farragut was finally ready to attack.

Mobile Bay was particularly dangerous because torpedoes—today called mines—rimmed the entrance to the harbor. As Farragut's fleet sailed past the Confederate forts on either side of the harbor, the lead ship hit one of the torpedoes and sank. A cry went out from another ship, warning of the dangers ahead. Farragut, just behind in the *Hartford*, replied with one of the most famous orders in military history. "Damn the torpedoes . . . go ahead . . . full speed!" Following Farragut's command, the ships stormed past the forts, and entered Mobile Bay, victorious once again.

After his second stunning victory, Farragut left active service. In 1866, he was named the first full admiral of the U.S. Navy. Two years later, he was asked to run for president, but declined, saying, "I have never for one moment entertained the idea of political life." In the years that followed, Farragut traveled widely and was given a hero's welcome wherever he went. Shortly before his death, he visited his father's birthplace on the island of Minorca. During the trip, he also met Queen Isabella II of Spain. She told the admiral, "I am proud that your ancestors came from my kingdom."

★ JUAN BAUTISTA ALVARADO

POLITICIAN

1809–1882

During his lifetime, Juan Bautista Alvarado y Vallejo saw Spain, Mexico, and the United States control the fate of his homeland of California. At times, he bristled under this outside control, believing Californians should rule themselves. That desire drove him to lead a short-lived revolt for independence. Alvarado then decided to work within the existing political system and serve as the constitutional governor of California, a post he held from 1836 to 1842.

Juan Bautista Alvarado was the son of José Francisco Alvarado and María Josefa Vallejo, who came from two influential military families of Spanish ancestry. His paternal grandfather, Juan Bautista Alvarado, arrived in California in 1769 with Gaspar de Portolá and Father Junípero Serra. These men had been sent to create Spanish bases along the California coast from San Diego to Monterey. They were part of the first group of Spanish colonists who settled Alta (Upper) California. The settlers built a chain of twenty-one missions and established presidios (forts) and pueblos until California became a part of the Mexican republic.

The colonial period in California ended in 1821 when Mexico won its independence from Spain. California was part of Mexico, but it remained largely independent and self-sufficient, as it had been under Spanish rule. Over the next several decades, California's local leaders took advantage of their distance from the center of Mexican government to make changes. Government institutions in California were re-formed, Franciscan friars were expelled, and mission lands were distributed for private use. The changes, however, sometimes created political unrest in California. And the Spanish face of California also began to change, as more Americans and European immigrants began to settle and trade there.

Alvarado was born in Monterey on February 14, 1809, when California was still part of the Spanish empire. His family belonged to the military class of Spanish colonists who called themselves Californios or *gente de razón*, meaning "people of reason." They considered themselves far superior to the Indians, Africans, and poor Mexicans who lived among them. After Alvarado's father died of a fever, the young boy was raised by his maternal relatives, the Vallejos, an important and respected upper-class family in California during the Mexican era. They lived in Monterey, the capital of Alta California. Alvarado grew up with his uncle, Mariano Guadalupe Vallejo, who was just a year older than he was. From an early age, the two boys were groomed for leadership.

When Alvarado was still in his teens, he became involved in California politics. His first official role came in June 1827, when he was named secretary of the *diputación* (legislature). Nine years later, he emerged as a key political figure in Alta California. For several years, some Californios

Alvarado's rebel force storms Monterey in 1836

had grumbled about the Mexicans sent as governors of California. They wanted to put local men in that position. Disappointed with Mexican rule, Alvarado organized a revolt against Governor Nicolas Gutierrez. He drew on the support of Californios and Anglo adventurers who felt excluded from the political process. In November 1836, Alvarado rallied a sizable rebel force and seized Monterey.

By January 1837, Alvarado had proclaimed California free from Mexican rule and declared himself governor. His uncle, Mariano Guadalupe Vallejo, became California's military commander. They then marched south, hoping to win the support of other communities. In general, the southern section of California resented the concentration of political power in northern California. But by the spring, they had won the backing of such towns as Santa Barbara and San Diego.

That June, the Mexican government sent a negotiator to try to end the rebellion in the California province. Alvarado stated his position for independence, arguing that California's governors should be native born, not "foreigners" from central Mexico. Finally in 1838, Mexico recognized Alvarado as official governor of the Department of California.

Alvarado's first major task as official governor involved secularization of mission lands. Secularization was the most controversial matter of the 1830s. It consisted of freeing Indians who worked almost as slaves at the missions, and then giving mission lands and herds to local residents. Alvarado endorsed more than two hundred land grants to Indians, Californios, and Anglos—more land grants than any other governor made during the Mexican era.

In his last four years in office, from 1839 to 1842, Alvarado reorganized the government structure and administration. He tried to make sure the government received all the taxes it was owed on goods brought into California. Alvarado also improved the educational system and how the missions were managed. In addition, he grappled with the growing number of foreign immigrants arriving in California. The newcomers, especially Americans, threatened the way of life the Californios had created—which had Californios at the top of the political and economic ladder.

By 1842, Alvarado was battling alcoholism, and Mexico prepared for a change in leadership in California. The Mexican authorities wanted to reunite the civil and military powers there under one person, and they chose Brigadier General Manuel Micheltorena for the job. He set out from Mexico with a force of soldiers and convicts to take control. When Alvarado left office at the end of the year, he had served longer than any other governor during the Mexican era.

After his retirement from politics, Alvarado attempted a second revolt from 1844 to 1845, but he failed to prevent the Anglo takeover of California. He and his family retired to Rancho San Pablo, east of San Francisco. He engaged in many unsuccessful financial ventures until his death on July 13, 1882.

PART TWO

EARLY AMERICAN BUSINESS AND CULTURE

★ VICENTE MARTÍNEZ YBOR
CIGAR MANUFACTURER, FOUNDER OF YBOR CITY
1818–1896

In 1886, France gave the United States a wonderful gift: the Statue of Liberty. Soon immigrants from southern and eastern Europe were streaming past this symbol of hope and freedom, and some of them ended up in Tampa, Florida. There, Vicente Martínez Ybor hired them to work in his cigar factory, and they lived in the industrial city Ybor built. Himself an immigrant, Ybor worked harder than most successful business owners of the era to make sure his employees earned solid wages and had good working conditions. In the process, he helped make Tampa one of Florida's major cities.

Ybor was born in Valencia, Spain, and by the 1850s he had entered the cigar business in Cuba, a Spanish colony at the time. For a period, one of his brands was the best-selling cigar in the world. Cuba had the perfect climate for growing premium cigar tobacco, but it also faced political unrest. In 1869, Ybor emigrated again, taking his cigar business to Key West, Florida.

By the mid-1880s, Ybor had outgrown his factory site in Key West and had no room to expand. Two friends told him about a spot they had found near Tampa that would be perfect for a new factory. Rail lines had been built into the city in 1884, and work was underway to expand the port there. Ybor saw that Tampa offered what Key West lacked: room to grow and easy access to both water and land transportation. The site also had a perfect climate and a good supply of fresh water.

In 1886, Ybor bought 40 acres (16 hectares) of land just outside Tampa. His dream was to build a factory as well as a town where his workers could live and play. City officials in Tampa were eager to help Ybor fulfill his dream because the city was still recovering from the economic turmoil brought by the Civil War. Tampa's leaders agreed to give him what he wanted most: complete control of both the planning and building of what would become Ybor City. Preparing the site, however, was not easy, as swamps had to be drained, and workers had to combat mosquitoes while keeping an eye out for alligators.

Ybor asked his close friend Gavino Gutiérrez to design his new industrial complex, and Gutiérrez borrowed from many different architectural styles. He designed brick factories with courtyards like the ones in Cuba; he gave the buildings iron balconies and railings popular in his native Spain; and he added sparse workers' cottages, which were common in the Old South. In the spring of 1896, the *Tampa Guardian* wrote about the main factory building: "There is no more substantial structure in the state of Florida. None but the very best material had been used in any part, and no expense spared to make it both handsome and convenient."

At his factory, Ybor hired workers from Cuba, Spain, Italy, and eastern Europe. He hoped that by treating them well, he could avoid the unrest other cigar makers faced from their employees. Ybor also offered the workers inexpensive housing in Ybor City, and he often opened his own home to them for celebrations. To investors and other manufacturers, he offered free land and well-built factory space. By the end of 1886, the factories of Ybor City had already produced a million cigars. Tampa was eventually home to two hundred cigar factories, earning it the nickname Cigar Capital of the World.

Despite Ybor City's prosperity, as the nineteenth century ended, labor unrest and political problems were on the rise. At this time, most of the workers were Cuban or Spanish. A struggle within Cuba for independence from Spain created bad blood between the Cubans and Spaniards. Political groups sprang up in Ybor City, supporting one side or the other in Cuba's growing revolution. Some of the groups were peaceful, but some were not, and strikes and demonstrations became common. Money that could have been used to strengthen the local community was instead sent to support the competing groups in the Cuban conflict.

Vicente Martínez Ybor did not see the ultimate result of the Cuban revolution—the Spanish-American War of 1898. The cigar king died in 1896. There was a funeral procession through Ybor City to honor its founder. Many workers marched, though not as one group. The mourners were instead divided into various ethnic and political factions, unable to leave behind their differences for even one day.

Ybor City continued to grow, but it never became the unified town that Ybor may have hoped for. The Spanish, the Cubans, and immigrants from Italy all lived separately, holding on to their national identities as long as they could. It would take several generations for Ybor City—now a part of Tampa—to be considered a true community and not just a workers' settlement.

★ JUAN CORTINA
RESISTER, HERO
1824–1894

In the borderlands between Texas and Mexico, the name of Juan Nepomuceno Cortina has often provoked wildly different reactions. To white Texans he was—and often still is—considered an outlaw who violently pursued his own selfish ends. But to Mexicans and many American Hispanics, he was a hero and a proud symbol of resistance to Anglo domination. The "Red Robber of the Rio Grande," as Cortina was called, is best known for his capture of Brownsville, Texas, on September 28, 1859. The story of Juan Cortina has not lost any power since then, in part because he continues to inspire Hispanics to defy the overt racism and discrimination of powerful Anglo-Americans.

Cortina was born on May 16, 1824, in Camargo, Mexico. His parents, Estefana and Trinidad Cortina, owned a prosperous cattle ranch. To prepare for his future duties as head of the family business, Cortina moved north of the Rio Grande, to lands near Brownsville claimed by both the United States and Mexico. During the Mexican-American War (1846–1848), he briefly fought against the Americans.

The U.S. defeat of Mexico made the Cortina lands around Brownsville part of Texas. Cortina settled there, and for almost a decade, he seemed to accept that he was now no longer Mexican but Mexican American. But over time, it angered him to see Anglo officials from Brownsville mistreating the Mexican Americans of the region. On July 13, 1859, he entered the city and happened upon one of his former employees being abused by the city sheriff. In a scuffle, Cortina ended up shooting the sheriff, firing the first shot of what was sometimes called the First Cortina War. With his actions that day, Cortina also launched his career as a heroic legend to Mexican Americans and an outlaw to Anglos.

Two and a half months later, on September 28, Cortina returned to Brownsville; released additional Mexicans who had been falsely imprisoned; and raised the Mexican flag, shouting "Death to the Gringos." Two days later, he issued a bold proclamation telling Texans, "Our object, as you have seen, has been to chastise the villainy of our enemies, which heretofore has gone unpunished. The[y] have connived with each other . . . to persecute and rob us, without any cause, and for no other crime on our part than that of being of Mexican origin." In a second statement a few months later, he called his Anglo enemies "flocks of vampires, in the guise of men."

Soon a variety of American military forces (some led by Colonel Robert E. Lee, the future commander of Southern troops during the Civil War), Texas Rangers, and militia were dispatched to catch or destroy Cortina. For a time, Cortina had success on the battlefield, and his army grew, as poor Mexicans from both sides of the Rio Grande joined his cause. But after losing a key battle in December 1859, Cortina returned to the Mexican interior. He remained there until Texas seceded from the Union, joining the Confederacy in its battle against the Union. With Texas now engaged in the Civil War, Cortina once again began to agitate in the border region. In May 1861, he undertook the Second Cortina War in the county of Zapata, but he was beaten and driven back into Mexico by Confederate captain Santos Benavides.

Once again in Mexico, Cortina shifted his attention to a new enemy. In December 1861, French troops arrived in Mexico, as France's emperor Napoléon III sought to control the government there. After fighting bravely for Mexico against the French, Cortina was appointed to the rank of general by Mexican president Benito Juárez. For a time, Cortina also aided Texans who supported the Union as they battled Confederate troops. In 1863, Cortina returned to his native region in Mexico and declared himself governor of Tamaulipas. He soon gave up the post, but claimed it for himself again in 1866.

After the Civil War, Cortina was still a wanted man in the United States. In 1870, some residents of Brownsville asked that he be pardoned for his earlier "wars," since he had supported the Union against the Confederacy. The effort failed, and in 1875, the growing American political influence inside Mexico led to Cortina's being summoned to Mexico City. The next year, he was arrested by President Porfirio Díaz. Though he was eventually released, Cortina remained in exile in Mexico City for most of the remainder of his life. He returned to the border briefly in spring 1890. According to one Mexican American scholar, Cortina was said to have died after taking poison on October 30, 1894, in his home state of Tamaulipas.

More than a century later, Cortina and his deeds still stir debate. In 2005, an Anglo journalist from Texas wrote, "No honest narrative of events can portray Cortina in a favorable light." Yet for many Hispanics along the Texas-Mexico border—and indeed throughout the United States—he remains a heroic example of resistance to mistreatment and inequality.

ESTEVAN OCHOA
BUSINESSMAN, CIVIC LEADER, MAYOR OF TUCSON
1831–1888

Before Tucson, Arizona, had an airport or an interstate highway or even a rail yard, Estevan Ochoa was the king of the city's transportation industry. He was born in Chihuahua, Mexico, into a rich mining and ranching family. As a boy, Estevan rode his father's freight trains throughout northern Mexico; the southwestern United States; and even to the start of the Santa Fe Trail in Independence, Missouri. As an adult in Tucson, Ochoa's shipping business made him one of the city's most prominent citizens, and he became its first elected Mexican American mayor.

In the mid-1800s, freighting, as shipping was also called, meant the hauling of goods by wagon train. These "trains" were crucial to the survival of small towns in the frontier regions of the Southwest. By that time, Ochoa had already begun a successful freighting company in New Mexico, and around 1860, he moved his business operations to Tucson. Arizona was then part of New Mexico, and Ochoa was chosen to serve on a committee that hoped to create a separate Arizona territory.

By the end of the Civil War in 1865, freighting was Arizona's most important business. Ochoa and his partner, P. R. Tully, ran a vast business empire. Tully, Ochoa & Company was not only a huge freighting business but also a kind of department store, supplying both Tucson and the remotest forts and ranches with everything from harnesses and wagons to shoes. Later, the company became involved in mining and sheep ranching. Ochoa was known for his honest dealings, as well as a keen business sense. "No other man," wrote the *Tucson Citizen* in 1874, "has given as much thought and attention to the development of the capacities of our country as Mr. Ochoa. He's always watching for something to introduce."

Estevan Ochoa and his wife, Doña Altagracia, brought grace and elegance to what had been a rough frontier town. During the 1870s, their home was Tucson's finest, and the couple entertained lavishly. Doña Altagracia dressed in silk and pearls and was followed about her mansion by a pet peacock, which fanned its plumes in front of startled guests and ate food from their hands.

The rise of Ochoa and of Tully, Ochoa & Company, is partly the story of an ambitious and talented man. But it is also the story of Tucson, a community in which Mexican Americans prospered. By 1860, most of California's native Hispanics had lost their great ranches and were struggling to earn a living. In Phoenix, Arizona, and in Texas, Anglo-Americans controlled politics and business, and they were not helpful either to the native Hispanics or to newcomers from Mexico.

In Tucson, however, Mexicans remained the majority of the population. Their businesses thrived, and many held positions of power. The Mexicans of Tucson—called the Tucsonenses—founded many new schools during the 1870s, both public and private. Ochoa himself helped lead the fight to found the public school system of Arizona. In 1871, he served in the territorial legislature, Arizona's lawmaking body at the time. As the chairman of the committee on public education, Ochoa introduced a bill that, for the first time, allowed the territory to collect property taxes to support the schools. Later, Ochoa personally supervised the construction of Tucson's first public school.

Ochoa's commitment to public education stemmed from his strong belief that Mexicans who wished to live and prosper in the United States needed a good education and an excellent knowledge of English. Learning English, he said, was as "indispensable as our daily bread." Only by learning English, he thought, could Mexicans compete with their American neighbors. Ochoa supported several public education bills that mandated English instruction in all Arizona schools.

The combination of loyalty and flexibility helped make Estevan Ochoa and other Tucsonenses so successful. They were Roman Catholic, spoke Spanish, and helped start private schools for their children. Yet they also learned English, supported public education, and worked closely with Anglo-Americans when necessary. Ochoa bridged the two cultures so well that in 1875 he was elected mayor of Tucson. He and other Mexican American leaders in the city were respected by both their own people and the local Anglo community.

By the end of the 1870s, Ochoa saw that the world of shipping was changing. Railroads were now crossing the United States, and the tracks were closing in on Tucson. Rather than fight the new development, which threatened his own business, Ochoa did what he thought was best for the community. He supported a bill that allowed the Southern Pacific Railroad to cross Arizona. In 1880, residents of Tucson eagerly greeted the workers laying down the track, and the first passenger train rolled into town that March. Ochoa, always the civic leader, presented a ceremonial silver spike to the president of the railway.

Soon, however, the railway took its toll on Tully, Ochoa & Company. Ochoa began to sell his equipment at a loss, hoping to stay in business. He died in 1888, in Las Cruces, New Mexico. He was much poorer than he had once been, but he never lost his dignity.

MARÍA AMPARO RUIZ DE BURTON

NOVELIST

1832–1895

★

Coming from a prominent Mexican family and married to a U.S. Army officer, María Amparo Ruiz de Burton knew both the Anglo and the Hispanic worlds of her time. She used her unique perspective and flair for writing to become the first Mexican American to write novels in English. Her best-known work, *The Squatter and the Don*, reflects some of her anger toward the U.S. government for denying land claims by Californios, the wealthy Mexican families that once dominated California.

María Amparo Ruiz was born in 1832 in Loreto, Baja California. Her grandfather José Manuel Ruiz had served as the governor of Baja and owned vast tracts of land near modern-day Los Angeles. The family, however, met the same fate as other Californios, who lost control of the area during the Mexican-American War (1846–1848). The U.S. Army occupied Baja and forced the surrender of its citizens. At the war's close, María and her mother took advantage of the terms of the Treaty of Guadalupe Hidalgo to move north to Monterey and become U.S. citizens.

In 1849, María married Henry S. Burton, a West Point graduate and lieutenant colonel in the U.S. Army. She had met him during the surrender of Baja California. Ruiz is thought to have been very beautiful, and some people have suggested that she was the subject of the popular song *The Maid of Monterey*. This romantic ballad was sung by Mexican war veterans in the early days of the state. Her marriage to Burton was not accepted by some Mexican leaders. They opposed a Roman Catholic "Californio" marrying a Protestant Anglo. And the marriage also seemed to test her identity as a Mexican American. After witnessing the U.S. invasion of her land, she wanted to marry an officer of the invading army. But these larger issues did not seem to diminish her love for Burton or adversely affect their marriage.

In 1852, the Burtons settled in San Diego, and Ruiz de Burton spent the rest of her life in the United States. She soon became fluent in English and part of the social elite. In 1861, while living on the East Coast, she attended the inauguration of President Abraham Lincoln. She also wrote many letters, showing the talent for writing that would later win her fame.

Ruiz de Burton's writings reflect her complex reality. Her first known work is *Who Would Have Thought It?* Published in 1872, it was a romance about life in New England during the Civil War. By the time she had written the novel, she was a widow and had returned to San Diego, California. She found that Rancho Jamul, the property she and her husband had purchased there, was occupied by strangers. These Americans were squatters—people who lived on land they did not own and then claimed it as their own. Ruiz de Burton was one of many Californios who confronted squatters after the U.S. takeover of California. Adding to the rightful landowners' problems were an unsympathetic court system and railroad companies that also sought the land.

The struggle of the Californios to reclaim their land became the subject of Ruiz de Burton's second and last novel, *The Squatter and the Don* (1885). She published the book under the name "C. Loyal," which stood for "Loyal Citizen," a nineteenth-century term used to close official letters in Mexico. In the book, Ruiz de Burton uses the character Don

Mariano to express some of her own feelings on how the Californios were treated: "I think but few Americans know or believe to what extent we have been wronged by congressional action."

Some modern critics dislike Ruiz de Burton's treatment of the working classes in her novel because she seems to suggest they are unethical. The rich, meanwhile, come across with great dignity. Still, *The Squatter and the Don* offers a unique perspective on issues of race, gender, class, power, and colonialism in nineteenth-century America. The book was reprinted in 1992 and 2004.

Although Ruiz de Burton came from wealth and succeeded as an author, she still suffered hardship. She lost legal battles to reclaim her land in both Ensenada, Mexico, and California and died penniless in Chicago in 1895. But through her writings, she made her mark by touching the lives of her readers.

★ TIBURCIO VÁSQUEZ
OUTLAW
1835–1875

To some Hispanics of California, particularly the poor, Tiburcio Vásquez was like a modern-day Robin Hood. Although a criminal, he seemed to be fighting for a higher cause—the rights of a people who lost control of their homeland to an invading nation. But the Anglos who ruled California saw Vásquez as a mere bandit, and in the end he paid for his crimes with his life.

Tiburcio Vásquez was born on his parents' modest ranch in Monterey County. At the time, California was still part of Mexico. Vásquez received a good education, and even as a teenager he was fluent in English as well as his native Spanish. In 1848, just as Vásquez entered his teens, the United States conquered Mexico and took control of California. That event shaped Vásquez's political attitude and his life. Years later, he wrote in a Los Angeles newspaper, "My career grew out of the circumstances by which I was surrounded as I grew into manhood. . . . I was in the habit of attending balls and parties given by the native Californios, into which the Americans, then beginning to become numerous, would force themselves and shove the native-born men aside, monopolizing the dances and the women. . . . A spirit of hatred and revenge took possession of me. I had numerous fights in defense of what I believed to be my rights and those of my countrymen."

In the spring of 1853, Vásquez attended a dance along with several companions. He and his friends felt slighted by the Americans there and got into a fight with several of them. A sheriff named William Hardmount arrived, a shot was fired, and Hardmount lay dead on the floor. The evidence of who fired the gun is not clear, but Vásquez was accused, and he bolted from the scene rather than face what would have been certain execution. At age sixteen, Vásquez was a wanted man, and he began a life on the run.

Vásquez's belief that Mexicans in California could never get a fair deal from the ruling Anglos ignited a passion inside him. He decided to organize like-minded young Mexicans to rob cattle and goods, mostly from those they considered "invading" Americans. He once said, "Given $60,000 I would be able to recruit enough arms and men to revolutionize southern California." During the winter and spring of 1856–1857, Vásquez and his group stole horses and rustled cattle, giving much of their take to poor Mexicans in the Salinas Valley. Vásquez wanted to help out these people, but he also expected them to hide him and his men in return.

In 1857, Vásquez was arrested in Los Angeles for horse stealing and was sent to San Quentin Prison. After his release in 1863, he returned to his parents' home but couldn't seem to stay out of trouble. By the early 1870s, he had returned to the life of a bandit, and soon he committed the crime that made him notorious across California.

In August 1873, Vásquez and his men robbed Snyder's General Store in Tres Pinos. During the raid, they gunned down three Anglos in the streets. Vásquez and his gang fled to southern California, with a posse of lawmen in pursuit. Now the bandit had a price on his head, as law officials offered $8,000 to anyone who captured Vásquez alive and $6,000 if he were brought in dead.

Vásquez continued to rob when he was not trying to evade the posse. For a time, his men hid in hills that are now called Vásquez Rocks. Then in May 1874, someone told law officials that Vásquez was hiding in a Los Angeles house owned by a man known as Greek George. The posse closed in on Vásquez and nabbed him as he tried to flee the house. Wounded during his capture, Vásquez supposedly told the posse to be kind, reminding them that bringing him in alive was worth more than killing him.

After his arrest, Vásquez granted interviews to newspaper reporters. He became a celebrity of sorts, and a local theater group performed a play of his life. Vásquez insisted that he had never killed anyone and that he tried to stop his men from killing, too. That claim, however, did not convince a jury of his innocence, and he was convicted for the three Tres Pinos murders. On the afternoon of March 19, 1875, he was hanged for the crime.

Today, Vásquez is the subject of Hispanic artists who see him as a hero. A California health center bears his name. Even some Anglos of Vásquez's day understood his appeal to downtrodden Mexican Americans.

LORETA JANETA VELÁZQUEZ
CONFEDERATE SOLDIER
1842–1897

Like a few women before her, Loreta Janeta Velázquez was so driven to go to war that she disguised herself as a man and became a soldier. When her true identity was revealed, she became a spy. Years later, she wrote about her exploits in a well-known memoir, the only detailed source of her incredible life. The only problem is that no one knows for sure if her tale is true. Velázquez was either one of the most amazing figures of the Civil War or one of the greatest hoaxers in American history.

According to her autobiography, *The Woman in Battle*, Velázquez belonged to a wealthy family from Havana, Cuba. Her parents sent her to New Orleans to be educated, and there she met and married a U.S. military officer known today only as William. By the time she was eighteen, Velázquez was married and had already borne three children, all of whom died as infants.

In 1861, when the Civil War began, Velázquez and her husband were living in Kansas. She teamed with her father-in-law, a Texan, to convince William to fight for the South. Velázquez had already devised her plan to dress like a man and fight as well. Her role model was Joan of Arc, the fifteenth-century French teenager who fought the English and is now a saint. Velázquez asked her husband's permission to go to war, but he refused it. So when William left for battle, she ignored his wishes. She headed for New Orleans, found a tailor to make her men's clothes, and assumed the identity of Lieutenant Harry T. Buford of the Confederate States of America.

Velázquez then went to Arkansas, where she recruited a volunteer force of 236 men. She took her small force to Pensacola, Florida, where her husband was stationed. She wanted him to lead the volunteers into battle with her by his side. "My desire was to serve with him, if possible," she later wrote. "But if this could not be done, I intended to play my part in the war in my own way."

William was astonished to see Velázquez and her volunteers. He confessed that he was proud of her ambition, but he pleaded with her to return to civilian life. Velázquez, however, was "wild about war" and wouldn't think of leaving. Shortly afterward, her husband was accidentally killed while loading his own gun. With his death, the young widow was now free to do what she had wanted for so long—fight on the battlefield.

Velázquez set off for Virginia, seeking a company to join. She was finally named a temporary commander under General Barnard Bee and fought in July 1861 at Manassas (in the North, it was called the First Battle of Bull Run). She wrote in *The Woman in Battle*, "The fiercer the conflict grew the more my courage rose. The example of my commanders, the desire to avenge my slaughtered comrades, the salvation of the cause which I had espoused, all inspired me to do my utmost; and no man on the field that day fought with more energy or determination than the woman who figured as Lieutenant Harry T. Buford."

Velázquez/Buford fought in several other battles, most notably the Battle of Shiloh in April 1862. By the next year, however, her army career had come to end. After she suffered a minor injury, the doctor attending her learned her true identity. She then decided she could be of more use to the South as a spy, a role she had briefly assumed after the fighting at Manassas. Playing the role of a pretty, intelligent woman—which she was—Velázquez gathered information about the Union.

When the Civil War ended, Velázquez traveled constantly, and for a time she worked in South America. Her autobiography appeared in 1876, and Velázquez's publisher assured readers that her story was true. But within two years, a former Confederate general named Jubal Early stepped forward to say that Velázquez was a fraud. He doubted her claims to be a soldier and spy.

Some modern historians have sided with Early. Velázquez could have gotten her details about the war from a number of books that appeared after its end. And in some cases, her details are vague, making it hard to verify their accuracy. Some historians are willing to grant that Velázquez may have fought as a man, as several hundred other women did during the Civil War. But they doubt her claim to have been a spy. Still, a few historians think that most of Velázquez's story is true, making her one of the most colorful figures in U.S. military history.

★ JUAN GUITERAS
MEDICAL RESEARCHER
1852–1925

For generations, yellow fever was a dangerous and deadly disease, seeming to strike randomly throughout the world's tropical and subtropical regions. Doctors wondered what caused the dreaded epidemics and why, in some villages, many died while others were unaffected. Juan Guiteras was one of the skilled researchers who visited hospitals in Cuba and the West Indies, trying to answer those questions and find a way to lessen the disease's lethal impact.

Guiteras had a special interest in Cuba's struggle with yellow fever. He was born on the island in 1852 and lived there until 1868, when his family left for political reasons. The Guiterases settled in the United States, and Juan attended the University of Pennsylvania in Philadelphia, continuing medical studies he had started in Havana. Guiteras graduated from the medical school in 1873, and later he taught at the university, specializing in tropical diseases. Guiteras also practiced medicine at the University Hospital.

Dr. Juan Guiteras (far right, leaning), August 1900

Members of the Commission on Infectious Diseases, Mariel, Pinar del Rio, Cuba, 1901

After years of research, Guiteras became the first scientist to suggest that children living in areas where yellow fever was common could develop an immunity to the disease. The immunity came after many mild bouts of yellow fever during childhood. These attacks were not life-threatening; in fact, the children often were barely sick. This theory became very important in learning how this disease was transmitted.

Guiteras came to agree with the theories of Dr. Carlos Finlay, another Cuban researcher. In 1881, Finlay suggested that an ordinary mosquito transmitted the disease. Before Finlay's groundbreaking research, doctors assumed that yellow fever was caused by "something in the air." Guiteras and Finlay used the mosquito theory to explain why yellow fever was common in some areas and not others. Epidemics were prevalent in Veracruz, Mexico, but not in Mexico City. The reason, the doctors believed, was that Veracruz was located at sea level, where mosquitoes could breed. Mexico City, on the other hand, lies more than 1 mile (1.6 km) above sea level—too high for mosquitoes and, consequently, for yellow fever. It wasn't until the end of the nineteenth century that Finlay's theories were accepted more widely.

The mosquito thought to carry yellow fever was common in Havana, Cuba. When the Spanish-American War broke out in 1898, large numbers of U.S. soldiers arrived in the city. Soon many of them were stricken with the disease. American and Cuban physicians began working together, visiting hospitals and diagnosing as many cases as they could. They noted all the details of individual cases, hoping to narrow the possible causes. Other diseases, such as typhoid and malaria, were also common in the Caribbean at that time.

Finally in 1900, a team of doctors led by Walter Reed proved the theories of Finlay and Guiteras. Yellow fever, they found, was caused by a virus transmitted by the bite of the female *Aedes aegypti* mosquito. With this knowledge, future epidemics could be prevented by eliminating the breeding grounds of these mosquitoes. Indeed, after this, the incidence of yellow fever declined, and hundreds of thousands of lives were saved.

After years spent studying and working at the University of Pennsylvania, Guiteras returned to Cuba in around 1900 and lived there until his death in 1925. For many of those years, Guiteras continued to study yellow fever and other tropical diseases, often sharing his research with experts in the United States.

★ GEORGE SANTAYANA
PHILOSOPHER
1863–1952

"Those who cannot remember the past are condemned to repeat it."

In a life divided between the United States and Europe, George Santayana was one of the most influential philosophers of the twentieth century. More than just a scholar, he was a poet who reflected on the meaning of life's experiences. As his famous quote above illustrates, he urged others to react to current events only after deep reflection on lessons learned by previous generations. He wrote that we must note the rhythms and patterns of the past in order to understand the present and the future.

Santayana was born in Madrid, Spain, on December 16, 1863. After spending his early years in Ávila, Spain, he moved to Boston in 1872 and lived there with his mother, stepbrother, and stepsisters. He attended the Boston Latin School and then Harvard University, from which he graduated with highest honors in 1886. After studying for a time in Europe, the young scholar returned to Harvard, where he taught from 1889 until 1912. Santayana was fluent in Italian and French as well as his native tongue and English, though he wrote his major works in the language of his adopted home.

Santayana's literary interests developed while he was still a college student, and in 1894 he published his first collection of poems. He also wrote a novel and essays examining the work of other writers.

Santayana's first philosophical essay was *The Sense of Beauty,* published in 1896. Four years later came *Interpretations of Poetry and Religion.* In 1905, he published the first of five volumes of *The Life of Reason,* which turned out to be his greatest work. In it, Santayana describes how all human thought and activity of any worth is tied to reason. *The Life of Reason* won praise around the world, and Santayana was credited with helping to shape a "golden age" of philosophy in the United States. His last major work, *Realms of Being,* was released in four volumes between 1927 and 1940.

In 1912, Santayana gave up his academic life at Harvard and moved to Europe. He lived in hotels, spending most of his time in Rome, Italy. As his work shows, there were two distinct sides to his character, formed by his connections with both America and Europe. He had, he said, a transatlantic mind: one pole being the ancient walled city of Ávila and the other the New World intellectual center at Harvard. He had allegiances to both of these very different places, yet also the sense that he did not quite belong to either. At times, that sense made him feel alone in the world. He called himself the "eternal stranger and traveler" and suggested that these two roles were perfect for a philosopher.

Starting in 1944, Santayana published a three-volume autobiography, *Persons and Places.* He discusses the different parts of his life in chapters with names such as "My Mother," My Father," and "Ávila." In the following excerpt from "I Am Transported to America," he notes a difference between his European way of thinking and the American way:

My eye, at the first moment of my setting foot in the new world, was caught by symbols of Yankee ingenuity and Yankee haste which I couldn't in the least understand but which instinctively pleased and displeased me. I was fascinated by the play of ... [carriage] wheels, crossing one another like whirling fans in the air, and I was disgusted by such a dirty ramshackle pier for a great steamship line. I think now that the two things expressed the same mentality. That pier served its immediate purpose, for there we were landing safely at it . . . what did it matter if it was ugly and couldn't last long? . . . As for the buggy, its extreme lightness . . . made speed possible over sandy and ill-kept roads. . . . The taste for [abstract ingenuity] marks the independence of a shrewd mind not burdened by any too unyielding tradition, except precisely this tradition of experimental liberty, making money and losing it, making things to be thrown away, and being happy rather than ashamed of having always to begin afresh.

★ ARTHUR SCHOMBURG
BIBLIOPHILE, ART COLLECTOR
1874–1938

Arthur Schomburg was a legendary bibliophile (book lover) and collector of African folk art. He was one of many African American intellectuals who gathered in New York City during the 1920s, forming an arts movement that came to be known as the Harlem Renaissance. With his life work, Schomburg gave blacks of both American and Hispanic heritage a greater sense of their roots and place in history.

The details of Arturo Alfonso Schomburg's early life are unclear, but it is known that he was born on January 24, 1874, in San Juan, Puerto Rico's capital. His father was a German-born merchant. His mother was a black laundress from the island of St. Croix, in the Virgin Islands.

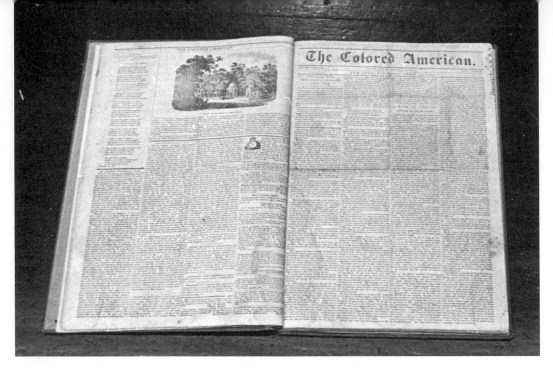

Rare editions of The Colored American *from Schomburg's collection*

With this mixture, he identified himself as an "Afroborinqueño," part African and part Puerto Rican.

Education was limited in San Juan during Schomburg's childhood. Schools charged tuition, which his family could not afford, though Schomburg was somehow able to attend elementary school for a time. He remembered his fifth-grade teacher once observing that "black people have no history, no heroes, no great moments," so he decided to devote his life to the cataloging and study of African artifacts.

After moving to New York City in 1891, Schomburg lived on the Lower East Side, a neighborhood famous for welcoming immigrants from many nations. By day, he held several different jobs, including bellhop and printer. After work, he attended night school at Manhattan Central High School. He soon became friendly with politically active Cubans and Puerto Ricans who lived in the city. Both Cuba and Puerto Rico were still colonies of Spain at the time, and some political leaders on the islands talked of revolution and independence. Schomburg sympathized with the colonized people of the

Caribbean who longed for their own nations. In 1892, he helped organize Las Dos Antillas ("The Two Antilles"), a political club that urged independence for Cuba and Puerto Rico. Through the club, he met other prominent Hispanic intellectuals of the time, such as José Martí, a leader of the movement for Cuban independence.

Las Dos Antillas disbanded in 1898, during the Spanish-American War. Schomburg began to shift his interest from Puerto Rico and Cuba to oppressed people everywhere, and he began to place more emphasis on his African, rather than his Hispanic, roots. Through travels to New Orleans, Spain, the Caribbean, and elsewhere, he consolidated a collection of some ten thousand items, including books (slave narratives, in particular), manuscripts, etchings, almanacs, journals, and pamphlets. Schomburg owned an important collection of almanacs published by Benjamin Banneker, the most prominent African American of the eighteenth century. In addition to his work as a printer, astronomer, and mathematician, Banneker helped survey Washington, D.C.

Schomburg's interest in black history led him to join a literary club, which further fueled his curiosity and helped him make new contacts. In 1911, Schomburg cofounded the Negro Society for Historical Research, which was devoted to black history. A few years later, he was inducted into (and later presided over) the American Negro Academy. Through all this, he supported himself and his family with a "normal" job at New York's Banker's Trust Corporation, having given up on an earlier desire to become a lawyer. In his free time, he focused on uncovering the richness of the African past, in the United States and beyond.

As his prominence as a historian and collector grew, Schomburg met and corresponded with a growing list of notable African Americans. As an essayist, he collaborated with such important African American scholars as W. E. B. Du Bois and Alain Locke. The subjects of his writing included the Puerto Rican artist José Campeche, the Haitian freedom fighter Toussaint-Louverture, and the Afro-Cuban general Antonio Maceo. Schomburg was also friendly with writers Claude McKay and James Weldon Johnson, who played key roles in the Harlem Renaissance, named for a New York neighborhood that was home to many African Americans.

In 1925, now himself part of the Harlem Renaissance, Schomburg wrote an article called "The Negro Digs Up His Past." In it he describes the importance of African Americans' using their history as a positive force, to overcome the negative past of slavery. "The American Negro," he wrote, "must rebuild his past in order to make his future. Though it is orthodox to think of America as the one country where it is unnecessary to have a past, what is a luxury for the nation as a whole becomes a prime social necessity for the Negro. For him, a group tradition must supply compensation for persecution, and pride of race the antidote for prejudice. History must restore what slavery took away, for it is the social damage of slavery that the present generation must repair and offset."

By this time, Schomburg's Brooklyn home was crammed with his pamphlets and artifacts. The contents were described as the "most useful of all collections of black history." In 1926, the New York Public Library's Division of Negro History received a $10,000 grant to buy Schomburg's collection. The library moved the works to a new branch in Harlem. In 1934, the Arthur A. Schomburg Collection of Negro Literature opened to the public. Schomburg served as its curator until he died in Brooklyn on June 10, 1938.

Today, the collection is part of the Schomburg Center for Research in Black Culture. It comprises more than five million items, including photographs, films, audio recordings, and institutional archives. Many of the center's records are available online. The exhibits continue Schomburg's goal of documenting the important contributions of Africans throughout the world's history.

★ WILLIAM CARLOS WILLIAMS
POET
1883–1963

Trained as a doctor, William Carlos Williams was also one of the greatest American poets of the twentieth century. Although educated in Europe and friendly with U.S. poets who lived there, Williams tried to reflect the language and lifestyles of typical Americans.

Much of Williams's life was spent in Rutherford, New Jersey, where he was born on September 17, 1883. While still in high school, he decided he wanted to be both a doctor and a writer. His interest in the arts was stoked by his mother, Elena, who had studied art in Paris. At home, she spoke Spanish to her children, and Williams gave a Spanish title to one of his first well-known collections of poems, *Al Que Quiere!* (*To Him Who Wants It!*).

Williams (center) discusses his play A Dream of Love *with actors Geren Kelsey and Lester Robin*

In 1906, Williams earned a medical degree from the University of Pennsylvania. He spent some time as an intern in New York City and did postgraduate studies at the University of Leipzig in Germany. In 1910, he opened a medical practice in Rutherford, which he continued until 1951. Hardworking in his practice and exacting in his writing, Williams wrote and published continually from 1909 until his death in 1963.

As a poet, Williams first experimented with new techniques popular in the United States and Great Britain during the 1910s. The poems were short, with short lines, and they avoided the strict meter and punctuation used in most traditional poetry. Over time, Williams chose to write about everyday items and the common people with whom he had contact in his medical practice. One of his best-known early poems is "The Red Wheelbarrow," published in 1923.

From that simple work, Williams eventually moved on to a mammoth five-volume poem called *Paterson*, about the people and places in a nearby New Jersey city.

In addition to poetry, Williams also wrote short stories, essays, plays, an autobiography, and novels. He won several important literary awards, including a Pulitzer Prize, which recognizes great achievements in American literature, music, and journalism. Williams was honored with the Pulitzer, as well as a gold medal from the American Academy of Arts and Letters, in 1963 just after his death.

Despite his mother's Puerto Rican roots, Williams was not seen as a Hispanic American writer until the last decades of the twentieth century. Most likely, before then his background was ignored because of his middle-class origins and his mixed ethnicity. Unlike the Puerto Rican writers Julia de Burgos and Jesús Colón, Williams was not born in Puerto Rico and did not write in Spanish. Some critics have stated that Williams sought to hide his Latino heritage. But Williams chose to write under his full name, which suggests he never denied his Hispanic roots on his mother's side.

Williams's influence continues as later generations discover his writing. He was especially important to a group of writers who emerged in the 1950s. He inspired poets such as Denise Levertov and Allen Ginsberg, and their writings are still popular. Through them and the poets they influenced, as well as through his own work, Williams's poetic styles and interests live on today.

BERNARDO VEGA
LABOR ACTIVIST
1885–1965

In his hometown of Cayey, Puerto Rico, Bernardo Vega saw at an early age the poverty that overwhelmed the lives of most of the island's peasant population. When the island came under U.S. rule, conditions did not change for most Puerto Ricans, and Vega joined the labor movement, hoping to improve conditions and wages for workers. He continued that work when he came to the United States, where he wrote a compelling portrait of Puerto Ricans and other immigrants trying to survive in New York City.

Vega was born in 1885, when Spain still controlled Puerto Rico. As a youth, he was drawn into the world of the *tabaqueros* (cigar makers). Near his home was a shop where the tabaqueros rolled cigars by hand. Especially appealing to the young Vega was the sound of the *lectores* (readers) whom the tabaqueros hired to read to them while they worked. The lectores read daily newspapers and novels as well as the political works of socialists such as Karl Marx. Marx and other socialists thought workers should own the factories where they worked—and eventually control the government. Thanks to these lectores, tabaqueros were among the best-educated and most politically aware workers in Puerto Rico, even if they could not read for themselves. Vega trained in cigar making and learned a lot about socialist ideals and political movements while on the job.

During the early period of U.S. rule, Puerto Rico remained a neglected colony. Vega and other tabaqueros saw that the U.S. companies now controlling Puerto Rico's economy, like the island's wealthier classes, had only their own interests in mind. No one looked out for the artisans and farmers who provided the labor for these companies. As a young man, Vega joined the Workers' Alliance, a political party seeking to defend workers' rights, and he wrote for Spanish-language newspapers.

Vega's interest in journalism eventually led him to purchase the newspaper *Gráfico* (*Illustrated*), a weekly publication that was aimed at workers and had been started by a group of tabaqueros. The newspaper described itself as a "*defensor de la raza hispana*" ("defender of the Hispanic race"). Along with a few other newspapers, *Gráfico* tried to create a unified identity among the various Hispanic nationalities living in New York City.

Vega's greatest contribution to Hispanic history and culture came with his memoirs, which he began to write in the 1940s. In English, the work is titled *Memoirs of Bernardo Vega: A Contribution to the History of the Puerto Rican Community in New York.* For many years, Vega had kept a detailed account of his experiences as a Puerto Rican immigrant, as well as those of other migrants during the early years of New York's Puerto Rican community.

Vega wrote about his own arrival in New York in 1916. He described how his ship passed the Statue of Liberty and the skyline that many passengers onboard knew from postcards they had seen. But others, he wrote, "had only heard talk of New York, and stood with their mouths open, spellbound."

For a brief time, Vega and other tabaqueros worked making munitions, as the United States was close to entering World War I. But soon Vega found a job at the El Morito Cigar Factory in Manhattan. There he worked with Spaniards, Cubans, and other Puerto Ricans, but there were no lectores to read to them as they labored.

The Memoirs of Bernardo Vega represents a priceless historical record of New York City's Puerto Rican community, especially during the decades between the two world wars and before the mass migration of the late 1940s and 1950s. During the 1950s, Vega returned to Puerto Rico and showed the completed manuscript of his memoirs to Cesar Andreu Iglesias, a friend who was a well-known Puerto Rican writer. He asked Iglesias to edit the manuscript for publication, but Vega died in 1965, before the project was complete. To honor his old friend's memory, Iglesias revived the project and published the edited manuscript in 1977.

In 1984, Juan Flores translated Vega's memoirs into English. In his opening comments, Flores notes the significance of this publication: "The English language edition of *Memoirs* is an event to celebrate, marking a new stage in the people's historical self-awareness. No book offers the millions of Puerto Ricans in the United States so many continuities and connections, so many recognizable and identifiable life experiences, so many incentives to recapture the buried past and to strike out against an unsatisfactory present." In the years since this edition appeared, however, some scholars have raised questions about the original Spanish editing and whether the memoirs are a true description of Vegas's life or a novel based on fact. Still, the book continues to provide a glimpse of a community and culture long ignored in the United States.

★ DENNIS CHÁVEZ

U.S. SENATOR

1888–1962

I would consider all of the legislation which I have supported meaningless if I were to sit idly by, silent, during a period which may go down in history as an era when we permitted the curtailment of our liberties, a period when we quietly shackled the growth of men's minds.

—Dennis Chávez, 1950

Dionisio (Dennis) Chávez's roots lie deep in the dry, dusty soil of New Mexico. He was born in Los Chávez, a place named for his ancestors. The Chávez name is common in New Mexico, but Dennis proved himself anything but common with his political career. Its highlight came in 1935, when he became the first

American-born Hispanic to serve in the U.S. Senate. (The first Hispanic U.S. senator was Octaviano Larrazolo, who served in 1928–1929.)

As a boy, Chávez moved with his family from Los Chávez to Albuquerque. At the time, New Mexico was still a U.S. territory; statehood would not come until 1912. For a while, Chávez attended public and Roman Catholic schools, but by the time he finished seventh grade, his family had hit hard times. To help out, Chávez dropped out of school the next year and began delivering groceries. After long hours at work, the boy went to the public library and read about U.S. history and politics. His reading shaped his desire to enter government service.

Starting in 1905, Chávez worked for the city of Albuquerque and became active in local politics, supporting candidates from the Democratic Party. In 1916, he ran for a local office but lost by several hundred votes. The same year, he served as a translator for Andieus Jones, an Anglo running for the U.S. Senate. Jones won the election, and he arranged for Chávez to come with him to Washington, D.C., as a Senate clerk.

In Washington, Chávez passed a special exam that let him enter the Georgetown University law school even though he did not have a high school or college degree. Chávez worked in the Senate by day and studied by night. In 1920, he returned to Albuquerque with his law degree and several years of practical political experience.

Back home in New Mexico, Chávez followed the classic pattern of many U.S. elected officials. He first set up a private law practice and then entered local politics, running in 1923 for a seat in New Mexico's House of Representatives. He won easily and served in the statehouse until 1924. One of the laws he sponsored provided free textbooks to students in public schools.

In 1930, Chávez began his career in national politics, winning election to the U.S. House of Representatives. Four years later, he challenged Bronson Cutting, a Republican, for his seat in the U.S. Senate. The race was hard-fought and bitter, and when Chávez barely lost, he and his supporters accused Cutting of using illegal tactics to win. The charge of fraud was still not settled when Cutting died in a plane crash in May 1935. Chávez was appointed to fill his seat, and in 1936 New Mexican voters chose him to complete the rest of Cutting's term. Chávez held that spot in the Senate until his death in 1962.

Senator Chávez worked hard to help the people of New Mexico. He championed several causes that directly affected both Hispanics and Indians throughout the Southwest. As the only Hispanic senator, he tried to end racial and ethnic discrimination. During the 1940s and 1950s, Chávez's work for fair employment laws and civil rights brought him national attention, at a time when many Americans ignored the discrimination that Hispanics faced.

Chávez also challenged Senator Joseph McCarthy and his supporters, who believed that Communists were trying to harm the U.S. government. Communists oppose the private ownership of property, a trademark of U.S. values. In the name of defending the United States, the McCarthyites wanted teachers and other public servants to prove their loyalty. Anyone who had ever attended a meeting led by Communists was considered a threat. At a time when McCarthy and his ideas were popular, Chávez spoke out for the right of all Americans to think and speak as they chose.

Although quiet and easygoing, Chávez never backed down from political challenges. And true to his humble roots, he tried to make life better for the poor and poorly treated. In 1988, President Ronald Reagan honored his achievements by declaring Dennis Chávez Day on what would have been his hundredth birthday. The president's proclamation said that Chávez fought for "the well-being of every American and displayed lasting concern for those in need."

A CHANGING NATION

Part Three

THE SPANISH-AMERICAN WAR AND ITS AFTERMATH

By the end of the nineteenth century, Spain's treatment of Cuba, its longtime Caribbean colony, had become an international scandal. Other European countries had finally become aware of the terrible living conditions most Cubans faced. Many citizens had been forced into concentration camps after 1895. In the United States, meanwhile, political and business leaders had been eyeing Cuba for decades. U.S. companies were deeply involved in the island's sugar trade, and President James K. Polk had once offered to buy the island from Spain.

During the 1890s, revolutionary Cuban groups tried to overthrow Spain's harsh rulers. They failed, but they did manage to take control of large parts of the island. The Spanish cracked down even harder on all Cubans, taking the island's revenues from the sugar plantations and using that money to arm themselves against Cuba's own people. Several U.S. newspapers began to devote a great deal of front-page space to the Spanish atrocities in Cuba. The articles were always one-sided, leading many Americans to feel Spain should be removed from Cuba.

William McKinley, U.S. president at the time, was unsure what to do. He wanted to weaken Spanish control in Cuba, but he disliked the rebels fighting for Cuban independence. And the president, like many members of Congress, wanted to avoid U.S. military involvement in Cuba—though he did not rule it out. Then a series of incidents put the United States and Spain on a path to war.

At the end of 1897, the Spanish promised to end their abuse of Cubans and reform the local government. Word soon leaked out, however, that Spain

The wreck of the U.S.S. Maine *in Havana Harbor*

did not plan to keep its promise. A Spanish diplomat further angered McKinley by calling him weak. On February 15, 1898, an explosion shook Havana Harbor. The U.S. battleship *Maine* had been sent to Cuba to protect U.S. citizens there and to show how serious the crisis had become. The mysterious explosion ripped through the ship, killing more than 260 men. William Randolph Hearst, a prominent U.S. newspaper publisher, quickly suggested that the blast was an act of war by Spain, and many Americans believed him. (Historians are now almost certain the blast was caused by an accident on the ship.) "Remember the *Maine*!" his newspapers' headlines screamed, and that battle cry led the United States to war in April 1898.

The Spanish-American War was short, but the results were far-reaching. After a decisive victory, the U.S. gained control of Cuba, Puerto Rico, the Philippines, and Guam to become a major international power.

The U.S. role in Cuba's future was settled with the Platt Amendment of 1901. The island received limited independence, because the United States reserved the right to send in its troops under various conditions. U.S. businesses also continued to dominate the economy. For more than fifty years, until the next Cuban revolution, Americans would have great control over Cuba's affairs. Puerto Rico had even less independence, as it remained a U.S. colony. In the decades to come, many immigrants from both islands would come to the United States, hoping to leave behind the hardships they found in their native lands.

★ THE RONSTADTS OF TUCSON

FEDERICO RONSTADT
1868–1954

LUISA RONSTADT ESPINEL
1892–1963

LINDA RONSTADT
1946–
MUSICIANS

In 1933, at the peak of her career as a singer, dancer, and actress, Luisa Ronstadt Espinel looked back on her childhood in Tucson, Arizona. Her memories were filled with family picnics and long days and nights of music. She remembered that her father "would accompany his songs on guitar and later tell us stories of when he was a little boy." Luisa's father, Federico (Fred) José María Ronstadt, passed to her his love of music. And the Ronstadt talents appeared again in the next generation, as Linda Ronstadt, Luisa's niece and Fred's granddaughter, became one of the greatest pop singers in the world.

Fred Ronstadt spent his childhood in Sonora, Mexico. His father, an engineer from Germany, had come to Argentina and briefly gone to San Francisco, California, before arriving in Mexico. There he met and married a Mexican woman from a prominent ranching family. The elder Ronstadt proudly served in the Mexican Army and raised his children in the traditions of his adopted country. Music was already a part of the Ronstadt family. As Fred later wrote in his memoirs, "My father was a lover of music and wanted me to start learning it as early as possible. . . . I was sent to the music class every afternoon after public school hours."

In 1882, Fred Ronstadt left his family in Mexico and moved across the border into southern Arizona. He already read and spoke English, and he continued to sharpen his skills in his new home. Fred settled in Tucson, which was an especially welcoming place for Mexicans. His first job was as an apprentice on the Southern Pacific Railroad. In 1888, when he was barely twenty years old, Fred started his own business manufacturing wagons, harnesses, and saddles.

Music was still important in Fred's life, and in 1888 he founded the Club Filarmónico. "We started out with eight or ten members," Fred recalled. "Some of them knew a little about music, but others didn't know a note . . . but in time, we sounded better." They sounded so good that they became the leading orchestra in town. They played weekly concerts and at holiday celebrations. The Club Filarmónico's greatest success came with a tour of southern California. The band gave well-attended concerts in Santa Barbara, Santa Monica, and Los Angeles.

Back in Tucson, the band gradually broke up as its members resumed their normal lives. Fred's carriage business turned into a hardware and supply store, the largest in southern Arizona. In 1919, one of Tucson's largest Spanish-language newspapers called Ronstadt one of the most respected leaders of the city's Mexican American community. Ronstadt told the paper he had once dreamed of earning enough money so he could return to Mexico. But as more family members joined him in Tucson and his business grew, he realized he would stay in Arizona his whole life. Still, he stated firmly, "not for a single moment did I forget my Mexican roots." And even as his business grew, Fred never lost his love of music. As his daughter Luisa Ronstadt Espinel remembered about her father,

Singer Linda Ronstadt

"[Music] was his whole life. . . . His business was a secondary consideration."

Luisa Ronstadt was born in 1892, at the height of the Club Filarmónico's success. As a young woman, she appeared in local theater and musical productions, but at an early age, she knew her ambitions would take her far from Tucson. She studied first in San Francisco, then in New York, Paris, and Madrid. She trained both as a classical musician and as a specialist in Hispanic folk music. She traveled around the world teaching others about the way of life of Hispanic country people.

During the 1930s, now known as Luisa Espinel, she appeared in several movies. By 1946, her acting career was over and she was living in Los Angeles. That year, she published a collection of Mexican folk songs. Some had originally come to Mexico from Spain, while others were unique to the culture Mexicans created on their own. Many were passed down to Luisa by Fred Ronstadt, so she called the collection *Canciones de mi padre (Songs of My Father)*.

More than forty years later, Luisa's niece Linda released an album with the same name. Her 1987 record *Canciones de mi padre* honors her father, Gilbert—Luisa's brother—her grandfather Federico, and the importance of traditional Mexican music to the Ronstadt family.

Linda Ronstadt was born in Tucson in 1946 and enjoyed a happy, fun-filled childhood there. Like her Aunt Luisa, her aspirations stretched far beyond southern Arizona. In 1964, Linda headed to Los Angeles to begin a singing career. Three years later, she and her band the Stone Poneys had a hit song, "Different Drum." It wasn't until the mid-1970s, however, that Linda Ronstadt emerged as one of the top female vocalists of the day. Her top hits included "You're No Good," "Tracks of My Tears," and "Heat Wave."

As her career progressed, Ronstadt repeatedly challenged herself by recording many styles of music. Fans who did not know about her Mexican heritage may have been surprised by *Canciones de mi padre*, but for her, it was natural to record songs she remembered her father singing and playing "during lazy Sunday afternoons" at the family's home in Tucson.

Ronstadt followed the release of *Canciones de mi padre* with a concert tour. She created what she called an old-fashioned evening of song and dance, something one might have seen in Mexico or the Southwest during the early 1900s. Ronstadt continued to sing Mexican songs in records and at concerts. She, like her aunt and grandfather before her, has cherished her Hispanic roots while remaining American. As she told a reporter in 2004, "I sing in my most authentic voice when I am singing either Mexican traditional songs or American standards."

LYDIA CABRERA
ETHNOLOGIST, NOVELIST, FOLKLORIST
1900–1991

The first Africans arrived in Cuba in the early 1500s, but it took four centuries for the culture they created there to reach beyond the island. The woman who almost single-handedly brought Afro-Cuban culture and religion to the world is Lydia Cabrera. Even after leaving Cuba to live in the United States, Cabrera continued to study and write about the Afro-Cuban traditions that had mesmerized her since her childhood.

Cabrera, the youngest of eight children, was born into a prosperous family in Havana, Cuba. She grew up among many Afro-Cuban servants, who taught her African myths, stories, and religious beliefs. This culture had remained alive even as the African slaves—brought to Cuba by the Spanish—learned to speak Spanish and adopted Roman Catholicism.

Often sickly as a child, Cabrera began her formal education with private tutors. Since legal and cultural barriers prevented her and other Cuban women from attending college, she continued her studies on her own. In 1927, Cabrera moved to Paris, France, to study art, her first passion, as well as Eastern religion. At the time, many Europeans had a growing interest in African art and the tradition of using stories and dance, rather than the written word, to keep a culture alive. Cabrera began to recognize the unique contribution of African cultures and customs to Cuban culture. Her interest was also fueled by the scholarly introduction to Afro-Cuban folklore that she had received from her brother-in-law, the anthropologist Fernando Ortiz. He had been a pioneer in the study of African culture in Cuba and was the first to use the Spanish term *Afro-Cubano*.

With the assistance of one of her former Afro-Cuban servants, Cabrera compiled the stories she had heard as a child. She published some in leading magazines, and in 1936 a French publisher issued the collected stories in French as Cabrera's first book, *Contes Nègres de Cuba* (*Black Tales of Cuba*). A Spanish version was released in Cuba four years later. By that time, Cabrera had returned to her homeland, determined to devote her life's work to the study of Afro-Cuban language, culture, and traditions.

Cabrera traveled back and forth across Cuba, searching for Afro-Cubans who could add to her knowledge. She worried that the old ways might die out, and she wanted to make sure she helped preserve them. One area of her expertise was Santeria, a mix of Catholic and native African religious beliefs and practices that developed among African slaves in the Caribbean. She earned the trust of the faith's practitioners. They had been suspicious of any attempts by outsiders to learn the secrets of their religious beliefs and practices. Cabrera was the first outsider to gain an inside view of the Afro-Cuban religion, and she presented her findings with respect for the cultural traditions of the people she studied.

Her large body of work constitutes the main source of information about the Afro-Cuban cultural tradition. Her 1954 book *El Monte (The Interior)* marked the pinnacle of her success as an ethnographer—someone who studies and records the culture of a particular ethnic group. *El Monte* helped spread information about the popular Afro-Cuban religion as reflected by Cabrera's unique insights into it. In 1958, she published *La Sociedad Secreta Abakua (The Secret Society of Abakua)*, a study of a secret society whose members were known as *nanigos*.

Cabrera also wrote works of fiction, weaving in legends and themes that reflect African origins or perspectives. Many of her stories tell of the hardships suffered by African slaves and use styles and themes that were common in the oral traditions of Afro-Cubans. Critics occasionally charged that she did not forcefully denounce the suffering that Cuban masters and government rulers inflicted on African slaves and their descendants. Others remained skeptical of her work because she did not practice the Santeria religion she studied.

After the Cuban revolution of 1959, Cabrera left Cuba and settled in the Miami, Florida, area. She continued to write about and study Santeria, which many Cuban exiles had brought with them to the United States. Cabrera was a pioneer in Afro-Cuban ethnography and anthropology, and her groundbreaking research contributed to a better understanding of Cuban culture and race relations on the island. When she died in Miami in 1991, she left an impressive legacy of more than one hundred books. Her work would greatly influence future research on Caribbean studies.

PATROCIÑO BARELA
WOOD-CARVER
c. 1900–1964

Raised to be a simple shepherd or to take on low-paying, temporary jobs, Patrociño Barela never learned to read or write. He spoke only broken English, and his Spanish was coarse. Perhaps life in the mountains of Taos, New Mexico, inspired Barela to express himself with his hands. Without ever taking a lesson, he began to carve sculptures out of wood. He combined an old Hispanic art form with his own unique style that struck some art critics as totally modern. In the process, he became the first Hispanic American artist to have his work shown at the world-famous Museum of Modern Art in New York City.

Barela was born around 1900. After his mother died in 1908, Barela and his father, a Mexican-born peasant, migrated north to Taos. Forced to earn his own living by the time he was twelve, Barela wandered from New Mexico to other parts of the West, taking jobs in mines, mills, rail yards, and in fields harvesting crops. As an adult, he was thin and short, barely reaching five feet tall. In 1930, he returned to Taos. He married the next year and then worked at menial jobs to support his growing family. His highest-paying job was as a wagon driver, hauling wood, dirt, and trash in a government jobs program.

At about this time, Barela became aware of *santero*, a centuries-old art of carving religious figures, which had survived in northern New Mexico. He saw an old *santo* (a carved figure of a saint) that was broken, so he decided to fix it for the parish priest. Once that was done, he began creating his own, carving pieces out of juniper and other local woods. As he told an interviewer in 1954, "The next night I start to do a piece. I work 'til about two o'clock in the morning. I have faces, arms and then lie down to sleep. The next night I work more."

Barela was not a churchgoing man. Pat (as he called himself) did not copy the traditional style of carving religious figures. Instead, he expressed his own experiences in his carvings. Many reflected his struggle to find meaning in a life that was marked by love for his children amid problems with his wife and a battle with alcoholism. He also used Bible stories for inspiration, as well as his own observations of the natural and human world around him. Barela's wooden sculptures have been compared to the stone relief carvings of medieval Europe. He carved figures in a basic way, focusing more on shapes than detail, giving them a powerful impact.

When Barela began his carvings, Taos was already home to many artists who were enchanted by the town's sunlight and mountainous beauty. But the Anglo artist colony in Taos took scant notice of Barela. His roots in the Hispanic folk tradition and his lowly employment made Barela easy to ignore. It was only by chance that he came to the attention of Ruth Fish of the Works Progress Administration (WPA), a government program created during the Great Depression of the 1930s. One division of the WPA was the Federal Art Project.

The project gave financial support to worthy artists who otherwise might not have been able to practice their art. With Fish's help, Barela received federal assistance for his carving (around $50 to $60 per month) while continuing to work other jobs to make ends meet.

In 1936, the WPA showcased some of the artists it helped at the Museum of Modern Art in New York. The show included some of Barela's carvings, and his work won unexpected acclaim. *Time* magazine called him the "discovery of the year." Some critics compared him to Henry Moore, a famous modern sculptor, and to other well-known artists Barela had never heard of. His works were compared to African primitives, which were also unfamiliar to him. He created his art based on what he felt inside himself.

Sadly, Barela's critical success did not lead to greater fame and fortune. Some art galleries asked to display his work, so they could sell them for top dollar. Barela, however, was content to just sell the pieces as he made them for whatever he could get, wrapping the carvings in simple brown paper. As he kept on carving, he continued to battle his alcohol addiction, and his physical health worsened. Alcohol may have played a part in the accidental fire that destroyed Barela's workshop. After the flames were finally out, Barela was found dead in the corner.

In his lifetime, Barela made more than a thousand carvings. He was the first Mexican American artist to receive national acclaim, and his work is still praised. And today, some of Barela's descendants in Taos carry on his legacy in the santero tradition.

JESÚS COLÓN
JOURNALIST, COMMUNITY AND LABOR ORGANIZER
1901–1974

In 1898, the United States won a fast and decisive victory in the Spanish-American War. With that victory came possession of the Spanish colony of Puerto Rico. Almost twenty years later, Puerto Ricans became U.S. citizens, and many residents of the island began emigrating to the mainland of the United States. Jesús Colón was one of them, and he became the first Puerto Rican to describe in English the discrimination and hardships his people faced as they adapted to life in their new home.

Colón was born on January 20, 1901, and raised in the tobacco-growing mountain region of Cayey, Puerto Rico. Growing up, he was exposed to the culture of the Puerto Rican *tabaqueros* (cigar makers). They were the best-educated of Puerto Rico's working class, thanks to their tradition of hiring *lectores* (readers) at the workplace. These lectores kept workers informed of local and international events by reading from newspapers. They also read novels and the political works of socialists such as Karl Marx. Marx and other socialists thought workers should own the factories where they worked—and eventually control the government. Colón embraced these ideas and carried them with him when he left for the United States at the age of sixteen.

Colón traveled as a stowaway in one of the steamships that brought early waves of Puerto Rican migrants to New York City. Arriving almost penniless, he knew that his mixed racial background, lack of formal education, and limited knowledge of English would make surviving in New York a major challenge. After working at a series of low-paying jobs, he decided to enroll in night school and complete high school.

In New York, Colón continued his contact with the socialist movement. That involvement, along with his own struggles, shaped his understanding of the social and economic conditions that made life so hard for Puerto Rican migrants and other workers. Colón became active in community and labor organizing, and he began writing for Spanish-language community newspapers. His journalistic craft blossomed from the trenches—from the "University of Life," as he once called it. In 1923, he began writing for the labor newspaper *Justicia* (*Justice*), the official publication of Puerto Rico's Free Federation of Workers. During 1927–1928, he was a regular columnist for *Gráfico* (*Illustrated*), a workers' Spanish-language newspaper owned by the Puerto Rican tabaquero Bernardo Vega. (Like Colón, he was a migrant from Cayey.) This work marked the start of a journalistic career that lasted almost five decades.

Colón combined journalism with his day job as a postal worker. For many years, he wrote for *The Daily Worker,* a newspaper of the Communist Party that was published in New York City. His columns in this and other newspapers focused on the lives and survival struggles of Puerto Ricans and other workers who battled prejudice and difficult work conditions. Colón admired the principles of democracy and equality promoted in the U.S. Constitution and Bill of Rights, but he believed that the U.S. economic system of capitalism betrayed those principles. Capitalism, Colón thought, created profound social inequality and kept power and privilege in the hands of a few.

He saw those same conditions at work in Puerto Rico. He once wrote about early conditions there under U.S. rule: "Our country, which had produced the varied products for our daily meals, was converted into a huge sugar factory with absentee owners caring absolutely nothing about the standards of living of the agricultural workers who comprise two-thirds of the Puerto Rican population. A man's sunrise to sunset labor under the burning tropical sun, cutting sugar cane, yielded one dollar and a half a day."

Colón was not just a journalist. He was a social commentator, a storyteller, and a master of using his own life to illustrate larger concerns. He used the word *sketches* to describe his short works, which focus largely on the daily experiences, issues, and problems faced by Puerto Ricans and other workers. He spoke out against civil rights violations, racism, and stereotypes of Hispanics that weakened their image of themselves and their community. He educated others about the competing goals and needs of different social classes and the ongoing inequality faced by African Americans and women. Colón was more than a writer. He believed in taking direct action to change society, and twice he ran for political office, though he lost each time.

In 1961, Colón compiled and published a selection of some of his writings, *A Puerto Rican in New York and Other Sketches.* On the whole, however, his work was unknown until the late 1960s and early 1970s, when scholars began examining the writings of different ethnic groups long ignored in America. Today, more than three decades after his death, Colón is considered one of the main influences of the "Nuyorican" literary movement. Based in New York, Nuyorican writers are largely the children and grandchildren of Puerto Rican immigrants. They draw on the two cultures they have directly experienced, Puerto Rican and American, just as Colón did.

★ DOLORES DEL RIO

ACTOR

1905–1983

During the 1930s and 1940s, Dolores Del Rio was perhaps the most famous and beloved Hispanic in the United States. Her dark hair and beautiful face made her a glamorous star in motion pictures. She and many other Hispanic actors of the day often had to play stereotypical roles—she was frequently the "exotic" love interest, foreign and sexy. But Del Rio's success came at a time when few minorities of any background achieved stardom in the world of popular entertainment.

María Dolores Asunsolo y López-Negrete was born on August 3, 1905. Her father was a banker, and she grew up in a wealthy household. When Dolores was four years old, her family fled Durango for Mexico City after the revolutionary Francisco

"Pancho" Villa threatened her father. Dolores began taking dance classes in Mexico City, and it was not long before she was dancing at festivals, social functions, and private parties. At age fifteen, she married Jaime Martínez del Río. She decided to capitalize the "D" of her new name and drop the accent over the "i," becoming known as Dolores Del Rio.

In the early 1920s, a U.S. film producer was honeymooning in Mexico. He saw Del Rio dance at a party given in his honor. Impressed with her beauty and performance, the producer invited her to come to Hollywood. In 1925, Del Rio made her acting debut with a small part in the movie *Joanna*. At the time, films were silent—although they might have a musical soundtrack, the actors did not talk. The next year, she got her first lead role, in *Pals First*, also a silent film, and soon she was labeled a "baby star," a young actor destined for stardom.

Del Rio's first "talking" picture was *The Bad One* (1930). After finishing that film, Del Rio had a nervous breakdown and did not work for almost two years. She finally accepted a feature role in *Girl of the Rio* (1932). The film was attacked by the Mexican government because of its negative portrayal of Mexicans and Hispanics. Two of her most famous films, *Bird of Paradise* (1932) and *Flying Down to Rio* (1933), followed, and *Photoplay* magazine declared Del Rio "the most perfect feminine figure in Hollywood."

Despite continued success, Del Rio became unhappy with her career in Hollywood. She returned to Mexico in the early 1940s. "I didn't want to be a star anymore; I wanted to be an actress," she explained in an interview. When she returned to work, her first Mexican film, *Flor silvestre* (1943), was slow to catch on with moviegoers. It took an intense advertising blitz to convince audiences to see the film. Once they did, they loved it—and Del Rio. She and her costar Pedro Armendáriz became "the first couple of Mexican cinema." The following year, Del Rio starred in *María Candelaria*, one of the most highly regarded Mexican films of the era. She once again received international acclaim after the film was screened at France's Cannes Film Festival in 1946.

A publicity photo of Dolores Del Rio for the movie Lancer Spy

Del Rio tried to return to Hollywood during the 1950s, but problems with the U.S. government kept her out. She had become friendly with Mexicans who were Communists. At the time, the U.S. government was highly fearful of Communists, since they opposed the U.S. political and economic systems. Del Rio said, "I love America and regard it as my very own," but she did not actually return to the United States to shoot a film until 1960. That year, she played a Native American mother in *Flaming Star*, which also featured the popular singer Elvis Presley. Four years later, she again played a Spanish woman in *Cheyenne Autumn*. Her last film role came in 1978, in a joint Mexican-U.S. production called *The Children of Sanchez*. Del Rio died in 1983 at her home in California.

ERNESTO GALARZA
LABOR ACTIVIST, PROFESSOR, AND WRITER
1905–1984

Ernesto Galarza straddled two worlds, achieving success in both. A respected scholar, he taught at several universities and wrote books that drew on his academic training as well as his personal experience. But Galarza was also involved in the day-to-day lives of Mexican American farmworkers. Like him, these immigrants had come to the United States seeking better lives. Galarza used his intelligence and drive to try to help poorly paid farmworkers of all ethnic backgrounds achieve better working conditions.

Galarza was born near the town of Tepic, Mexico. Following the outbreak of the Mexican Revolution, he fled to the United States with his divorced mother and two uncles. The family settled in Sacramento, California. Ernesto learned English quickly and excelled in school while working odd jobs. His mother and one uncle died during the Spanish influenza epidemic of 1918, leaving twelve-year-old Ernesto and his surviving young uncle alone in their new country. Still, he continued to work and go to school. After graduating high school, he attended Occidental College, where his senior thesis became his first book: *The Roman Catholic Church as a Factor in the Political and Social History of Mexico* (1928).

The next year, Galarza graduated from Stanford, one of the nation's top universities, with a master's degree in Latin American history and political science. By this time, he was already speaking out on the role of Mexican workers in the

United States. He wrote, "I would ask for recognition of the Mexican's contribution to the agricultural and industrial expansion of western United States. . . . From Denver to Los Angeles and from the Imperial Valley to Portland, it is said, an empire has been created largely by the brawn of the humble Mexican."

Following his graduation from Stanford, Galarza married Mae Taylor and moved to New York City to pursue a doctorate in history at Columbia University. During the 1930s, the couple ran a progressive school in Queens, New York, until Galarza took a job in 1936 with the Pan American Union, now part of the Organization of American States. The group promoted peace and unity in Latin America. By 1940, he was head of the Division of Labor and Social Information and had written numerous publications on Latin American issues. He was particularly concerned with improving education and workers' rights.

In 1947, Galarza finished his doctorate, becoming one of the first Mexican Americans to earn this advanced degree. He then left the Pan American Union and returned to California. For the next fifteen years, he held leadership positions with the National Farm Labor Union and the National Agricultural Workers Union. Galarza recruited union members and led strikes in California and Louisiana. Opposing him were wealthy agricultural interests—individuals and companies with influential political friends. The work that Galarza and others did prepared the ground for the later successful organizing efforts of Cesar Chávez and the United Farm Workers.

Galarza also testified frequently in the U.S. Congress against temporary guest workers, known as *braceros*. Under the bracero program, U.S. farmers could hire short-term Mexican labor to undercut or replace domestic workers. The presence of braceros, Galarza saw, made it harder for Mexican Americans and other farmworkers to win better wages and working conditions.

Galarza left his union work in the early 1960s. He devoted himself to writing and teaching at universities in the San Francisco Bay area. He also worked with Mexican Americans in the barrios, poor urban neighborhoods. He helped them form community groups that would give them the political power to make sure their needs were met. Improving public education was one of his main concerns.

As a writer, Galarza published many books and hundreds of articles and pamphlets on agriculture, labor, and Latin American history. His work in the 1960s and 1970s focused on larger issues affecting agricultural labor. He looked at the power of agribusiness—large companies that owned huge farms and ran them like factories, and that had largely replaced the smaller family farms of old. His first well-known book was *The Merchants of Labor: The Mexican Bracero Story*, which appeared in 1964, the same year that the bracero program he hated so much finally ended. His next book, *Spiders in the House and Workers in the Field* (1970), explored the legal tactics and backroom deals that growers used to fend off unions.

In 1971, Galarza wrote what remains his most popular book, a memoir called *Barrio Boy*. Critics have praised its intimate look at the author's changing image of himself, from a Mexican to a Mexican American. *Barrio Boy* is assigned reading in high schools and colleges throughout the United States. He also wrote stories and poems in Spanish to be used in bilingual classes. In 1979, Galarza was the first Hispanic American nominated for the Nobel Prize for literature, the world's greatest award for an author.

Throughout his life, Galarza saw his knowledge of both his native and his adoptive cultures as an asset. That knowledge helped him work successfully in Latin America, in the fields among farmworkers, and in academic settings. At the end of his life, he was living in San Jose, California, trying to improve public education, and still working to create better opportunities for Mexican Americans.

SEVERO OCHOA
MEDICAL RESEARCHER, NOBEL PRIZE WINNER
1905–1993

Within the human body, chemical reactions take place all the time. As a young man, Severo Ochoa developed an interest in science that led him to study those chemical processes that make human life possible. His research helped him win the greatest honor offered to scientists, the Nobel Prize.

Ochoa was born at Luarca, Spain, on September 24, 1905. His father, also named Severo, was a lawyer and businessman. The family moved to Málaga, and Ochoa received his bachelor's degree at a local university in 1921. During his school years, Ochoa read the works of Santiago Ramón y Cajal, a great Spanish scientist. Ramón y Cajal won recognition for his study of the human nervous system and has been called the father of neuroscience.

As Ochoa later wrote, "Through his writings and his example he did much to arouse my enthusiasm for biology."

Ochoa next attended the Medical School of the University of Madrid, hoping to study with his scientific hero. Ramón y Cajal, however, retired before Ochoa began his classes. Still, he was able to study with other notable scientists in the years to come as he focused on biochemistry and physiology (the study of the function of living matter). He earned his medical degree in 1929, then went to Heidelberg, Germany, to work with Otto Meyerhof, who had won a Nobel Prize in 1922. With Meyerhof, Ochoa studied the biochemistry and physiology of muscle.

In 1931, Ochoa returned to the University of Madrid to teach physiology. He held this job until 1935 and also found time to do research in London. In 1936, he worked again at Meyerhof's laboratory in Heidelberg. Ochoa's research now focused on enzymes, which help initiate biochemical reactions in the body. His work took Ochoa back to England for a time, where he studied the function of vitamin B_1 (thiamine) in the body.

In 1941, with World War II raging in Europe and the United States not yet in the war, Ochoa accepted a position at the Washington University School of Medicine in St. Louis, Missouri. Once again, he had the chance to rub shoulders with some of the world's top researchers, as his colleagues included Carl and Gerty Cori, future Nobelists. In 1942, Ochoa moved to the New York University (NYU) School of Medicine, where he served as a professor of pharmacology and biochemistry. In 1954, he was named chairman of the Department of Biochemistry, and two years later he became a U.S. citizen.

During those years at NYU, Ochoa continued his work with enzymes. His greatest discovery came in 1955, when he and his research assistants found an important enzyme inside bacteria. The enzyme was polynucleotide phosphorylase, and Ochoa discovered that it had an important use in the study of RNA, a nucleic acid. RNA takes the genetic code found in another nucleic

Dr. Ochoa at work in his lab

acid, DNA, and turns it into proteins used by cells. With his new enzyme, Ochoa was able to create RNA outside the body, where he and other scientists could study its function.

In honor of his breakthrough, Ochoa shared the 1959 Nobel Prize for Medicine and Physiology with Arthur Kornberg, who had found a way to create DNA in a test tube. Ochoa became the first Hispanic American to win that award.

Ochoa continued to do research in the United States before returning to Madrid to teach. He received many awards and honorary degrees for his life's work. None, however, were as significant as his Nobel Prize, the recognition of his great contribution to our understanding of how the body works.

JOSÉ LIMÓN

DANCER, CHOREOGRAPHER

1908–1972

If words were adequate to describe fully what the dance can do, there would be no reason for all the mighty muscular effort, the discomfort, the sweat, and the splendors of that art. For it has always existed to give us that which nothing else can.

—José Limón

For José Limón, dance was a way to explore the passion and excitement of life in a physical, visible way. Inspired by early masters of modern dance, he created his own style that drew on his Mexican background, highlighting the strength of his large, powerful body. In the process, he helped increase the prominence of male dancers. By time of his death in 1972, Limón had left his mark on the world of dance, and his influence continues today.

José Arcadio Limón was born in 1908 in Culiacán, México. His father was a musician, and José studied music as well, though he originally showed more talent for the visual arts. He wrote, "It was taken for granted by everyone, including myself, that I was destined for a painter's career." While Limón was still a child, his family left Mexico for Arizona, before finally settling in Los Angeles. There, Limón pursued his artistic studies at the University of California at Los Angeles (UCLA), but he left the school in 1928 to begin an art career in New York.

Limón quickly lost patience with New York's art scene, as his style seemed to be out of favor. In 1929, he happened to attend a modern dance concert held by Harold Kreutzberg, and the show enthralled him. Limón later wrote, "I did not want to continue on this earth unless I learned to do what that man was doing." The next year, at age twenty-two, he began to study dance with the Humphrey-Weidman Company. Limón proved to be a quick learner—within a month after his first class, he danced in a Broadway musical. He would continue to dance in concerts and plays, and sometimes performed duets with Doris Humphrey, one of his instructors.

Limón also did his first work as a choreographer, creating the moves that dancers perform onstage. In his choreography, he drew from the Spanish and Mexican dances he'd seen as a young boy. These Hispanic dances suited his large build and were popular with audiences in New York and on the West Coast. The first major piece he created, *Danzas Mexicanas,* was performed in 1939. He based the dances on five symbolic figures of Mexican history, including the Indio (Native American) and the Conquistador.

Limón kept busy throughout the 1930s as a dancer and teacher. In 1943, he was inducted into the army and served in the Special Services Division as an entertainer. When World War II ended, Limón felt his skills had dulled after not practicing modern dance for more than three years. At thirty-seven, he thought he should either give up dancing or, as he put it, "work harder than ever and get myself back. I chose the latter course." In 1946, Limón formed his own company, the José Limón Dance Company. Humphrey was the company's artistic director, and she created works that showcased Limón at the height of his career. These included *Lament for Ignacio Sanchez Mejias* (1947) and *Day on Earth* (1947). Critics called Limón the greatest male dancer of his generation.

Limón connected with his Mexican roots in *La Malinche* (1949), which recounts the story of conquistador Hernán Cortés and his Indian lover. In 1949, he also debuted what many consider to be his masterpiece, *The Moor's Pavane*, based on Shakespeare's play *Othello*. The dance continues to be performed by ballet and modern dance companies around the world. In 1951, Limón and his company traveled to Mexico City, where Limón created more pieces based on Mexican themes and rhythms. He worked with his own dancers and a local company. "I found I had much in common with the Mexican dancers," he later said. "They [also] use dance to talk about human experience."

Although he had become a U.S. citizen, Limón often returned to Mexico, where he quickly became a major celebrity. His fame also spread around the world, as the U.S. government chose him and his company to represent the best of American art at concerts in Central and South America, Europe, and Asia. As always, he displayed an impressive stage presence and the ability to connect with the public at large, not just fans of modern dance.

During the 1960s, Limón devoted himself to teaching and creating dances for his company. He rarely danced in public, but in 1969, in his last performance, he danced the lead role in his classic *The Moor's Pavane*. By this time, Limón was already partway through a five-year battle against cancer, a struggle he ultimately lost in 1972. His name lives on through the company he founded and through his works. In 1997, he was inducted into the National Museum of Dance Hall of Fame, a tribute to his innovative techniques and the range of human emotions he conveyed through dance.

LUIS ÁLVAREZ
PHYSICIST, NOBEL PRIZE WINNER
1911–1988

During World War II, the United States and Great Britain assembled an amazing team of scientists to work on a secret weapon that could win the war. Called the Manhattan Project, this wartime effort led to the development of the atomic bomb, the most destructive force ever unleashed by humans. One member of the Manhattan Project was Luis Álvarez. In the years after the war, he continued to study atoms, the particles found within every solid, liquid, and gas in the universe, as well as the even tinier subparticles within them. His work earned him a Nobel Prize as well as other scientific honors.

Álvarez could trace his roots to Spain through his grandfather, who emigrated from there to Cuba during the nineteenth century. Álvarez's father, Walter, was a physician and teacher in California who eventually became a medical journalist. As a boy, Álvarez worked with the tools in his father's workshop and created electrical circuits. Later in life, he remembered his father's suggestion to take time alone, with his eyes closed, to think of new problems to solve. "I took his advice very seriously," Álvarez later wrote, "and have been glad ever since that I did."

After completing high school in Rochester, Minnesota, where his father had taken a job at the famous Mayo Clinic, Álvarez enrolled at the University of Chicago. He originally wanted to study chemistry, but he disliked his classes. As a junior, he took a class about light and soon switched his major to physics.

He later wrote that "it was love at first sight" with his new scientific interest. Álvarez received his bachelor of science degree in 1932, then remained at the University of Chicago to earn a master's degree (1934) and a doctorate (1936) in physics. He focused on optics, the study of light.

Álvarez then left Chicago to begin his teaching and research career at the Radiation Laboratory of the University of California at Berkeley. Along with optics, Álvarez was fascinated by atomic particles. He continued his education on his own, reading at the school's library and scribbling out ideas. Álvarez never accepted that his first theory or solution was the right one and always pushed himself to consider other possibilities. Other professors at Berkeley called him "the prize wild idea man" because of his far-ranging interests and scientific creativity.

In 1940, shortly after World War II began in Europe, Álvarez went to the Radiation Laboratory of the Massachusetts Institute of Technology (MIT). He worked on several projects for the U.S. military involving radar. He and his assistants used microwaves, a form of energy, to develop a system that helped pilots land their planes at night and during bad weather. He also worked on projects to track planes in flight and to improve bombing systems.

In 1943, Álvarez left MIT and went back to the University of Chicago, where he worked with physicist Enrico Fermi. Álvarez helped Fermi design the world's first nuclear reactor, a key part of the Manhattan Project. The next year,

Álvarez went to Los Alamos, New Mexico, where the first atomic bombs were built. He helped create the detonator for one type of atomic weapon, and he was chosen to observe the first military use of an atomic bomb.

On August 6, 1945, a B-29 bomber plane carried the bomb, which was nicknamed Little Boy. Álvarez flew in another plane and watched as Little Boy drifted down over the Japanese city of Hiroshima. About 2,000 feet (610 meters) above the ground, the bomb exploded, unleashing a bright light, a huge mushroom-shaped cloud, and the destructive force of 20,000 tons of explosives. The blast and the deadly radiation it released killed about one hundred thousand people, and Álvarez was shocked by the bomb's devastating power. But as he wrote to his young son Walter, "What regrets I have about being a party to killing and maiming thousands of Japanese civilians this morning are tempered with the hope that this terrible weapon we have created may bring the countries of the world together and prevent further wars."

After the war, Álvarez returned to his teaching post at Berkeley and remained active there until 1978. His work in optics during those years later led to new consumer goods, such as improved binoculars and a zoom lens for video cameras. He also continued to study particles, seeking new ways to detect them and accelerate their movement. During the 1950s, one device used to spot particles was called a bubble chamber. Álvarez improved its performance and went on to discover new particles. That work led to his winning the Nobel Prize for Physics in 1968. When receiving his award, Álvarez was quick to share the credit for his important work: "We all appreciate that the Prize must be given to a person, rather than to a group, but we are all honest enough with each other to understand just how much of a group effort our work really was."

Later in his life, Álvarez won attention in a new scientific realm. In 1980, he visited Italy with his son Walter, now a geologist at the University of California. They discovered a large amount of the rare element iridium in an ocean canyon. Iridium is more common on meteors and asteroids than in layers of rock. A chemical dating process showed that the rock was about 65 million years old—dating back to the same time that dinosaurs were thought to have become extinct. Álvarez and his son suggested that 65 million years ago, a gigantic asteroid, at least 6 miles (9.7 km) wide, struck our planet. The impact itself and the thick cloud of dust it created—so dense that it blocked sunlight—could have drastically changed Earth's environment, leading to the dinosaurs' extinction.

For many years, scientists rejected the Álvarezes' theory. In 1990, however, scientists discovered a submerged crater near the Yucatán Peninsula in Mexico. The crater was 65 million years old and 185 miles (298 km) in diameter. Scientists estimate that the asteroid that created the crater would have been about 10 miles (16 km) in diameter when it hit. One of the largest craters ever discovered on Earth, it contained iridium, leading some scientists to think that the Álvarezes' theory about the dinosaurs could be correct. In recent years, however, some scientists have claimed that the Mexican crater was not the site of the dinosaur-killing asteroid, and others still don't accept the original theory. The debate continues today.

Álvarez died of cancer on September 1, 1988. The science world mourned the loss of a great physicist who was also a great inventor—he held twenty-two patents, including one for a machine that helped golfers train indoors. One colleague called Álvarez that rare professional who "seemed to care less about the way the picture in the puzzle would look when fitting everything together than about the fun of looking for the pieces that fit."

THE BRACEROS AND THE MOJADOS

Twice during the twentieth century when the United States faced a severe shortage of farmworkers, it looked to Mexico for help. The U.S. government hired special workers called *braceros*. The word came from the Spanish *brazo*, meaning "arm." The braceros used their arms and hands to pick crops; in English, they might be called "hired hands."

The first bracero program began in August 1942 and ended in 1947. During that period, about 220,000 workers entered the United States under the program. The second period was by far larger and longer. It ran from February 1948 to December 1964, and 4.5 million Mexicans entered the country on temporary work permits. The U.S. and Mexican governments worked together to run both programs.

Workers from Mexico had a great impact on the growth of the American Southwest even before World War II (1939–1945). In fact, workers had crossed the long border between Mexico and the United States since the beginning of the nineteenth century. Only in 1917, when the United States entered World War I (1914–1918), did the Mexican government ask U.S. officials to provide workers such basic needs as housing, medical care, and sick pay. The United States, however, rejected the idea of any formal agreement, though it let U.S. farmers ignore some existing restrictions on immigration so "guest" Mexican farmworkers could enter the country.

A bracero harvests carrots in Arizona, 1942

During the boom years of the 1920s, many Mexicans migrated north and found jobs on their own. But when the Great Depression struck in the 1930s, the Mexican government faced a huge problem. Mexicans who couldn't find work on American farms returned to their homeland. Because the laborers were not eligible for funds from U.S. aid programs, Mexico had to pay the high cost of supporting them.

In 1942, the United States once again needed Mexican workers. The country had just entered World War II, and several million American men were preparing to go off to battle. At the same time, men and women farmworkers flocked into cities to work for the defense industry. U.S. farmers clamored for help harvesting their crops and begged the government to enter an agreement with Mexico. This time, however, the Mexicans insisted that the U.S. government provide for the basic needs of the guest workers. U.S. officials agreed, and the bracero program was born.

For U.S. farms, the first bracero program was a success. The Mexicans were good workers and eager to come to the United States. Wages were much higher than in Mexico, and many families benefited by having at least one worker in the bracero program. The typical bracero was a man in his mid-thirties. He usually could not read or write Spanish and spoke no English. The program offered him the only hope of supporting a large, extended family.

The bracero would stay in the United States with one employer for six months. Then he would return to his home and apply to come back for the next harvest season. Because American employers liked experienced workers, they would hire the same braceros year after year. Railroad companies also used the braceros—by 1945, about 67,000 of them were working on U.S. railways.

Although employers supported the program and many Mexicans earned more than they could at home, the bracero program had critics. Housing for workers was far below American standards. When the program began, chicken coops and railroad cars were used to house workers. Finally, the government built camps, but these provided only the most basic shelter. According to the agreement between the United States and Mexico, "The worker shall be paid in full the salary agreed upon, from which no deduction shall be made in any amount." Yet in some cases, employers subtracted a daily fee for food, even if the workers did not eat anything.

World War II ended in 1945, and the need for braceros fell. The program ended in 1947, but Mexicans still entered the United States, often illegally. These illegal workers were called *mojados*—Spanish for "wetbacks"—because they often entered the United States by crossing the Rio Grande. The term later became an insulting name for any Mexican entering the country without legal papers. No one knows how many mojados entered and reentered the country during the 1940s. Most either had not been accepted into the bracero program or just wished to avoid government red tape. But the mojados rarely had trouble finding work. Plenty of U.S. growers willingly took the risk of hiring illegal aliens just so they could pay them far lower wages than they would have to pay either braceros or American workers.

Braceros line up for a meal, 1963

Southwestern fruit and vegetable growers called on the U.S. Congress to introduce a new bracero program, and one finally went into effect in 1948. The new program gave Mexico less input on how the program was run and workers were selected. When the Korean War broke out in 1950, the United States once again faced a wartime shortage of workers, and Congress extended the program. After the war ended in 1953, Congress extended it again, first for one year, then—at the urging of the growers—over and over.

By the early 1960s, Mexican American officials were speaking out loudly against the bracero program. Evidence showed that the program led to poverty-level wages and horrible working conditions for both Mexican Americans and braceros. Several lawmakers pointed out that the program was in effect a handout to the growers, who made higher profits thanks to the low wages they paid. Labor groups accused the growers of using Mexican farmworkers to keep unions out of agriculture.

In 1964, Congress finally ended the bracero program. The way was now paved for union organizers to demand better working conditions for Mexican American farmworkers. Growers began using new machinery to pick and process their crops, which eventually led to lower prices for consumers. The arrival of mojados, though, did not stop, and these illegal immigrants continue to stir debate in Congress and across the United States.

PART FOUR

AN AMERICAN WAY OF LIFE

138

★ THE AMERICAN G.I. FORUM

HECTOR PÉREZ GARCÍA
PHYSICIAN, CIVIL RIGHTS ORGANIZER
1914–1996

MACARIO GARCÍA
WAR HERO
1920–1972

Mexican Americans served bravely during World War II. Many who suffered from discrimination and underemployment in the United States entered the U.S. Army. Some were not even U.S. citizens, but they made themselves and other Hispanics proud. Unfortunately, when the fighting ended, Mexican American veterans returned home to the same prejudice they had left behind. That prejudice affected Macario García, who had received the highest military honor fighting for the United States. The experiences of Macario and others angered Hector Pérez García (no relation), who had served overseas during the war. In 1948, he founded the American G.I. Forum to confront the problems Mexican American veterans faced.

Both Garcías were born in Mexico and then later moved with their families to Texas. Both battled poverty and prejudice. By the time the United States was fully involved in World War II in 1942, Hector García had become a medical doctor—a rare achievement for Mexican immigrants in Texas at that time. He volunteered for the army and fought bravely in combat before the army decided to use his professional skills in the medical corps. Unlike Dr. García, Macario was not well educated—he had not finished high school—and he was drafted into the army. He showed no fear on the battlefield and was credited with a single-handed assault of two German machine-gun sites, killing six enemy soldiers and wounding several others. Back in the United States, President Harry Truman awarded him the Congressional Medal of Honor.

Macario García, however, found that being a decorated war hero did not end the discrimination he had to endure. A restaurant owner in Texas refused to serve him because he was Mexican. García got into a fight with the man, the local sheriff was called, and Garcia was arrested. News soon spread about the medal winner who was sent to jail because he fought for his legal rights. At his trial, García was found innocent, and he went on to gain his U.S. citizenship in 1947.

By now, Dr. García was back in Texas, and he knew about the insults Macario García and other Mexican American veterans had experienced. Injured veterans did not receive medical care they had been promised and had trouble finding jobs. Then in 1948, a Texas undertaker refused to bury the remains of Felix Longoria, a Mexican American soldier killed in the Battle of the Philippines. Dr. García had come home from the war tired of seeing pain and poverty and cruelty. He did not want more conflict. But, as he told his family, "I do not seek to fight unless it's completely right." Helping Mexican

American veterans secure what they had earned, Dr. García believed, was one fight that was right.

In 1948, the doctor organized the American G.I. Forum specifically to help Mexican American vets get what they had earned through their military service. He served as chairman of the board and organized more than a hundred chapters in Texas alone. Soon there were G.I. Forum members all over the country, and the organization expanded its focus, speaking out on civil rights issues in general, not just the problems of veterans. The G.I. Forum was soon recognized as an important Mexican American organization.

During the 1960s, Dr. García became an expert on the problems of Mexican migrant workers. He called for an end to the bracero program, which brought Mexican workers into the United States. With his rising prominence as a Mexican American leader, he was named as an alternate U.S. ambassador to the United Nations, becoming the first U.S. citizen to address that body in Spanish. He advised three U.S. presidents, and, in 1984, he received the Presidential Medal of Freedom, America's highest civilian honor.

Dr. García died in 1996, but the American G.I. Forum lives on. Its thousands of members speak out for improved veterans' benefits and on critical issues important to Mexican Americans. Local and state groups encourage members to work within their communities for social and political change.

DESI ARNAZ
ENTERTAINER AND ACTOR
1917–1986

In 1950, Desi Arnaz and his wife, Lucille Ball, had an unusual idea: Create a half-hour TV show based on their life. They approached the Columbia Broadcasting System (CBS), one of the major TV networks of the day, and convinced them to air the show. Soon, the exploits of a Cuban bandleader and his red-haired, nutty wife became the top show in the United States, and *I Love Lucy* remains one of the most beloved TV shows of all time. With the show, Arnaz helped define the TV situation comedy (sitcom), created an entertainment empire, and brought Hispanic Americans onto the small screen.

Desiderio "Desi" Alberto Arnaz y de Acha III was born in Santiago, Cuba. His father was the mayor of Santiago, and both sides of Arnaz's family had money. In 1933, after a revolution forced the ruling Cuban government out of power, the family moved to Miami, Florida. Arnaz, who played guitar and sang, soon joined the orchestra of Xavier Cugat, one of the leading Latin bandleaders at that time. After playing with Cugat, he played in his own band in clubs throughout the United States.

By the end of the decade, Desi Arnaz was on his way to becoming a star. In 1939, he played a major role in the Broadway play *Too Many Girls*. When the play was made into a movie, Arnaz re-created his stage role, and during the filming fell in love with one of his costars, a comic actress named Lucille Ball. Within a year, they were married and living in Los Angeles. During the

1940s, Ball continued to work in films and also did radio while Arnaz toured with his band. To keep their long-distance marriage thriving, the couple spent thousands of dollars every year on phone calls and telegrams.

Working together on a TV show was one way for Arnaz and Ball to have a somewhat more normal family life. And the sponsors of Ball's successful radio program, *My Favorite Husband,* had proposed making a television program loosely based on that show. Arnaz and Ball created their own company, Desilu, to produce the show. In the original TV show, Arnaz and Ball appeared as Larry and Lucy López. Some changes were soon made, and their characters became Ricky and Lucy Ricardo, while two new characters—Ethel (Vivian Vance) and Fred (William Frawley) Mertz, the upstairs neighbors and landlords—were added.

Always a businessman, Arnaz resolved to do things his own way. He insisted the new show, called *I Love Lucy,* be filmed in Los Angeles rather than New York, where CBS wanted it shot. Arnaz also worked with Karl Freund, a cameraman he had met while making films, to devise a three-camera system to film the show. This let them film a single scene from different angles and cut back and forth between the characters. This approach, as well as taping in front of a live audience, are still common features of the TV sitcom. Arnaz also worked out a unique business deal for him and his wife. They agreed to make less money up front and keep all the money the show made after its original run. That decision would make Arnaz and Ball very wealthy.

The plots of *I Love Lucy* are now familiar to generations of TV viewers. Desi Arnaz played Ricky Ricardo, a Cuban bandleader based on

Arnaz himself. His thick Spanish accent made it hard for others, including Lucy, to understand him, and provided some of the show's humor. When his sometimes-wacky wife upset him, Ricky unleashed his anger in rapid-fire Spanish. Lucy often riled her husband with her efforts to get into show business or such crazy schemes as stealing an elephant. Ricky's most famous lines, usually repeated from one episode to another, were "Lucy, I'm home" and, when demanding that Lucy provide a full account of her misadventures, "You've got some 'splainin' to do."

I Love Lucy made Arnaz and Ball international stars. They tickled funny bones while showing that a marriage could survive almost anything. As one critic put it, they managed to "convince viewers that *any* wife might . . . glue a beard on her face in a campaign against her husband's moustache." Thanks to the success of the show, Arnaz became the first Hispanic television star in the United States.

The popularity of *I Love Lucy* led to the growth of Desilu Productions. Arnaz, head of the company, began to use profits from the success of *I Love Lucy* to produce other TV programs. A major success for Desilu was the series *The Untouchables,* about the adventures of Elliot Ness and his "G-men" (FBI agents) in their fight against Al Capone and other gangsters. At one point, Desilu was bigger than some of the major motion-picture studios, such as Warner Bros. and MGM.

I Love Lucy first aired on October 15, 1951. Starring in the show and running Desilu became a drain on the couple, and weekly episodes of *I Love Lucy* ended in June 1957. But, for the next few years, Arnaz and Ball made some hour-long specials featuring their beloved characters, and reruns from the early seasons also aired. The last show appeared in 1961, a year after Arnaz and Ball divorced. In 1963, Arnaz decided to retire from television, and he sold his share in Desilu to Ball. He died in 1986, but on television, he lives on as Ricky Ricardo, enduring the challenges and charms of life with Lucy.

ANTONIA PANTOJA
SOCIAL ACTIVIST
1922–2002

Growing up poor in Puerto Rico, Antonia Pantoja might not have seemed a candidate for an influential life. But her grandmother, Pantoja later said, always told her she had a "special destiny." That special destiny turned out to be promoting education among Puerto Ricans and improving life in the Puerto Rican communities that began growing in the United States after World War II. Her nonstop efforts reflected one of her core beliefs: "One cannot live a lukewarm life. You have to live life with passion." By the time of her death in 2002, Pantoja was one of the leading Hispanic activists in the country.

Antonia Pantoja was born in San Juan, Puerto Rico. Despite her family's poverty and the absence of her father, Pantoja used her natural intelligence and will to succeed to receive a good education. She was supported and encouraged by her grandmother and others. Her grandfather also shaped her thinking. He worked in a cigar factory and organized the other workers to strike for better wages. From him, she later said, she learned about "the rights of people to organize . . . to fight for the problems that affected them."

In 1942, Pantoja received a teaching degree from the Normal School of the University of Puerto Rico. For two years, she taught in rural schools on the island, then she decided to leave while the United States was fighting in World War II. The trip to the mainland was hazardous because enemy submarines sometimes lurked nearby. But Pantoja made the trip safely and began a new life in New York City. Like thousands of other Puerto Ricans, she came in search of new opportunities and a better life.

Pantoja worked first in factories. She was determined to improve her English and to explore the rich cultural life of the city. In 1952, with the help of a scholarship, she graduated from Hunter College with a degree in sociology. Two years later, she obtained a master's degree in social work from Columbia University.

During the 1950s and 1960s, life was hard for Puerto Ricans in New York. Most could not speak English, had little or no education, and worked in the worst-paying jobs. Puerto Rican families often lived at the poverty line, crowded together in small apartments. In addition, the children of these families faced one of the highest dropout rates in the United States. The community lacked organization and political power. Looking around and seeing this despair, Pantoja vowed to make a difference for the better.

Even while still at Columbia, Pantoja took time from her studies to found the Hispanic Young Adult Association. In 1958, she and other activists founded the Puerto Rican Forum, her first professional effort to begin dealing with the "Puerto Rican problem," particularly within education. In 1961, she founded Aspira, her most lasting contribution to social work. The name came from the Spanish word for "aspire," and Pantoja hoped her efforts would help Puerto Ricans aspire to achieve great things. The organization sought to help Puerto Rican students enter college and receive financial aid. Through Aspira's efforts, Puerto Ricans began to push for reforms, seeking courses more relevant to Puerto Rican students, classes for adults, and better relations between schools and their local communities. Aspira started as a New York organization but eventually went nationwide and expanded its focus to include all Hispanic youth.

One of Pantoja's top concerns was bilingual education. In 1972, Aspira sued the City of New York in federal court over its policy of teaching only in English. The court ruled in favor of Aspira in 1974, and the city was ordered to begin bilingual education and English-as-a-second-language programs for Latino students. In 1970, Pantoja also founded Universidad Boricua, the country's first college controlled by Puerto Ricans, located in Washington, D.C. She became head of the university after earning a doctoral degree in 1973 from Union Graduate School in Ohio. She also established the Puerto Rican Research and Resource Center in Washington, D.C.

Health problems led Pantoja to move west, and in 1978 she took a teaching job at San Diego State University's School of Social Work. There she created the Graduate School for Community Development. Returning to Puerto Rico in 1985, Pantoja continued her leadership by establishing Producir, an organization to help small businesses in neglected areas. During the 1990s, she returned to New York City to resume her work in the Hispanic community.

During her life, Pantoja received numerous awards, including the Presidential Medal of Freedom, the highest honor given to a civilian. Just before her death she published her autobiography, *Memoir of a Visionary: Antonia Pantoja* (2002), a moving account of her life, aspirations, and achievements. Antonia Pantoja was a brilliant and effective community activist, social worker, educator, and one of the true pioneers in advocating for better education for Puerto Ricans and all Latinos in New York.

TITO PUENTE
MUSICIAN
1923–2000

In the world of Latin music, Tito Puente was considered royalty. He won the nickname *El Rey del Mambo*—"The King of Mambo." Mambo is a form of dance music that he helped popularize. He was also sometimes called the King of the Timbales, or simply El Rey. A musician, bandleader, and composer, Puente drew both Hispanic and Anglo fans to his concerts with his sizzling rhythms that blended jazz and Afro-Cuban music. In his later years, a new generation of fans learned about Puente's music when rock guitarist Carlos Santana recorded some of his songs. Puente is one of the most important figures in the history of Latin music.

Tito was born Ernest Anthony Puente, in Spanish Harlem, a Hispanic neighborhood in New York City. His parents settled there after leaving their native Puerto Rico. Tito showed a flair for music at an early age, and he listened to big-band jazz stars such as Duke Ellington. Another of his heroes was the popular drummer Gene Krupa. Tito wanted to learn drums, too, and he became a master of the timbales, two small tom-toms mounted on a stand. He also learned to play the standard drum kit with its assortment of drums and cymbals, as well as piano, vibraphone, and saxophone.

Tito combined his natural musical talents with a strong drive to succeed, and he was already playing gigs—concerts or dances—as a teen. He dropped out of high school at age fifteen to play professionally in Miami Beach, Florida, and then worked with a young Cuban pianist named José Curbelo. By the time World War II began, Puente was playing his timbales at the front of the stage instead of the back, where most percussionists played. He also played standing, instead of sitting down. His musical talents and charming personality demanded that he play front and center. For a time, he played with Machito and His Afro Cubans. That band's musical director, Mario Bauza, was one of the first musicians to combine Latin rhythms with jazz, and he greatly influenced Puente's later style.

Puente's career stalled during World War II, when he entered the navy. After the war, he used a special government program for veterans called the G.I. Bill to attend the world-famous Juilliard School of Music. There he learned how to write music and how to arrange it, which means deciding how a band would play a certain tune. By 1948, he was leading his own band. With this group of talented musicians, Puente took the energy of Cuban dance music and expanded it well beyond what anyone before him had done. At the famous Palladium Ballroom in New York City, Puente played Cuban dance music called mambo, and it made him a star. He then went beyond the traditional dance styles, adding the complex melodies, harmonies, and orchestral arrangements of modern jazz. Puente led both his Palladium big band and a smaller Latin jazz group known as the Latin Ensemble.

During the 1950s at the Palladium, Puente was crowned El Rey del Mambo. His hit records of the decade include *Puente Goes Jazz* and *Dance Mania*. He continued to play and record through the 1960s, then watched the rock group Santana have a hit in 1970 with his song "Oye Como Va." Carlos Santana and his band helped bring Puente and Latin jazz to a new audience. After that, during his shows, Puente was often asked by audience members to play "that Santana song," which he did with great pleasure. Puente and Santana later performed together in concert.

Puente went on to showcase his talents on both television and the big screen. He appeared on *The Bill Cosby Show* and played some of his own music in the 1992 film *The Mambo Kings*. In 1979, he won the first of four Grammy Awards, the highest honor in the music business, and he also received a star on the Hollywood Walk of Fame. Throughout his professional career, Puente made 119 recordings and was loved around the world. He died shortly after completing his last album, *Por Fin/At Last*. His manager, reflecting on Puente's work for that recording, noted that the master musician was sick while he made it. Still, "the solos he did on the album are just incredible." Puente remained El Rey until the very end.

★ CELIA CRUZ
SINGER
1925–2003

Watching Celia Cruz perform was a treat to both the ears and the eyes. She came onstage wearing one of many wigs, her trademark high-heeled shoes, and a colorful, billowing dress. Then out of her mouth came sizzling Spanish word, sung to the dance music of the Caribbean, a product of the region's mixed heritage of European and African culture. One Cuban American writer described Cruz as "a grandmother-like figure with a mammoth voice who could dance like a teenager." She became known throughout the world as the Queen of Salsa, the vibrant dance music she sang with such energy.

Cruz was born in the Santo Suarez neighborhood of Havana, in October 21, 1925. She started singing as a child and studied music theory, piano, and voice at the National Conservatory of Music. Her father wanted her to become a teacher, but as a teenager Cruz began singing on some of the radio talent shows popular in 1940s Havana. She won a contest and met musicians and producers who helped launch her musical career. Cruz left her studies and toured with a female dance group. In 1950, she joined La Sonora Matancera as the lead singer and recorded her first of many songs with the band.

Havana during the 1950s was a vibrant city for wealthy tourists who came to gamble and hear Cuban entertainers. Cruz and La Sonora Matancera played in the lavish hotels and clubs, providing the danceable, driving soundtrack for Americans and other foreigners looking for a good time. At times, she also performed without the band, developing the colorful stage appearance that became her trademark and helped make her a star. But the party atmosphere ended for both Cubans and tourists when Fidel Castro took control of Cuba in 1959. His Communist government shut down the casinos and threw out the American-owned businesses that dominated the island's economy. Many Cubans fled the country, and Cruz soon became an exile as well. On July 15, 1960, Cruz and La Sonora Matancera left for a concert tour of Mexico. The singer would never return to her homeland.

Cruz continued her successful musical career in Mexico, and she also began to appear in films. By the end of 1961, she decided to go to the United States, eventually settling in New York City. When Castro's government later refused to grant her an entry visa to visit her dying mother, she vowed she would not return until Cuba gained its freedom.

At the time, New York's Hispanic communities were filled with the sounds of different styles of dance music that came from the Caribbean and South America. What came to be called *salsa* (sauce) was a mixture of the Cuban music called *son* and dance styles from Puerto Rico. During the late 1960s and the 1970s, Cruz played a crucial role in New York's salsa boom, recording both solo and with the top artists of the day. She worked with a number of Puerto Rican musicians, such as singer Johnny Pacheco, bandleader Tito Puente, and trombonist Willie Colón.

In the world of Latin music, Cruz was a rarity: a woman who could match the musical skills of her male partners while easily outshining them on the stage. Cruz was also an example of the diversity of the Hispanic community in the United States. With her African roots, she became a symbol of pride among people of different languages and colors. And as salsa's popularity grew, Cruz began to work with a wide range of musicians outside the Hispanic community, including stars such as Patti LaBelle and David Byrne.

The most important partnership of Cruz's life was with trumpeter Pedro Knight. They met while both were performing with La Sonora Matancera, and they married in 1962. Although some show-business couples find it hard to stay together, given the pressures of their field, Cruz and Knight were admired for their steadfast loyalty to each other and joy in each other's company.

During her career in the United States, Cruz recorded more than seventy albums, and hits such as "Yerberito Moderno," "Burundanga," and "Quimbara" topped the record charts. Cruz also acted in ten films, with roles in *The Mambo Kings* and *The Perez Family*. She received numerous awards for her music, including several Latin Grammys. In 1994, President Bill Clinton granted her the highest honor bestowed on an artist in the United States, the National Endowment for the Arts Medal. Well into her seventies, she proved she was able to keep up with the times—and with musicians young enough to be her grandchildren—when she recorded the rap-infused *La Negra Tiene Tumbao*. The record earned her a Grammy for Best Salsa Album of 2002.

Onstage, Cruz was known to shout out *azúcar* (sugar). She used it to call for extra energy with her band and the audience. By referring to sugar, she also looked back to the main crop of her homeland and to the African slaves brought there to raise it.

CÉSAR CHÁVEZ
LABOR ORGANIZER
1927–1993

César Chávez knew what it was like to work long hours in the hot sun, picking crops as a migrant farmworker. Seeing and feeling for himself the difficulties of the job led Chávez to fight for better working conditions for Mexican American farmworkers. During the late 1960s and early 1970s, Chávez became the most important Mexican American U.S. labor organizer and activist. He was also a leader in the larger struggle for civil rights and workers' rights for all Americans, making him the most prominent Mexican American of the day.

Chávez was born near Yuma, Arizona, where his family once owned a farm as well as a small store. But during the Great Depression of the 1930s, the Chávezes could no longer afford to pay their taxes, and they lost the farm and their business. They joined other area farmers who had once owned land but now had to travel across the West, looking for work on other farms. The Chávez family ended up in California's Imperial Valley. Contractors who worked for large landowners there had promised them good wages. Instead, César and his family ended up earning less than they were promised and lived in a one-room shack made of metal. The Chávezes found jobs picking cotton, grapes, and carrots, following the seasons from one camp to another.

As a result, Chávez never stayed in one school for very long. He once said he had attended at least thirty elementary schools, some "for a day, a week, or a few months." His formal education ended after eighth grade. From his family, however, he learned two of his most important lessons: the value of hard work and the need to care for poor, suffering people.

At age seventeen, Chávez joined the navy, enduring what he later called "the two worst years of my life." He then went back to California, where he married Helen Favela, whose parents also had roots in Mexico. Although he returned to migrant work, Chávez found time to read. His favorite topic was history, and he studied the way past politicians and activists had sought solutions during times of crisis. He was especially drawn to the writings of Mahatma Gandhi, a great thinker

and political leader from India. Gandhi had led the call for India's independence from Great Britain, but he wanted to achieve that goal through nonviolent means. Nonviolence became a key part of Chávez's thinking as well.

By 1950, Chávez and his family were living in a Hispanic neighborhood in San Jose called *Sal Si Puedes* (*Get Out If You Can*). But too many Mexican Americans could not flee the poverty of the city because of the low wages they made on the farms. In 1952, Chávez met Fred Ross, a leader of the Community Service Organization (CSO). The group helped farmworkers and other poor people by finding them housing, medical care, and legal services. Ross helped Chávez start to shape his own philosophy. He began to take an active role in the struggle to improve migrant workers' miserable conditions. Most worked long hours under the sun for low wages. Their jobs were never secure—they could be fired at any time—and they received no medical benefits. By the time he was thirty-three, Chávez was organizing families in the grape fields and persuading growers to increase wages.

Chávez eventually became a leader of the CSO, but he left the organization when it resisted his efforts to organize the grape pickers. He then used some of his own money to create the National Farm Workers Union. The union's name was later changed to the United Farm Workers Union (UFW). Chávez brought together Hispanics while also opening up the ranks to Filipinos and the small community of black farmworkers. By the mid-1960s, he had become a beloved folk hero to the poor and to the boisterous student movement. But to some California business owners and the politicians who defended their interests, Chávez was a hated enemy.

Chávez was known for organizing marches that attracted substantial media attention. He also went on hunger strikes in order to achieve his objectives. In 1968, for instance, he drank only water for twenty-five days. This fast came during a bitter struggle to win recognition for labor unions on the huge farms of the West. Chávez asked Americans to not buy grapes unless the package had a label that said they had been picked by union workers. The boycott won national attention and even spread to Europe. During this time, Chávez began to work with important national politicians, such as Senator Robert F. Kennedy, the brother of former president John F. Kennedy. Chávez helped organized Mexican Americans as a potent political force in California and on the national scene.

As the battle for the union went on, Chávez spoke at rallies across the country. He said, "Our strikers . . . have been kicked and beaten and herded by dogs, they have been cursed and ridiculed, they have been stripped and chained and jailed. . . . But they have been taught not to lie down and die nor to flee in

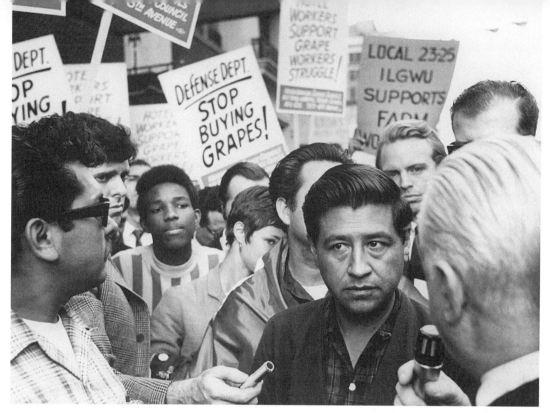

Chavez is interviewed during a demonstration in 1969

shame, but to resist with every ounce of human endurance and spirit." This was the beginning of La Causa (The Cause), as his movement came to be known. Chávez formed alliances with religious associations, other minority groups, and student organizations. He sent UFW members from the countryside to cities in order to boycott and picket. Civic resistance became his main tool. In order to achieve the movement's goals, he repeatedly reminded everyone that resistance needed to be peaceful. Chávez once remarked, "The rich have money but the poor have time."

By 1970, the UFW had won a partial victory, gaining union contracts with most of the major grape growers. Still, in the years to come, Chávez battled with other unions for control of the fields and continued to bring national attention to the farmworkers' difficult lives. In 1972, he went on another long fast. The next year, the U.S. Congress passed a law that made it easier for the UFW to hold and win elections among the workers.

Unlike other labor leaders of the era, Chávez combined activism with a concern for the environment. That mix made him appealing to the environmental movement of the 1980s and 1990s. His struggle to improve labor conditions was also a fight against pesticides. Throughout the 1980s, Chávez led a boycott to protest the use of toxic pesticides on grapes. This boycott was far less successful than earlier ones. In 1988, Chávez went on another famous fast—his "Fast for Life," which lasted thirty-six days. The Reverend Jesse Jackson, a prominent African American leader, continued the fast after Chávez concluded it. Other celebrities followed suit, including actors Martin Sheen, Edward James Olmos, Danny Glover, and Whoopi Goldberg.

As Chávez aged, America moved away from the era of idealism and reform that he had helped create during the 1960s. The Chicano movement, which sought to give Mexican Americans more political power, began to dwindle, and Chávez's role in the larger Hispanic community seemed unsure. Was he simply a Mexican American leader, or could he also present himself as a champion of the various Latino groups, such as mainland Puerto Ricans, Dominican Americans, and Cuban Americans? And were these groups interested in what he had to say?

As the UFW lost influence as a force for social and political change, Chávez focused on speaking at university and international forums. These talks were less about struggle than about presenting himself as a past hero from an increasingly distant age. But plenty of people still remembered Chávez and the importance of his work. After his death in 1993, more than fifty thousand marched to his funeral. They honored him at the sites in Delano, California, where he had done his first and last fasts. He is buried in La Paz, California, home of the UFW headquarters. A foundation in his name was established in Glendale, California, in 1993 to educate people about his life and legacy.

★ LAURO FRED CAVAZOS
EDUCATOR, GOVERNMENT OFFICIAL
1927–

Lauro Fred Cavazos devoted his public life to education, and he took a particular interest in the high dropout rates of Hispanic students. Cavazos had a chance to directly tackle that problem when he served as the head of the U.S. Department of Education. With his appointment to that position in 1988, he became the first Hispanic American to serve in a presidential cabinet.

A sixth-generation Texan, Cavazos was born on January 4, 1927, on the King Ranch, a sprawling cattle and horse ranch in south Texas. Cavazos began his education in a tiny one-room schoolhouse and eventually attended Texas Tech University, where he earned bachelor's and master's degrees in zoology. He later went to Iowa State University, where he received a doctorate in physiology. Subsequently, Cavazos taught at the Medical College of Virginia and at Tufts University School of Medicine in Boston. He was appointed dean at Tufts, serving in that position from 1975 to 1980. During his career, he consulted with the World Health

Organization and other leading worldwide health groups regarding medical advancements. Cavazos also wrote numerous articles and served as an editor for various medical journals.

Cavazos returned to Texas in 1980 to accept the presidency at his first alma mater, Texas Tech. He was the first Hispanic American and graduate of the university to rise to that position. Cavazos also served as president of the school's Health Science Center. In his dual role at the university, Cavazos became a distinguished leader in education and medicine.

In 1983, the League of United Latin American Citizens (LULAC) named Cavazos Hispanic Educator of the Year, and it later gave him its Hispanic Hall of Fame award. In 1984, President Ronald Reagan honored Cavazos for his leadership in the field of education. Four years later, Reagan tapped Cavazos to serve as secretary of the Department of Education. The move seemed unusual since Reagan was a Republican and Cavazos belonged to the Democratic Party. But it showed the president's faith in his new secretary's abilities, as well as a desire to reach out to Hispanic voters, who traditionally voted Democratic.

In 1989, Reagan left office and was followed by another Republican, George H. W. Bush. He kept Cavazos as his secretary of education. In that role, Cavazos fought to reform education and increase educational opportunities for all American children, but especially Hispanic Americans. He started programs to fight drug abuse and worked to raise the expectations of parents, students, and teachers so that children might have brighter futures.

Political pressures from Republicans who disliked Cavazos led him to resign in December 1990. But after leaving Washington, D.C., he remained a leader in the fields of medicine and education. He returned to Tufts University Medical School, where he still serves as professor of family medicine and community health.

★ RUBEN SALAZAR
JOURNALIST
1928–1970

Ruben Salazar's love of words and interest in politics led him into journalism at a time when few Hispanic Americans excelled in that field. By the time of his death, Salazar was the leading Mexican American journalist in the country. The questions that surrounded his death—at the hands of Los Angeles police—reflected one of the issues that drove Salazar's later career. He hoped to uncover injustice against Mexican Americans and make sure they received the rights and protection they deserved.

Salazar was born in Ciudad Juárez, Chihuahua, Mexico. When he was an infant, his family crossed the Rio Grande into Texas. Growing up in El Paso, Salazar was a good student, fluent in Spanish and English. After high school, he joined the army, serving in Germany. When his tour of duty ended, he attended the University of Texas at El Paso and received a bachelor's degree in journalism. As a student, Salazar worked at the *El Paso Herald-Post.* After graduating, he landed a reporting job at the *Santa Rosa Press Democrat.*

Salazar showed a flair for investigative journalism, digging deep for facts rather than relying on the official statements of politicians and others. For one story, he went undercover, posing as a drunk so he could see firsthand the conditions Mexican Americans faced in an El Paso jail. Salazar spent most of his time covering the suffering of the Mexican American community in the barrios, institutions, and prisons around El Paso. His boss called him one of the best reporters on the paper.

Salazar's focus on the struggles of *la raza,* the Mexican American people, continued as he took on new jobs in California. He moved from Santa Rosa to work for the larger *San Francisco News,* then to the powerful newsroom of the *Los Angeles Times.* Salazar joined the *Times* in 1959, when it was just beginning to assert itself as a major newspaper. The paper was also beginning to pay more attention to the needs and desires of the large Mexican American community in the region. Salazar worked that beat for several years. Then, in 1965, he covered the Vietnam War. Like many journalists of the era, he seemed to support the war at first. But after covering the war for about a year, he became sickened by the slaughter he saw. He also came to see that many poor African and Hispanic Americans were dying in the fighting.

In 1966, the *Los Angeles Times* brought Salazar back from Vietnam and made him chief of its office in Mexico City. He was the first Mexican American ever to take such a major role at any U.S. newspaper. In 1968, Salazar returned to Los Angeles and was assigned to cover the growth of the Chicano movement. Throughout the 1960s, Mexican Americans had called for greater civil rights in political participation, with protests and sometimes violence adding weight to that call. Salazar covered these troubled times and the goals of Chicano activists. In one 1969 article, he wrote, "The Spanish language is part of [Mexican] culture which should not be tampered with. Having colonized the Southwest, Spanish-speaking people refuse to abandon their traditions because of the advent of Anglo-American culture."

Salazar's outspoken support of some aspects of the Chicano movement brought him unwelcome attention from local law enforcement and the Federal Bureau of Investigation. His bosses at the paper began to encourage him to tone down his language. Yet people who knew him said Salazar was a journalist first, not an activist. Still, he saw injustice around him, and his experience in Vietnam had also shaped his thinking. He would pursue the truth, as he always had as a journalist, and speak out about what he learned.

In 1969, Salazar was offered the position of news director at KMEX, a Spanish-language television station. The job would give him a chance to do what he believed all journalists should do: "The press's obligation is to rock the boat." Not wanting to lose Salazar completely, the *Times* offered him a weekly column to explore Chicano affairs. Suddenly, he was in a position to reach millions of Chicanos through the nightly news while maintaining his controversial column in the *Times*.

On August 29, 1970, a large march was scheduled by the National Chicano Moratorium for the Los Angeles area. The group opposed the Vietnam War. The news media showed up, as thirty thousand protesters walked the streets. Salazar was on hand to record the Chicano perspective. The march was tumultuous, and the police made a strong showing. What happened to Salazar that day is still uncertain. At one point, he entered a bar, and Los Angeles Sheriffs Department officer Tom Wilson stepped inside and fired a tear-gas grenade launcher, hitting Salazar in the head. The killing was ruled a homicide, but Wilson was never prosecuted. Salazar had angered Los Angeles police with his continuing coverage of their harsh treatment of Mexican Americans. Some

Chicanos claim Salazar's death was a deliberate effort by the police to silence what some people saw as a dangerous and powerful voice. Others have argued that the killing was an unfortunate accident, fueled by the wild scene at the protest itself.

To some Chicanos, Salazar was a martyr, a hero who gave his life for a great cause. He became the subject of books, films, and paintings. His wife and his journalist friends, however, say Salazar would have rejected the label of martyr. He was always a journalist first. But not just any journalist. As one friend later wrote, "He was not the first Latino reporter or even the first Latino columnist, but he was the best and the bravest."

Today, he is remembered by the Ruben Salazar Library in Santa Rosa, California, and there are scholarships and educational awards in his name throughout the United States.

PANCHO GONZALES
TENNIS CHAMPION
1928–1995

★

That first racket of mine, to me, was the eighth wonder of the world. . . . I never let it out of my sight. I took it to bed with me to protect the strings and warping frame from the temperature changes of the room. To find the proper grip . . . I shook hands with it all day. . . . Sometimes I even talked to it, I'd say, "Good morning Señor Tennis Racket." And in my own falsetto [high voice], the racket would respond "Good morning, Señor Gonzales."

—Pancho Gonzales

Richard "Pancho" Gonzales was, to say the least, an unlikely tennis champion. At a time when tennis was still a gentleman's sport played mostly at private clubs, Gonzales stunned tennis fans by scrapping his way to the top with the feisty determination of a boxer. His resolve and skill made him one of the most popular tennis stars of his day and earned him a place in his sport's hall of fame. He was also the first nonwhite player to excel in the game.

Born in Los Angeles to Mexican-born parents, Gonzales was the first person in his family to play tennis. As he admits in his autobiography, he was a wild kid with more restless energy than his hardworking parents could handle. When he told his mother he really wanted a bike, she said, "'Too dangerous. I'll get something safer.' She went to the May Company and bought me a tennis racket." Pancho took the racket to a public tennis court nearby and began hitting a beat-up tennis ball he found lying on the ground. From that moment on, as he later recalled, "I was madly in love." Tennis became his life.

Gonzales never took formal lessons. He learned by watching others play and then practicing. And he won by hitting the ball harder than anybody else, particularly on his serve. He won his first tournament in 1939, while still in junior high school. That same year, the *Los Angeles Times* sports editor wrote a column titled "Southern California—Cradle of Tennis Champions." The column mentioned Gonzales, and it led to his being introduced to Perry T. Jones, an important man in California tennis at the time. Jones saw the eleven-year-old play and was impressed with his skills. Less impressive was Gonzales's attendance in school—he often skipped classes to practice his game. Since Gonzales missed so many classes, Jones refused to let him play in local tournaments. Still, Gonzales was able to compete with other boys his age, and he became one of the best young players in California.

Gonzales dropped out of high school to concentrate on tennis, then served in the U.S. Navy from 1945 to 1947. After leaving the service, he began playing tennis seriously again and was soon ranked as one of the top twenty players in the United States. One tennis magazine wrote early in 1948, "It is our opinion that the six-foot-three powerhouse from Los Angeles is one year away from the top." It turned out the magazine was right. Gonzales improved steadily throughout the summer, then in September, he won the U.S. Singles Championship at Forest Hills, New York. He followed that with another tournament win early in 1949. Since focusing on tennis full time, Gonzales had won on the full variety of surfaces used for tennis courts—clay, grass, and artificial—and proven himself a dashing champion.

His stunning success came with a price, though. Gonzales himself admitted that he lost focus on his game after all the acclaim and attention he received following the Forest Hills win. In 1949, he trained poorly, gained weight, and lost his edge. Sportswriters began calling him "the problem child of tennis." As he battled with both the media and himself, he began to lose crucial matches. Just a year after his win at Forest Hills, no one expected him to repeat as champion there. They expected Gonzales to prove what many tennis experts had said all along—that his victory in 1948 had been a fluke.

But just as he had done the year before, Gonzales saved his best game for the biggest tournament. He breezed through the early rounds, then faced Ted Schroeder in the final. Schroeder, a former champion at Forest Hills himself, was favored to win. Gonzales, however, defeated him in a grueling five-set match to

Gonzales holding Men's Amateur Singles trophy, 1948

retain his championship. His favorite part about winning, he later recalled, was seeing the next cover of *American Lawn Tennis* magazine. A picture showed him smiling broadly, with his wife, Henrietta, at his side. The caption read, "The Last Laugh."

The next year, Gonzales turned professional, and starting in 1953 he won the first of eight U.S. Professional Championship titles. At the time, however, the most important championship events, such as the Forest Hills tournament and England's Wimbledon, were only open to amateurs. Gonzales could not compete for those titles, though he usually defeated the amateur

Gonzales playing at Wimbledon, England, 1969

champs once they turned pro. In 1961, Gonzales retired, but his fierce drive to compete—and win—led him back to the court in 1964. Another retirement soon followed, and then another return to the game he loved.

At age forty, Gonzales was eager to compete against men half his age. The draw was that the era of "Open" tennis had begun, meaning that both pros and amateurs could play at the top four "Grand Slam" events. Gonzales did not win any of these events, but he still showed his brilliant style of play. In 1969, he played one of the most memorable matches of all time. Gonzales and highly ranked Charlie Pasarell played a marathon 112-game battle that went on for more than five hours. In the end, "old man" Gonzales came out on top.

Gonzales continued to play major events until 1972. That year, at forty-four, he became the oldest man to win a tournament in the Open era. Then Gonzales retired for good, though he continued to play in senior events and taught in both Las Vegas, Nevada, and California. Since his death in 1995, many tennis experts have praised his perseverance. In 2002, Pasarell told a reporter, "He was the toughest competitor who ever played. He just fought and fought."

★ ROLANDO HINOJOSA-SMITH
NOVELIST, PROFESSOR
1929–

The son of a Mexican father and an Anglo mother, Rolando Hinojosa-Smith has spent much of his life in south Texas. The region's culture, just like Hinojosa-Smith, is the product of mixed Mexican and American roots, and Hinojosa-Smith reflects that dual heritage in his writings. For more than thirty years, he has been one of the most respected Chicano authors, and the appeal of his fictional creations has crossed over to the world of Anglo literature.

The son of Manuel Guzmán Hinojosa and Carrie Effie Smith, Rolando was born in Mercedes, Texas. He is often known simply by his father's last name, Hinojosa. His father's family traced its roots in Texas to the mid-eighteenth century, when the region was still part of Mexico, then a colony in the vast Spanish empire.

Rolando Hinojosa-Smith showed an interest in writing while still in high school, but his first professional work did not appear for almost another thirty years. At age seventeen, he joined the army. After finishing one tour of duty, he started college, but he was soon called back to service during the Korean War. Afterward, he went to the Caribbean as director of the army's newspaper. When his military service ended, he earned his bachelor's degree at the University of Texas at Austin, then began teaching in Brownsville, Texas. Hinojosa's life in Texas was interrupted again in 1960, when he left to study at New Mexico's Highlands University, where he received a master's degree. From there, he went to the University of Illinois to complete a doctorate in 1969, then once again returned to his native state to teach.

While studying and teaching, Hinojosa found time to write, and in 1971 he completed his first novel. *Estampas del valle y otras obras* (*Sketches of the Valley and Other Works*) won the Quinto Sol Prize, the highest honor for a Chicano novel. The story is set in Belken County, a fictional place Hinojosa created so he could explore the region where his family lived, the lower Rio Grande. His characters—through monologues, dialogues, letters, and interviews—provide a realistic, often humorous, view of life and customs in the region. Hinojosa created a history for these people and their home based on facts recollected from oral accounts, written documents, interviews, and the history of his own family.

Estampas del valle was the first in a series of novels set in Belken—or, more specifically, the equally fictional Klail City—and Hinojosa called his series the Klail City Death Trip. His second novel, *Klail City y sus alrededores* (translated as *Klail City*) appeared in 1976 and won the prestigious Casa de las Americas prize, awarded to the best novel in all of Latin America. Hinojosa was the first Hispanic author to receive that prize. In this and other novels he continued developing the lives and times of the characters introduced in the first book.

In 1976, Hinojosa once again left Texas, to head the Chicano Studies Department at the University of Minnesota. Belken County, however, remained on his mind, as he published *Korean Love Songs from Klail City Death Trip*, a selection of poems based on his experiences in the Korean War. Written in English, that work showed his interest in expressing himself in both of his languages. Hinojosa returned to Texas in 1981 to teach at the University of Texas at Austin, where he has remained ever since, still writing his novels about the people of Klail City. His work also includes short stories and articles.

Although his writing has brought him fame, Hinojosa enjoys teaching. "I have the best job in the world," he said in 1997. "I teach where I want to teach, at my old alma mater, and then I get to write. I also get to travel. People invite me to come give talks and readings. I'm doing what I want to do." Hinojosa's books have been read around the world, reflecting the praise he earned from the *New York Times*: "Although Hinojosa's sharp eye and accurate ear capture a place, its people and time in a masterly way, his work goes far beyond regionalism. He is a writer for all readers."

★ JAIME ESCALANTE
EDUCATOR
1930–

Few high school math teachers have so much impact that they inspire Hollywood films about their accomplishments. But in his work with inner-city Hispanic students, Jaime Escalante proved he was no ordinary math teacher. Escalante believed in the power of education to transform one person, and the power of a community to work together for a common goal. The fame Escalante won because of *Stand and Deliver*, the film based on his experiences, made him one of the best-known and most respected teachers in the United States.

Escalante was born in La Paz, Bolivia. He was the son of two teachers, Zenobio and Sara Escalante. His mother taught him the geometric concepts of circumference and symmetry by explaining the ideas while peeling an orange. This little game stuck with Escalante, and he would take a similar approach to teaching when he entered the classroom. As a young student, he loved to work on puzzles and enjoyed challenging himself by solving chemistry problems that were beyond his grade level. Later, as an older student, he taught physics and mathematics classes to help support his mother and his brother and sisters.

Escalante taught for nine years in Bolivia until he decided to emigrate to the United States. He first studied at the Universidad de Puerto Rico, but he soon moved his family to Pasadena, California. He enrolled at Pasadena City College and earned an associate of arts degree in electronics in 1969. Three years later, Escalante received a bachelor's degree in mathematics from

California State University at Los Angeles. While studying, he held a number of jobs to support his family, including working as a busboy and a cook. He finally took a better-paying job at an electronics factory.

Teaching was Escalante's great passion, second only to his family. Although he was earning a good salary in the electronics industry, he decided to quit his job in 1974. He became a mathematics teacher at Garfield High School in East Los Angeles, an area with a high concentration of Latinos. Escalante taught calculus, trigonometry, and algebra to students who faced daily challenges. Poverty, gangs, drugs, and violence were always present, and few students considered education a high priority. During his time at Garfield High School, Escalante worked hard to develop a mathematics program in which an increasing number of students took the advanced placement (AP) exam in calculus each year. In his classrooms, he used sports as a way to teach, the way his mother had once used an orange. He associated something forbidden in math—dividing by zero—with a basketball infraction—an illegal defense.

Escalante saw that the language of math was confusing to many students. The goal, he said, was to "use the words with which the kids are familiar."

In 1982, eighteen of Escalante's students took the AP exam and passed. However, the company that gave the test thought the scores were wrong. Since few Hispanics traditionally took the test, let alone did so well, company officials assumed Escalante's students might have cheated. Escalante encouraged the students to retake the test, and the Latino community in Los Angeles rallied around them as they worked to prove their innocence. All of the students who retook the exam passed, proving to the testing company and the world that Latinos were intelligent and capable. With Escalante's constant cry of *Ganas* (desire), they had mastered calculus, a course usually reserved for Anglo students from middle-class or higher backgrounds.

News of the students' accomplishments spread throughout the worldwide Latino community, and a newspaper article about Escalante caught the eye of Cuban-born filmmaker Ramón Menéndez. He created *Stand and Deliver* to show the challenges that Escalante and his students encountered in their struggle to prove their innocence. Actor Edward James Olmos played Escalante, and the film also featured Hispanic actors Lou Diamond Phillips and Andy Garcia. The movie and a 1988 book, *Escalante: The Best Teacher in America*, spread his name worldwide. For his exceptional efforts in the classroom, Escalante was awarded the Presidential Medal for Excellence in Education and inducted into the National Teachers Hall of Fame.

Escalante left Garfield High School in 1991 and began teaching in Sacramento, where he stayed until 1998. During those years, he also appeared on the Public Broadcasting System series *Futures with Jaime Escalante*. The show, aimed at students, featured him explaining possible careers in math and science. Escalante was proud that many of his former students went on to hold science and engineering jobs.

★ MARISOL
SCULPTOR
1930–

During the early 1960s, the New York art world was buzzing over pop art, a new style that was influenced by popular culture. Marisol, a sculptor who goes by just her first name, was part of this new art scene. Andy Warhol, the "king" of pop art, referred to Marisol as "the first girl artist with glamour." But as her large body of work has shown, Marisol is more than a pretty face. Her work goes beyond pop art, drawing on older European traditions and folk art. She uses her work both to make people smile and to make them think about deeper social and political issues. Today, some of the world's greatest museums proudly display her art.

Marisol at work on a sculpture

Marisol Escobar was born in Paris, France, to a wealthy family from Venezuela. She spent most of her youth traveling and remembers "my brother and I, with suitcases and trunks, and staying in hotels." Her family returned to Venezuela from time to time, and Marisol was educated at boarding schools there and in Europe. She attended high school in Los Angeles, where she took her first serious art classes. At nineteen, she moved to New York City to study art at the Art Students League and other schools in the city. She had long been interested in folk art and pre-Columbian art—the art of the Mayan, Aztecs, and other Indians of Central and South America. She made her first wood and clay figurines to imitate this style. As her artistic vision grew, her work came to be seen as a cross between popular art and folk art.

Art lovers soon viewed Marisol as a witty, inventive sculptor, and by the end of the 1950s her work was winning rave reviews. In addition to making pieces out of wood and metal, she added everyday objects, things other people had thrown away, like shoes or a baby carriage. She later said, "All my early work came from the street. It was magical for me to find things." Her quirky pieces attracted much attention, especially during the 1960s. People seemed to crave slightly eccentric personalities, and Marisol filled this need. She worked with great seriousness and purpose, but in public she could be a little zany. Once she showed up for a panel discussion at New York's Museum of Modern Art wearing a white Japanese mask. She kept the mask on throughout the evening, until finally the audience clamored for her to take it off. As Marisol did so, the crowd saw that her face was made up to look just like the mask.

Although Marisol created many figurines, she also did larger sculptures. One, *The Party*, features fifteen partygoers all wearing bits and pieces of Marisol's own clothes and all bearing her face. Another sculpture that is highly personal for her is *Mi Mamá y Yo*. The piece has been shown around the world, but Marisol keeps it in her personal collection. *Mi Mamá y Yo* features a young girl—representing Marisol as a child—holding up a parasol to shield her lovely mother. Marisol's own mother died when the artist was eleven, and the image comes from a family photograph.

Over the years, Marisol has experimented with new themes. During the early 1970s, she did a series of pieces featuring fish. Later, she did portraits of artists she knew, based on their photographs. And she did her own versions of paintings by famous artists, including sixteenth-century Italian master Leonardo da Vinci. By the 1980s, she was depicting scenes from the history of her adopted homeland, the United States.

Marisol's work has found a home in such important museums as New York's Metropolitan Museum and the Museum of Modern Art. Her pieces are also on display in Germany, Japan, and Venezuela, and many museums have featured her work in special shows. Throughout her career, Marisol has tried to make audiences think about the people and situations around them. Her work, one critic said, illustrates that Marisol "feels both [the audiences'] absurdity and their pain and encourages us to do the same."

★ ROBERTO GOIZUETA
BUSINESSMAN, HUMANITARIAN
1931–1997

Coca-Cola has been called the world's most valuable brand name, and Coke is the largest beverage manufacturer on the planet. Some of the company's success can be traced to the leadership of Roberto Goizueta. During his years as chief executive officer (CEO) at Coke, Goizueta helped introduce several popular new products. Those products helped Coke shake its image as a stodgy, old-fashioned company and led to new profits. With his success, Goizueta also shattered old ideas about the role of Hispanics in the workplace. For years, some Anglos thought Hispanic Americans lacked the skills to lead a large company and that Hispanics served only as cheap labor. Goizueta showed how wrong those stereotypes were.

Roberto Crispulo Goizueta was born in Havana, Cuba. His father owned a sugarcane business and could afford to send Goizueta to Cheshire Academy, a private school in Connecticut. To help improve his English, Roberto watched the same old American movies over and over. Goizueta continued his studies at Yale University, where he graduated in 1953 with a bachelor's degree in chemical engineering, then returned home to help with the family business.

In 1954, he answered a want ad in the paper—and it changed the direction of his life. The ad was from an American company looking for a bilingual chemical engineer or chemist. That American company was Coca-Cola, and Goizueta was hired in July. He was sent to Nassau, Bahamas, where he was named area chemist for the Caribbean.

When a long-simmering revolution in Cuba ended in 1959, Fidel Castro removed the pro-American government that had been in power. The next year, Goizueta and his family left Cuba with $200 and one hundred shares of Coca-Cola stock and moved to Miami. Still with Coca-Cola, he was put in charge of the company's Latin American operations, part of his climb up the leadership leader. In 1964, he was transferred to company headquarters in Atlanta, Georgia, where he was named vice president of technical research and development. Goizueta was later elected president of the soda giant and then chairman of the board and CEO. His rise to the top was based on his tenacious work ethic, generosity, and effectiveness.

As CEO, Goizueta concentrated on increasing sales, both domestic and international. He made changes within the company, and he used catchy slogans—such as "Coke Is It!"—in the company's advertising campaigns. Reshaping Coke sometimes meant taking risks by introducing new products, such as Diet Coke. Goizueta also began using a type of corn syrup instead of sugar in the drinks to reduce manufacturing costs. But one of his gambles turned out to be a colossal blunder. In 1985, the company introduced New Coke, made with a different formula than the old Coke. Most consumers hated the taste of New Coke, and they jammed the company's telephone lines to complain. Goizueta, however, turned a mistake into a plus for the company. He reintroduced the traditional flavor three months later under the new name Classic Coke, which helped the company beat its market rival, Pepsi, in earnings for the first time since the 1970s.

During Goizueta's sixteen years as president, the market value of Coca-Cola increased from $4 billion in 1981 to more than $150 billion in 1997, the largest increase in the history of the company. At the pinnacle of his success, Goizueta was named CEO of the year by *Chief Executive* magazine. His business talents also brought him great personal wealth. At the time of his death, his fortune was estimated by *Forbes* magazine to be $1.3 billion.

Still, Goizueta never forgot his origins or his mother language. He made a point of keeping his name Roberto, rather than changing it to Robert or Bob. And Goizueta received the Herbert Hoover Humanitarian Award of the Boys Club of America, which recognized his efforts and generosity on behalf of those in need and his work to make the Hispanic community stronger. Goizueta participated in many other charity programs, such as the Points of Light Initiative, an organization he helped found to promote volunteer service. He also started his own foundation, which helps children, supports at-risk families, and creates educational opportunities. At Emory University, Goizueta donated $1.5 million to the school of business, which was named in his honor.

Goizueta's life is the tale of an ambitious young man who pursued his dream of leading one of the most powerful firms in the world despite lacking a formal business school education. And he tried to live by the words he gave in a 1995 speech on leadership: "At the end of the day, you have to be true to yourself. You have to be loyal to your own expertise . . . and your own demanding code of honor. I believe that if working in the Coca-Cola system means anything, it means doing what is right. Not necessarily what is correct— no one is correct all the time. But doing what is right."

RITA MORENO
ACTOR, SINGER, DANCER
1931–

Winning an Academy Award (also called an Oscar) is the highest honor for a film actor in the United States. Television has a similar award for outstanding work, the Emmy. Few people win both awards, but Rita Moreno did. But her talents—and the honors—don't stop there. Moreno has also won a Tony, for her work on Broadway, and a Grammy, the highest honor in the music business. She is the only person to have won all four of these major awards. With her acting, singing, and dancing, Moreno has proven herself to be one of the most talented entertainers in the world.

Rita Moreno was born Rosita Dolores Alverio in Humacao, Puerto Rico.

Her family was made up mostly of small independent farmers called *jíbaros*. At age five, she left Puerto Rico to join her mother, who was working in the garment industry in New York City. Soon, little Rosita was taking dance lessons and showing her talents onstage. At age seven, she was performing at a local nightclub, and then she danced and sang at Macy's department store and at private parties. At eleven, she was dubbing Spanish-language versions of American films. And just two years later, she landed her first Broadway role, which brought her to the attention of Hollywood talent scouts. Early in her film career, she often played stereotypical Hispanic females or women from other dark-skinned ethnic groups. Rosita longed for the day when she could play larger roles that really let her show her talents.

While performing professionally as a singer and dancer, she continued taking acting lessons. In 1950, she returned to the big screen in several films. Louis B. Mayer, head of the Metro-Goldwyn-Mayer (MGM) film studio, suggested that she shorten her first name from Rosita to Rita. She also took the surname of her mother's third husband. She would henceforth be known as Rita Moreno. One of her bigger film parts came in 1956, in the film version of the Broadway musical *The King and I*. While working on that picture, she met Jerome Robbins, a famous choreographer—a person who creates dances. Robbins later asked Moreno to star in *West Side Story*, a Broadway play he was developing. Moreno was too busy to take the lead role of Maria as Robbins wanted. But in 1961, she appeared as Anita in the film version of the musical, and *West Side Story* made Moreno a star.

West Side Story is a modern retelling of the Shakespeare play *Romeo and Juliet*. Two lovers, one Anglo and one Puerto Rican, are caught up in a rivalry between local gangs. Moreno's performance of the musical number "America" was one of the highlights of the film, and her performance earned her an Oscar for best supporting actress. Hoping that such recognition would open new doors, Moreno instead found that most of the scripts sent to her after *West*

Side Story were like the films she had made before. They merely called for her to replay stereotypical Latin spitfires. She turned to the theater for a broader range of roles, but she never completely abandoned films.

From 1971 to 1977, Moreno appeared on *The Electric Company*, a children's television series. Her work on the soundtrack album for the show earned her a Grammy in 1972. In 1975, Moreno received a Tony for her performance in the Broadway show *The Ritz*. In 1977, she won an Emmy for her work on *The Muppet Show*, a program with broad appeal to both kids and adults. She won a second Emmy in 1978 for playing Rita Capkovic, a recurring character on *The Rockford Files*, a comedy-detective show.

Rita Moreno holding her best supporting actress Oscar, 1962

During the early 1980s, Moreno was nominated for several more Emmys, and she won rave reviews for her work as a nun on *Oz*, a cable television drama that ran from 1997 to 2003. She also continued to make movies, appear onstage, and sing in nightclubs. In 2004, President George W. Bush recognized her long and successful career by giving her the Presidential Medal of Freedom, the highest honor a U.S. citizen can receive.

Throughout her career, Moreno has called for greater diversity in the roles offered Latinos in films, on television, and onstage. Her success in every field she entered has inspired many young actors of different ethnic groups to pursue their dreams.

ROBERTO CLEMENTE
PROFESSIONAL BASEBALL PLAYER
1934–1972

Baseball coaches and fans say the best players have key tools of the game: These greatest of the great can run fast, hit for both power and a high batting average, field their position, and throw with speed and accuracy. Roberto Clemente was just shy of being one of these prized players, as his home run totals did not match those of true power hitters, but few batters have ever put more fear into opposing pitchers. For more than fifteen years, he roamed the outfield for the Pittsburgh Pirates, running down fly balls and gunning down hitters foolish enough to try to take an extra base. At the plate, he was a lifetime .300 hitter, the sign of batting greatness, and he was the first Hispanic elected to the Baseball Hall of Fame. But besides his great athletic ability, Clemente is remembered for his generous spirit—and also for the tragic plane crash that took his life after the 1972 season.

Roberto was born in Carolina, Puerto Rico, the youngest of five children in a poor family. Early on, Roberto ran track and field and threw the javelin, excelling in both sports, but his true love was baseball. At age seventeen, he signed a contract with the Santurce Cangrejeros in the Puerto Rican League. His rare combination of skills—hitting, fielding, and throwing—drew scouts from Major League Baseball teams to watch him play. One scout impressed with Clemente was Alex Campanis of the Brooklyn Dodgers, who later called him "the greatest natural athlete I have ever seen." The Dodgers signed Clemente in 1954, giving him a ten thousand dollar bonus.

The Dodgers knew Clemente was a budding superstar, but they did not have a spot for him yet on their major league roster. They sent him to their minor league team in Montreal, Quebec, and tried to keep Clemente's profile low so other teams would not see how good he was. Being hidden upset Clemente, since he knew he was good enough to play. The Dodgers' strategy did not keep the Pittsburgh Pirates from drafting him at the end of the 1954 season. When Pittsburgh began its season in 1955, Clemente was on the major league roster, and he soon became the team's starting right fielder.

Clemente faced a time of adjustment in the big leagues. He was dark-skinned, and Jackie Robinson had only recently broken baseball's "color barrier," the unofficial rule that kept minorities out of the game. Clemente still faced prejudice from both players and fans and was also isolated because he spoke little English. At times, he was misquoted and ridiculed by the media. Throughout his career, Clemente remained proud of his Puerto Rican roots. He returned home every winter, to play ball and work with poor children and made sure his three children were born on the island.

Clemente had an unimpressive rookie year, but starting the next season, he had the first of thirteen years with a batting average above .300. During the

1960s, Clemente joined the ranks of Henry "Hank" Aaron and Willie Mays as one of the top players in the National League. He had more than 200 hits four times (1961, 1964, 1966, and 1967), hit over .350 twice (1961 and 1967), and led the league in batting four times. The highlight of the decade was 1966, when he hit .317 and had career highs in home runs (29) and RBIs (119). That performance earned him the National League Most Valuable Player award. Clemente appeared in twelve All-Star Games and won twelve Gold Glove Awards for fielding. He played in two World Series. He hit .310 against the New York Yankees in the 1960 series, which the Pirates won. The highlight of his postseason play came in 1971, when he helped the Pirates beat the Baltimore Orioles in seven games. Clemente was named the series' Most Valuable Player.

On September 30, 1972, in the last game of the season, Clemente got his 3,000th hit. He was only the eleventh player to reach that level of batting greatness, and the first Latino player to do so. Sadly, this was his last game. Just before Christmas that year, deadly earthquakes struck Managua, the capital of Nicaragua. With his usual concern for others, Clemente personally directed a relief mission, flying to Managua on a plane loaded with food and supplies. The plane never got past the San Juan, Puerto Rico, coastline, crashing into the ocean. All of baseball and Latin America mourned the death of Roberto Clemente, a great player who died while performing a humanitarian service.

In Puerto Rico, the island held a three-day period of mourning for its favorite sports hero. The Baseball Writers Association of America took an unusual step and waived the rule requiring that five years pass after a player's career ended before he could be considered for the Hall of Fame. Clemente was elected to the hall in 1973. Soon after, Major League Baseball created the Roberto Clemente Award, an annual award given to a player who best demonstrates sportsmanship, community involvement, and team contribution.

TRINI LÓPEZ
ENTERTAINER
1937–

The world of pop music was changing in 1963. Rock groups such as the Beatles and the Beach Boys were on the edge of superstardom, and folk music—once confined to coffeehouses and protest rallies—was also becoming more popular. That year, Trini López appeared with his own unique blend of folk, rock, and Latin music. His hit "If I Had a Hammer" made him an international star, and other musicians appreciated the way he gave folk music a danceable beat.

Trinidad "Trini" López III was born in a poor Hispanic neighborhood in Dallas, Texas. His parents had immigrated to the United States from Moroleón, Mexico, seeking work. His father secured a job at Southern Methodist University, while his mother cared for the growing family, taking in laundry to make ends meet. With six children, money was always tight.

When Trini was about eleven, his father bought him a cheap guitar and taught him how to play traditional Mexican songs. López learned quickly, and he soon began playing American popular tunes as well. As a teenager, he helped support the family by playing music on street corners and in Dallas restaurants. He dropped out of high school after the eleventh grade to perform full time.

López recorded his first single, "The Right to Rock," in 1955 with a local record producer. The producer asked López to change his name to something more Anglo, but the musician refused. "The Right to Rock" got some airplay in Dallas, and it led to a recording contract with the Cincinnati rhythm-and-blues (R&B) studio King Records. López joined such popular acts as the Platters and James Brown. King released several R&B and bluegrass songs with López, backed by the label's studio musicians. As the only Latino performer for a mostly black record company, López did not fit in. He was also frustrated with not being able to record his own songs. He soon left King Records and moved to Los Angeles.

After a year in Los Angeles, López landed a regular performance at PJ's, a popular nightclub. Record producer Don Costa saw his act and recommended him to Frank Sinatra, who signed López to an eight-year contract with Reprise Records. López was eager to record in a professional studio again, but Costa wanted to record the first album at PJ's, where, he explained, they could "create all of the excitement that you're creating here in person on record." López agreed, and his first album, *Trini López at PJ's,* was recorded in 1963. The set included López's signature blend of folk, blues, gospel, and traditional Mexican songs, performed with an up-tempo beat.

The album featured Trini singing well-known songs such as "When the Saints Go Marching In" and "This Land Is Your Land." But the one true hit on the record, the one that made López a star, was "If I Had a Hammer." The song, written by Pete Seeger, had recently been recorded by the folk group

Peter, Paul, and Mary. But López gave the song new energy, and he stressed the positive message of the chorus: "I'd hammer out love between my brothers and my sisters / all over this land." The lively guitar playing made the song a hit in the United States, where it reached number three on the record charts. It eventually became a number-one hit in more than twenty countries. Perhaps the most remarkable aspect of the song's success is its simplicity. It was recorded during a weeknight set, when López did not use a bass player so he could save money: just two people, López and his drummer, performed.

With the success of "If I Had a Hammer" and his first album, López began to tour, packing in crowds. He soon produced another album, *More of Trini López at PJ's,* and had another hit, "Kansas City." Outside the United States, López hit the record charts with songs such as "La Bamba" and "America." He never shied away from his Mexican American heritage, performing his own version of "Cielito Lindo" and "Corazón de Melón" in his live act. Reprise released many of these Spanish-language standards as singles in Latin America and Spain.

By early 1964, López was a worldwide sensation. He performed for eighteen days in Paris, sharing top billing with the Beatles. He appeared on Dick Clark's popular television show *American Bandstand,* and the Gibson guitar company released two "Trini López" signature models. He had one other hit, "Lemon Tree," in 1965, and a year later "I'm Coming Home, Cindy" made a brief chart appearance.

As the 1960s wore on and the mood of the country darkened, López's happy versions of Mexican and American folk songs lost their appeal. He tried acting, appearing in television shows and several movies, including *The Dirty Dozen.* That career did not last, but López has continued to record albums and perform, despite never re-creating his early success.

ROSARIO FERRÉ
WRITER
1938–

As a Puerto Rican writer, I constantly face the problem of identity. When I travel to the States, I feel as Latina as Chita Rivera. But in Latin America, I feel more American than John Wayne. To be Puerto Rican is to be a hybrid. Our two halves are inseparable; we cannot give up either without feeling maimed.

—Rosario Ferré

Rosario Ferré has felt the pull of two cultures—Hispanic and Anglo—for most of her life. She began her career as a writer and scholar, working in her native Spanish. Later, she upset many Puerto Ricans when she began writing fiction in English, though that decision brought her skills to a wider audience. The daughter of a former governor of Puerto Rico, Ferré has taken a strong interest in the island's political relationship with the United States. Despite her political and journalistic writings, she is best known for her creative work and has been called "Puerto Rico's leading woman of letters."

Ferré was born to well-to-do parents in Ponce, Puerto Rico. They sent Rosario to high school and college in the United States. For a time, she thought about being a dancer or perhaps a nun, but she finally settled on writing as a career. While still in high school, Ferré published her first professional work in a Puerto Rican newspaper. After graduating from Manhattanville College in

1960, she returned to Puerto Rico. She married the son of a socially prominent family and had three children.

In the late 1960s, Ferré began graduate studies in literature at the University of Puerto Rico. There she met a visiting professor named Angel Rama, an important Latin American scholar of the day. He encouraged both Ferré and her cousin Olga Nolla, also a writer, in their efforts to publish a literary magazine. The result was *Zona carga y descarga* (*Loading and Unloading Zone*), which appeared in the 1970s. It marked the coming of age of a new generation of island writers who challenged conventional wisdom about literature and other topics.

At that time, Ferré's father, Luis, was governor of the island. He hoped that Puerto Rico would become a U.S. state. His daughter, however, favored independence, and she was also outspoken on other issues, such as equal rights for women. Ferré expressed her views through her magazine and in her first two books—*Papeles de Pandora* (*Pandora's Papers,* 1976), a collection of poems and short stories, and *Sitio a Eros* (*Place to Eros,* 1980), a book of essays with a feminist viewpoint. These writings caused an uproar among the island's established cultural and political leaders. Because of her feminist themes and because she published in Mexico, where Ferré resided briefly after she divorced her husband, she became well known throughout Latin America.

In 1983, Ferré moved to the United States and earned a doctorate from the University of Maryland, where she also taught. She returned to Puerto Rico in 1991. Although she has written often on women's issues and the need for greater equality, Ferré has felt the tension between being a feminist and a more traditional wife and mother. She said in 2001 that she did not begin writing fiction until after her youngest child turned twelve, and that with her second husband, she has struggled to meet both his and her own needs.

Ferré's Spanish-language fiction includes several collections of popular folk tales such as *Los cuentos de Juan Bobo* (*The Juan Bobo Stories,* 1981) and also poetry, novels, and short stories. *Maldito amor y otros cuentos* (*Damn Love and Other Stories*), a collection of novellas, was published in 1985; two years later, it appeared in English as *Sweet Diamond Dusts*.

Ferré stepped into controversy in 1995 when she wrote her novel *The House on the Lagoon* in English. Many island writers and intellectuals decried her use of English, since Spanish has traditionally been an important way to affirm the island's cultural identity. The book, however, was a critical success and was chosen as a finalist for the National Book Award. Other novels in English followed, including *Eccentric Neighborhoods* (1998) and *Flight of the Swan* (2001). These books helped Ferré reach a wider audience and have her work known outside the island. She continued to publish in Spanish as well, including a biography of her father, *Memorias de Ponce* (*Memories of Ponce,* 1992); a collection of journalistic pieces, *A la sombra de tu nombre* (*Under the Shadow of Your Name,* 2001); and a bilingual book of poems, *Duelo del lenguaje/Language Duel* (2003).

Ferré's transition from Spanish to English was an important move. It was an acknowledgment of Puerto Rico's political situation: despite some residents' desire for independence, most favor remaining part of the United States, as either a commonwealth or a state. Ferré even changed her views on this subject, emerging in 1998 as a supporter of statehood. And her switch to English also showed an awareness of the cultural importance of that language, which is spoken and read widely by millions of the Hispanics who live in the United States.

PART FIVE

MAKING THEIR MARK

★ MARTIN SHEEN
ACTOR AND ACTIVIST
1940–

Martin Sheen had a strong interest in politics long before he became famous for playing a political leader on TV. And he didn't play just any leader—on *The West Wing*, Sheen starred as Josiah Bartlett, the president of the United States. Off the set, Sheen has often made news for attending rallies that protested nuclear weapons, poverty, and U.S. military involvement overseas. At one peace rally in 2005, Sheen told fellow protesters, "I think you know what I do for a living, but this is what I do to stay alive." Sheen has credited his Roman Catholic faith for his strong commitment to peace and fighting social injustice.

"Martin Sheen" is the stage name of Ramón Estevez, son of a Spanish father and an Irish mother. From an early age, Ramón knew he wanted to act, a career choice his father opposed. The elder Estevez wanted his son to go to college. Ramón reluctantly took the entrance exam for his hometown college, the University of Dayton (Ohio). As he later explained, "Unknown to anyone, I purposely failed the exam, scoring just 3 percent out of a possible 100. My father got the message, but still would not bless my dream." Ramón set off for New York, where he chose the Anglo-sounding Martin Sheen as his name, so he would not be cast solely in Hispanic roles.

Like many young actors, Sheen struggled to get his career off the ground and often had to work at odd jobs. Finally, the parts came. First, there were roles on TV shows such as *The Defenders* and *East Side, West Side*. Then in 1964, he landed a part in *The Subject Was Roses*, an award-winning Broadway play. By the late 1960s, Sheen had an increasing number of jobs in television and film, so he moved his family to Los Angeles, the heart of those industries.

Sheen's first big film role came in *Badlands* (1973). Although the movie had a low budget, Sheen caught the eye of critics with his portrayal of a young murderer in love. The next year, he had the title role in the TV movie *The Execution of Private Slovik*, a true story based on an incident in World War II. Sheen was nominated for an Emmy Award, television's highest honor, for his work. His major works of the late 1970s and 1980s includ *Apocalypse Now*—one of his personal favorites—*Gandhi*, and *Wall Street*. Sheen told one interviewer that his work on *Gandhi* in India, a land with pockets of extreme poverty, renewed his interest in his Catholic faith. He also credited Terrence Malick, the director of *Badlands*, for shaping his spiritual views.

Sheen's commitment to Catholic teachings on peace and social justice led to his participation in protests. Since 1986, he has been arrested dozens of times for speaking out. Often, the arrests came after he trespassed at nuclear power plants or test sites for nuclear weapons. In his career, he has played roles that

Sheen speaks out against the war in Iraq in March 2006

complement his activism. On *The West Wing*, for instance, Sheen and his fellow actors often depicted events similar to the day's headlines.

But not everyone enjoys *The West Wing* or Sheen's political views. In 2003, the United States invaded Iraq, and Sheen quickly protested the war. Political supporters of the war and of President George W. Bush attacked Sheen's ideas. Some even tried to persuade NBC, the network that broadcast *The West Wing*, to take him off the show. The experience, he told one interviewer, led him to believe that "once you follow a path of nonviolence and social justice, it won't take you long before you come into conflict with the culture, with the society. You can't know what is at stake or how much it is going to cost you until you get in the game."

Along with his dedication to political action and acting, Sheen is known for his strong love for his family. He is proud that all four of his children have acted, with Charlie Sheen and Emilio Estevez making the biggest splash in Hollywood. Both starred in a number of movies during the 1980s and 1990s, and Charlie has also excelled on television. As a strong pacifist, the elder Sheen worries about the world his children's children will inherit, which helps keep him focused on the world beyond Hollywood. Yet whatever his worries, he says, "I still believe in . . . the basic human goodness present in all of us."

★ RITCHIE VALENS
ENTERTAINER
1941–1959

Ritchie Valens lived at a time when Mexican Americans had not yet created a strong identity for themselves and prejudice was still common. Pushed by a love of rock music, Valens learned to play guitar, and his talent helped him overcome barriers and win fame. His recording of "La Bamba," a traditional Mexican tune, inspired other Mexican Americans of southern California to form bands. Valens was a groundbreaker and model for a young generation of Hispanics eager to perform—and succeed.

Ritchie Valens was born Richard Steve Valenzuela in Pacoima, California. Listening to such early rock 'n' roll musicians as Elvis Presley, Little Richard, and Chuck Berry led him into the world of entertainment.

Through the mid-1950s, Valenzuela played guitar at local parties and occasional dances, both solo and with a group, the Silhouettes. Eventually, the San Fernando performer became known as "the Little Richard of the Valley," and his talent was brought to the attention of Bob Keane, a Los Angeles record company owner and music producer.

In 1958, Keane recorded Valenzuela on the Del-Fi recording label. Valenzuela's records first appeared in regional record stores, then spread across the country as his sound won fans. Keane proposed that the teenager shorten his professional name to Valens for broader, more mainstream acceptance, and Valenzuela agreed. His first hit record, "Come On, Let's Go," sold five hundred thousand copies. By the next year, he had played a small part in a rock 'n' roll movie called *Go, Johnny, Go* and appeared on *American Bandstand*, the premier television show for rock and pop music. Valens also gave concerts in Hawaii, New York City, and elsewhere. By all accounts, he was a talented, confident, well-mannered youth. He learned his trade quickly and well, and he showed enormous potential.

In January 1959, Valens left for a tour of the Midwest as a headliner with Dion and the Belmonts, Buddy Holly, and the Big Bopper. By this time, Valens had two more hit songs. Appearing on the same 45 rpm record were "Donna" and "La Bamba." The first was a love song he had written for his girlfriend. "La Bamba" was an old tune that had gained popularity throughout Mexico with traveling musical shows. When recorded music and movies developed, it became known through the rest of Latin America. "La Bamba" moved north into the United States as Mexicans entered the country looking for work—reaching rural labor camps and urban neighborhoods. Valens gave the song a rock sound that proved popular with teens, even if they didn't understand the words.

The tour with Valens and these other rock stars was called the Winter Dance Party. The acts traveled the upper Midwest, plagued by a bus whose heater and engine performed poorly. By the time they got to the Surf Ballroom in Clear Lake, Iowa, on Monday, February 2, Buddy Holly decided to charter a small aircraft to ferry himself and two others to their next show in Minnesota. Following the Clear Lake show, Valens, the youngest musician of the group, persuaded one of Holly's musicians to flip a coin for space on the plane. Valens won the toss and took his seat, but minutes after takeoff, the plane crashed in subfreezing temperatures. Ritchie Valens died three months shy of his eighteenth birthday. "La Bamba" and "Donna" remained popular after Valens's death, and his untrained style of rock later influenced many "garage" bands. Their members, like Valens, lacked formal training, but they loved the energy and emotional release rock 'n' roll provided.

In 1987, Luis Valdez, a Mexican American playwright and director, was drawn to the Valens story. He directed a Hollywood movie of the entertainer's life called *La Bamba*, starring Lou Diamond Phillips as Valens. The film, which has remained popular since its release, includes the band Los Lobos playing the title song on-camera in a Mexican style and off-camera in Valens's rock version. That version became a number-one hit, marking the first time that a song sung entirely in Spanish hit the top of the rock-music charts. The record also showed the lasting appeal of Valens's approach to the song.

In 1990, Valens was awarded a star on Hollywood's Walk of Fame, and the following year he was inducted into the Rock and Roll Hall of Fame. In 1993, the U.S. Postal Service issued a stamp in his memory, and the next year Pacoima's Recreation Center was named for its famous son; a fair is held there every May to celebrate his memory.

JOAN BAEZ
SINGER, ACTIVIST
1941–

For almost fifty years, when people have met to protest a war or demand social change, Joan Baez has likely been there. Either alone with her guitar or backed by a band, Baez has used her silken soprano voice to sing for causes she believes in. She came out of the protest-song school of folk singing, influenced by such giants as Woody Guthrie and Pete Seeger. Over her career, she has expanded to embrace a number of musical styles, from country to traditional Spanish folk. But her powerful voice has remained constant, as has her belief in the power of people to make the world a better place.

Baez was born on Staten Island, New York, but growing up she spent time in several places, including California and Iraq. Her father, Alberto, was a Mexican American physicist who moved around for his career. Joan's mother, also named Joan, was a Scottish-born drama teacher. By 1958, the family was living in the Boston, Massachusetts, area. Cambridge, just outside of Boston, was filled with coffeehouses where young folk musicians gathered to sing and play guitars. After attending one performance, Joan devoted her free time to learning to play guitar and sing traditional folk songs. Soon, she was performing in those Cambridge coffeehouses.

Baez caught the attention of a music promoter, and he booked her to play at a Chicago club. By the summer of 1959, she was playing at Rhode Island's Newport Folk Festival, one of the largest folk festivals in the United

States. After performing there again the following year, Baez received several offers to record an album. She chose to work with Vanguard, a small label known for recording liberal folk singers. By the end of 1960, Baez's self-titled debut was in record stores across the country.

Baez was pleasantly surprised to hear that her record was selling well. Soon, she was on the road playing concerts. While in New York City, she met a scruffy young folk singer named Bob Dylan. For several years afterward, Dylan and Baez were linked romantically and professionally. Baez recorded some of his songs, bringing them to a wider audience.

By 1963, Baez had recorded her third album and was appearing before crowds of twenty thousand people. She appeared at the 1963 March on Washington led by civil rights leader Martin Luther King Jr., and her political activism was growing. Yet Baez was also still popular with mainstream audiences, and she was asked to sing at a gala for President John F. Kennedy. After Kennedy was assassinated, the event went on as scheduled. Baez surprised some of the important Washington figures in attendance when she sang Dylan's "The Times They Are A-Changin'." The song challenged traditional ideas and the power of the people who ruled the country.

The 1960s were a turbulent era in U.S. history, and Baez sang and protested across the country. She took part in the Free Speech Movement founded in California and helped launch the Institute for the Study of Nonviolence.

Baez condemned the war in Vietnam and became an active supporter of César Chávez, who was trying to unionize migrant Mexican farmworkers.

Baez also expanded her musical interests, recording several albums influenced by country music. For a time, she recorded in Nashville, the capital of the country music scene. Her best-selling song ever, "The Night They Drove Old Dixie Down," was recorded during this time, and she reunited with old friend Bob Dylan for a widely praised tour, the Rolling Thunder Revue. In 1974, she released *Gracias a la Vida*, an album sung entirely in Spanish. She dedicated it to her father who, she wrote, "Gave me my Latin name and whatever optimism about life I may claim to have." Baez also recorded her own songs and those from a growing pool of young American writers, such as Jackson Browne and Stevie Wonder.

For many Americans, the age of protest came to a close with the end of the Vietnam War. But Baez has remained active in the peace movement, often traveling to and performing in the world's most violent areas. She spoke out for human rights and against the death penalty. In 1985, she performed at Live Aid, a worldwide series of concerts that raised money for Africa. Into the twenty-first century, Baez remains active onstage, in the recording studio, and at protest rallies. As she once said, "My concern has always been for the people who are victimized, unable to speak for themselves and who need outside help."

★ ANGEL CORDERO JR.
JOCKEY
1942–

Thoroughbred racehorses are the most expensive and valued animals in the world. Especially prized are the offspring of champions, as owners hope the young horses will inherit their parents' talents. Angel Cordero Jr. seems to have inherited some talents from his father, or at least learned well from his example. Angel Sr. was a well-known jockey and trainer in his native Puerto Rico, and Angel Jr. became one of the greatest jockeys in the world. In a career that spanned more than thirty years, Cordero Jr. won 7,057 races worth more than $164 million in prize money. His record includes victories at the greatest horse races in the United States, including the Kentucky Derby.

Cordero rides Coin Silver during a workout in 2005

Angel Tomás Cordero Jr. was born in Santurce, Puerto Rico, in 1942. As early as age five, Angel would go to the track with his father to work and learn about horse racing. At age seventeen, Cordero began racing in Puerto Rico, riding his first winner in 1960. When he turned twenty in 1962, he traveled to New York City to become a professional jockey. Cordero was known as an avid competitor with a passion for winning. He was also a fan favorite, especially at the track in Saratoga, New York. He won the racing title there thirteen times, with eleven straight wins, and was considered the king of Saratoga riding. In 1968, he led all U.S. jockeys in wins.

Starting in the 1970s, Cordero emerged as a champion jockey at some of horse racing's greatest events. In 1974, riding Cannonade, Cordero won the Kentucky Derby. This grueling 1.25-mile (2 km) race has been run since 1875 and is the first "jewel" in the series known as the Triple Crown of horse racing. The other two races are the Belmont Stakes, held in New York, and the Preakness, which is run in Baltimore. In 1976,

Cordero won the Derby and the Belmont Stakes riding Bold Forbes. The jockey considered the Belmont victory his greatest race ever, with his horse winning by just a neck. Cordero won the Preakness twice, in 1980 and 1984. And in 1985, riding Spend A Buck, he won the Kentucky Derby for a third time.

From 1977 to 1990, Cordero's mounts won over $5 million each year, and in 1982, he set a record for jockey earnings when he won over $9 million. In 1982 and 1983, he received the prestigious Eclipse Award, the most respected award in horse racing. It recognized his impressive record of victories and his commitment to the sport and to Thoroughbreds.

In 1988, at age forty-six, Cordero was inducted into the Thoroughbred Racing Hall of Fame, but, because of his competitive drive, he continued to race for another four years. His famous racing career came to a stop only after a fall at Aqueduct (in New York) nearly cost him his life. On the advice of his doctors, he announced his retirement in 1992 and returned to Puerto Rico. Following in his father's footsteps, Cordero became a trainer. His first victory as a trainer came in July 1994, when Holy Mountain won the Lexington Stakes at Belmont Park. He also became a jockey agent and one of the foremost authorities on horse racing.

Cordero was always disappointed with the way his career ended. So, in 1995, he defied his family's wishes and rode in several races, including one at the Breeders' Cup, a series of major races held at the end of each racing season. Ten years later, Cordero once again climbed into the saddle to ride in a professional race. At age sixty-three, he rode Indian Vale at Philadelphia Park, as part of a fund-raising effort for victims of Hurricane Katrina, which had devastated New Orleans earlier that year. Racing fans turned out to cheer on the former champion one last time. Cordero did not win, but he was glad for the warm reception he received. "The fans still remember," he said after the race.

LOS ANGELES' PACHUCOS AND THE ZOOT SUIT RIOTS OF 1943

Two cultures clashed on the streets of Los Angeles in June 1943, the result of ethnic tensions that had been building for years. On one side were the *pachucos*, gang members from the Mexican American community. These young men had already grabbed attention with their zoot suits—high-waisted baggy pants and long suit coats with very broad shoulders. The suits all but screamed "I am different" to Los Angeles' Anglo community, and they earned the gang members the nickname "Zoot Suiters." On the other side were U.S. Navy sailors, waiting to be shipped out for war service in the Pacific. The violence that broke out in the "Zoot Suit Riots" stunned the city and the nation and highlighted the intense prejudice Mexican Americans faced in California.

Los Angeles had been tense since the summer before, when a Hispanic boy was found murdered in an area known as Sleepy Lagoon. Police decided the killer had to be from one of the city's many Mexican street gangs, and they promptly arrested twenty-three Mexican American boys. The police beat some of them, trying to pry loose a confession of guilt, and, during the trial, several witnesses made shockingly racist statements. When twelve gang members were found guilty of murder in January 1943, many in the community felt that the boys' only crime was that they were Mexican.

The pachuco gang members were the children of migrant workers who had come to the United States to do farm and railroad work. These immigrants had fled desperate poverty in Mexico and were happy for any job. Many of their children were born in the United States and so were U.S. citizens. They were less tolerant of the bad housing, bad schools, and bad jobs most Mexican Americans faced. These young people were also stung by the anti-Mexican prejudice that was so common among Anglos in Los Angeles. The pachucos and their girlfriends wanted a way to express their frustration and bitterness, and they found it in their outrageous clothes and hairstyles.

The Los Angeles police, however, did not see the Zoot Suiters as just rebellious teens. They considered anyone wearing a zoot suit to be a gang member—though this was not true—and saw all pachucos as a threat to social order. The sailors and other military men on leave in Los Angeles viewed the wildly dressed Mexicans as un-American and therefore good targets. These servicemen were, as one of them later testified, itching to fight.

Tensions rose throughout May 1943, and there were small clashes here and there. Then, on June 3, a fight broke out between a sailor and a Zoot

Suiter, and the sailor's jaw was broken. A group of sailors armed themselves with clubs, belts, and chains and went out looking for revenge. They beat up any Zoot Suiters they saw, and by the next night, any Mexican was considered fair game. The Mexicans began to fight back, and soon several thousand civilians were helping the servicemen in this growing battle. The police did not arrest the sailors and, at times, joined in the violence against innocent Mexicans. One reporter saw an officer attack a Zoot Suiter after he left a pool hall. The Mexican had refused to enter a police car and asked why he was being arrested. The officer "answered with three swift blows of the night-stick across the boy's face and he went down. As he sprawled, he was kicked in the face."

As the rioting went on for almost a week, Spanish-language newspapers asked for calm, while English-language papers seemed to egg on the military attackers. What began as street fights turned into a major race riot, and the violence spread to other cities in California. The national press began to report the story, and soon riots broke out in Chicago, Detroit, and Philadelphia. The U.S. military finally stepped in and ordered all servicemen to remain in their barracks. At the same time, Los Angeles officials made it illegal to wear zoot suits.

The violence had angered officials in Mexico because some Mexican citizens living in Los Angeles were victims of the violence. Embarrassed U.S. officials began investigating and found that sailors had indeed attacked unarmed people and that neither the local police nor military officials had done anything to stop the violence. Both the Mexican and the Anglo communities of Los Angeles began looking at the causes of the Zoot Suit Riots. A committee appointed by Governor Earl Warren realized that the harsh conditions many Mexican American youths faced had played a part, as had prejudice against the pachucos. Officials hoped that improved education and job training would give Mexican American youths a better chance to feel part of society and make them less likely to join gangs. The committee also called for "an educational program throughout the community designed to combat race prejudice in all its forms."

★ REINALDO ARENAS
WRITER
1943–1990

As a teenager, Reinaldo Arenas embraced the changes Fidel Castro promised for Cuba. Arenas took up arms against the old pro-American government before finding his true calling as a writer. Soon, Arenas's work and his sexuality would lead to conflict with Castro's revolutionary government. Arenas then openly opposed Castro, both in Cuba and after fleeing to the United States. Meanwhile, his writing won him a worldwide reputation.

Born in 1943 near Holguín, Cuba, Arenas was raised in extreme poverty. As an adult, he claimed that one of his first memories was being forced to eat dirt because his family lacked food. At age fifteen, he joined the revolutionary army of Fidel Castro, who said the government he envisioned for Cuba would eliminate the kind of harsh conditions Arenas had known. Arenas moved to Havana, Cuba's capital, in 1962 and worked at the national library. He also attended college, studying literature, philosophy, and economics. Although he never earned a degree, Arenas used his time in the capital to write and publish his first novel, *Celestino antes del alba* (1967). The book was published two decades later in English as *Singing from the Well* (1987), and it was the first of five works sometimes called Arenas's Pentagonia. *Celestino antes del alba* is a defense of individual freedom in a world of misery, ignorance, and intellectual barbarism. The book upset some Cuban officials, who wanted the island's writers to focus on social goals and not question government policies or attitudes. After this, Arenas could not openly publish in Cuba.

Arenas further stirred the anger of Castro's government with his next book, *Le monde hallucinant* (1968), called in English *Being an Account of the Life and Adventures of Friar Servando Teresa de Mier.* He smuggled the work out of Cuba, and it was published in France and later in Mexico. This novel, considered one of his best, retells the life of Fray Servando Teresa de Mier, a Mexican friar of the late eighteenth century. The monk's unusual views on the Roman Catholic Church upset church leaders, and he spent years either in jail or wandering in exile. Arenas's book drew obvious parallels to the politics of Cuba in the 1960s, since Castro did not tolerate ideas that strayed from his own. The book was considered an attack on revolutionary ideals.

Arenas's homosexuality was also a concern to Cuban officials. Although homosexuality was not officially illegal under Castro, the government did not approve of it. Homosexuals were sent to forced labor camps, and in 1970, Arenas landed in one where he was forced to cut sugarcane.

Arenas tried unsuccessfully to escape the island twice. The first time, he tried to flee by floating out to sea on a tire. The second time, he was almost shot. He hid in Lenin Park for nearly two months and was then taken to the Castillo del Morro prison in 1974. The government was upset that he had published abroad without getting approval. After two years of torture and many attempts at suicide, Arenas confessed to the false charges of sexual abuse and was released. Afterward, he was forced to hide his writings. While writing *Otra vez el mar* (*Farewell to the Sea: A Novel of Cuba*), Arenas had to bury his drafts of the book in the yard or hide them on the roof of his house. The government continually found the book and destroyed it, forcing Arenas to rewrite it no fewer than four times. The book did not appear in print until 1982, after Arenas had left Cuba.

In 1980, Castro decided to let thousands of Cubans who disliked his government leave the island for the United States. These exiles sailed on boats that left from Mariel Harbor, and their experience is often called the Mariel boatlift. Arenas decided to use the boatlift as his way out of Cuba. He ended up in New York City, where once again he faced poverty, as he had during his childhood. But now he at least had the freedom to write and publish whatever he wanted, and he often used that freedom to attack Castro and his rule.

Arenas founded the journal *Mariel* in the 1980s and wrote many articles for it until it closed down. In 1987, he was diagnosed with AIDS (acquired immunodeficiency syndrome). At the time, the disease was not as treatable as it is today, and Arenas rushed to complete those works he did not wish to leave unfinished. As death drew near, Arenas committed suicide on December 7, 1990. In a note written to a Spanish-language newspaper, Arenas said, "My message is not a message of failure, but rather one of struggle and hope. Cuba will be free, I already am." His autobiography, *Before Night Falls,* was published after his death and was later adapted into a movie of the same name. By some accounts, the book was not always accurate as to the facts of Arenas's life; as with his fiction, he was more concerned with his thoughts and emotions than with realism.

As a Latino writer, Arenas is mostly remembered for his passion for literature and his political activism. His works express the thoughts and feelings of many people held down by their governments. His writings also question the traditional roles of men and women and defend homosexuality, freedom, and tolerance. Despite the fact that his literary career was not recognized until after his death, Arenas is regarded today as one of Cuba's best authors.

MARIO MOLINA
SCIENTIST, NOBEL PRIZE WINNER
1943–

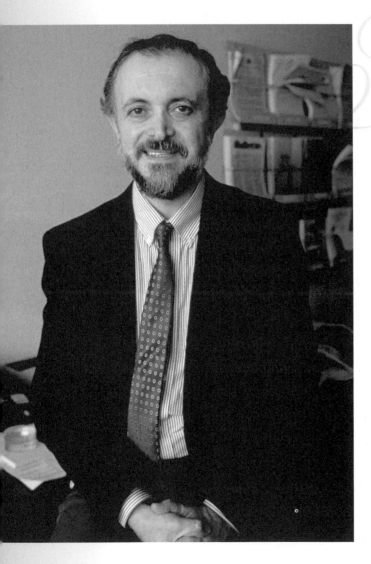

The ozone layer sits above Earth's surface, where it acts to filter out deadly radiation from the sun. During the early 1970s, Mexican American chemist Mario J. Molina became interested in certain chemicals produced on Earth that drift up into the ozone layer. He and a research partner found that the chemicals destroy the ozone layer, threatening the safety of humans and other life. For his work exploring the ozone layer, Molina received the 1995 Nobel Prize for Chemistry.

Molina was born in Mexico City in 1943. He came from a wealthy background. His father was a lawyer who later served as Mexico's ambassador to Ethiopia, Australia, and the Philippines. The young Molina's budding interest in chemistry was supported by his parents, who let him convert one of the family's bathrooms into a crude laboratory. Molina was also encouraged by his aunt Esther Molina, a chemist in the sugar industry. With her help, Molina later recalled, he carried out "more challenging experiments along the lines of those carried out by freshman chemistry students in college." At age eleven, Molina attended boarding school in Switzerland, then returned to Mexico for high school. He already knew that his classmates were baffled by his keen interest in chemistry. But, he later said, "I explained to them that for me, it was very, very interesting, and I had a lot of fun. I think they understood then."

In 1960, Molina enrolled in the chemical engineering program at the National University of Mexico. After graduation, he headed to Germany for additional training in mathematics, physics, and other areas, and then spent several months studying in Paris. Molina returned to Mexico as an assistant professor at the National University, where he established the first graduate program in chemical engineering. In 1968, he left for the University of California (UC) at Berkeley to pursue a doctorate in physical chemistry.

During the 1960s, Berkeley was a center of radical political thinking. That atmosphere led Molina to reflect on the significance of science and technology to society. Some of his first work was with lasers, and Molina was upset to think that some lasers were being designed for use as weapons. "I wanted to be involved with research that was useful to society, but not for potentially harmful purposes."

After completing his doctorate, Molina moved to the University of California at Irvine and began working with Sherwood Rowland. The two scientists shared an interest in the chemicals in Earth's atmosphere and in environmental studies. Molina chose to study chlorofluorocarbons (CFCs). These chemicals were found in spray cans, air conditioners, and other common items and were often released into the atmosphere. In 1974, Molina and Rowland published an article in *Nature* that suggested a connection between CFCs and destruction of the ozone layer. The mass media eventually picked up the CFC story.

The effect of CFCs on the ozone layer became a publicly debated issue, and Molina was in the middle of it. He had to balance his position as an impartial scientist with the need to communicate with the media and policy makers. He and Rowland spoke to the U.S. Congress about potential controls on CFC emissions, which eventually led to the Montreal Protocol on Substances That Deplete the Ozone Layer. This international agreement, first drafted in 1987, set a timetable for ending the use of CFCs and other chemicals that harm the ozone layer.

In 1975, Molina became a faculty member at UC–Irvine and established his own atmospheric science laboratory. During those years, his wife, Luisa, began working with him. She also worked with him when he left the university in 1982 to take a job at the Jet Propulsion Laboratory, part of the National Aeronautic and Space Administration (NASA). There, the Molinas drew connections between a hole in the ozone layer over Antarctica and CFCs, which was later confirmed.

In 1989, Molina returned to teaching, becoming a professor at the Massachusetts Institute of Technology (MIT). He was appointed as a scientific adviser to President Bill Clinton in 1994, and, the next year, he and Rowland shared the Nobel Prize for Chemistry with Dutch scientist Paul J. Crutzen. The award recognized Molina and Rowland's first discoveries of the harmful effects of CFCs on the ozone layer.

In the years that followed, Molina spent less time in the lab and more in the classroom. He also returned regularly to Mexico City to work on environmental concerns. In 2002, he and his wife coedited *Air Quality in the Mexico Megacity: An Integrated Assessment*, a compilation of the research done there. Molina also established the Molina Fellowship in Environmental Science to bring young scientists from emerging nations to MIT to study environmental sciences. He hopes that these scientists will return to their countries and tackle complex environmental concerns.

★ ANTONIA COELLO NOVELLO

U.S. SURGEON GENERAL

1944–

The highest medical official in the United States is the surgeon general. As the country's top doctor, the surgeon general tracks health trends and encourages Americans to exercise, eat right, quit smoking, and generally take better care of themselves. Hispanics have often struggled with their own health problems, and in 1990 they saw someone particularly sensitive to their issues step in as surgeon general. That year, Antonia Coello Novello became the first Hispanic—and the first woman—to hold that important medical position.

Antonia Coello was born in Fajardo, Puerto Rico. From infancy, she had a problem in her colon, so she spent much of her young life surrounded by doctors and nurses.

She knew from an early age that she wanted to one day become a doctor. After high school, Antonia enrolled at the University of Puerto Rico, and she received her undergraduate degree in 1965. She then earned her master's degree at Johns Hopkins University in Baltimore and returned to Puerto Rico to attend medical school. She graduated in 1970, the same year she married Joseph Novello, another doctor.

Antonia Novello was soon back in the United States, studying at the University of Michigan and Georgetown University. She concentrated on pediatrics, the medical treatment of children, and especially kids with kidney diseases. After finishing her studies in 1975, Novello spent two years in private practice in Virginia.

In 1979, Novello took her first government job, with the Public Health Service Commissioned Corps. As part of this work, she held several different positions at the National Institutes of Health (NIH). In 1986, she was named deputy director of the National Institute of Child Health and Human Development (NICHD). Always known for her energy, Novello took time during her years at NIH to earn another college degree, teach part-time at Georgetown, and advise lawmakers on health issues. In 1987, she added another new item to her busy plate, serving as coordinator for AIDS (acquired immunodeficiency syndrome) research for NICHD. In that job, she developed a keen interest in the treatment of children with AIDS.

While at NICHD, Novello led a study team that issued a report on the health of Hispanic Americans. The study said that fewer Hispanic Americans had health insurance than any other ethnic group. Hispanics had higher rates of diabetes, high blood pressure, and certain kinds of cancer. To make matter worse, they were being hit hard by AIDS as well. The report also noted that there were too few Hispanics in the health professions.

By the time the study was released in 1990, President George H. W. Bush had named Novello the U.S. surgeon general. Novello said she was shocked

Novello demonstrates proper hand washing to prevent the spread of the flu

when she was offered the job. "Life has made you believe that you have to have connections, that you must be at the right place at the right time and have the right friends. None of those things happened to me. This is why, when the call came, I thought it was a joke and I almost didn't answer it."

As surgeon general, Novello continued to focus on health issues affecting children and minorities, with AIDS a particular concern. She made headlines with sharp attacks on the tobacco industry for seeming to promote smoking among children. She also led the first national workshop on health care in America's Hispanic communities. The result of that was a report called *One Voice, One Vision: Recommendations to the Surgeon General to Improve Hispanic/ Latino Health*. In it, Novello wrote, "Speaking with one loud voice, we can begin to make America listen to us as never before." One thing Hispanics needed to call for was better health care.

The report appeared in 1993, the same year Novello left her job as surgeon general. In the years that followed, she worked at UNICEF, an agency of the United Nations that addresses children's health. In 1999, she became commissioner of health for the State of New York.

★ RICHARD RODRIGUEZ
WRITER, TEACHER
1944–

When Richard Rodriguez entered his first-grade class, he knew perhaps fifty words of English. Thrown into a world where he could barely understand what was said around him, Rodriguez felt alone. Through his and his parents' efforts, Rodriguez slowly perfected his English, and he went on to earn college degrees. In 1982, he published an autobiography, *Hunger of Memory: The Education of Richard Rodriguez*, which describes his efforts to learn English and to feel like an American. Those efforts, however, distanced him from his Mexican roots. Rodriguez has continued to write books and articles, emerging as a thoughtful voice on many issues, including the role of ethnicity in a nation comprised of people from so many different backgrounds.

Rodriguez was born in California. His parents were Mexican immigrants who spoke Spanish at home. As Rodriguez wrote in his autobiography, his early school experience shaped his ideas about education and, specifically, bilingual education. How would his life have been different, he asks, if he'd attended a school where Spanish was spoken? His early years might have been happier and more secure, but his entire education would have suffered, he decides. When a child goes to school, Rodriguez argues, he must leave his family's world behind. School is "public," and family is "private." Spanish was his private language—the language he used at home—and English was public. The great lesson of school, he believes, is to gain a public identity. As Rodriguez said years after his book was published, "It was my teacher's role to tell me I was an American. The notion that you go to a public institution in order to learn private information about yourself is absurd."

In *Hunger of Memory*, Rodriguez describes some of his early struggles to master English. "I was unable to hear my own sounds, but I knew very well that I spoke English poorly. My words could not stretch far enough to form complete thoughts. And the words I did speak I didn't know well enough to make into distinct sounds." His struggles made school a painful experience in the beginning. But some pain is necessary, Rodriguez later realized, to acquire the education needed to prosper in the larger world.

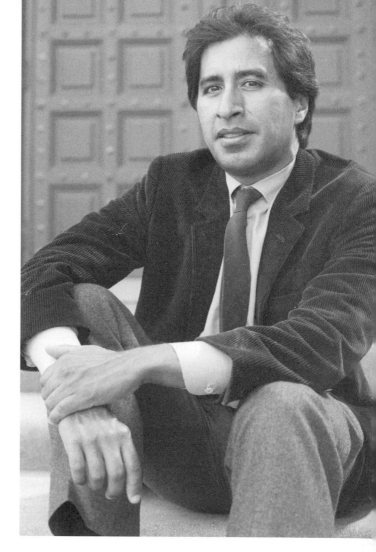

Going on to college, Rodriguez graduated in 1967 with an English degree from Stanford University, then received his master's degree from Columbia University two years later. In 1972, he continued his studies on a Fulbright scholarship, an academic honor given by the U.S. government to professors and top graduate students. He later pursued further studies in English literature at the University of California at Berkeley.

Hunger of Memory marked Rodriguez's rise to prominence as a writer. The book was widely praised, though some Hispanics disliked his attack on bilingual education. These critics believed that teaching students in both Spanish and English was a way to preserve Hispanic culture. Years after the book was published, Rodriguez was still arguing with the supporters of bilingual education, repeating his belief that "you can't use family language in the classroom."

After publishing *Hunger of Memory*, Rodriguez went on to write thoughtful essays for many magazines. In 1992, he released his second book, *Days of Obligation: An Argument with My Mexican Father*. In it, he continues to explore his feelings on being Mexican American in a mostly Anglo world. Ten years later, he published *Brown: The Last Discovery of America*. Rodriguez saw it as a companion to his first two books. Together, he saw them all as a look at modern America through the perspective of his own life. And though he discusses his own ethnic background, Rodriguez did not want to be seen as a purely Hispanic writer. "I owe my existence to so many other influences," he told one interviewer. "The notion that you would find me on a bookshelf somewhere far in the corner with other Hispanic writers denies . . . the [Anglo and African American] writers who shaped me."

Rodriguez branched out beyond the written word to present his essays on public radio and television. In 1997, he won a Peabody Award, which recognizes excellence in radio and television journalism. He was singled out for the way he "confronts the camera, and converses directly with the viewer, thereby drawing us into the unique slices of American life that comprise his subjects." Today, Rodriguez continues to work in three media—print, radio, and television—bringing his deep insights to all facets of the world around him.

★ EDWARD JAMES OLMOS

ACTOR

1947–

When Edward James Olmos began his performing career, he was a singer, not an actor. The teenager led a group called Eddie James and the Pacific Ocean, and he decided to do some acting as a way to improve his singing. Instead, Olmos found out he had some talent, which led to his career as an award-winning actor in television, films, and theater. But acting was not his only passion: Olmos also became involved in political causes, and he has tried to take on artistic projects that reflected his social concerns.

Olmos was born to a Mexican-born father and Mexican American mother in East Los Angeles, California. The neighborhood had a large Latino population, but it also had other ethnic groups, including Russians,

Koreans, and Chinese. The diversity of the neighborhood, and the way the different groups got along so well, shaped Olmos's views as an actor and as an activist.

When he was a student at Montebello High School, Olmos formed the band Pacific Ocean. While playing regularly at nightclubs, he attended East Los Angeles College and California State University. It was there that he met his first wife, Kaija, the daughter of actor Howard Keel, with whom he eventually had two sons. For a time, Olmos did odd jobs to support his family while trying to keep his music career alive and break into acting.

His big break came in 1978, when he landed the role of El Pachuco, the narrator in the play *Zoot Suit*. The play was based on the true story of young Mexican Americans who were falsely accused of murder in Los Angeles during World War II. For his role, Olmos drew from his childhood experiences, and his performance won wide acclaim. Los Angeles critics named him the best new performer of the year. The play then went to Broadway, where Olmos was nominated for a Tony Award, the top prize in professional theater.

Over the next few years, Olmos appeared in several movies, including the horror film *Wolfen* and *Blade Runner*, a science-fiction classic. In 1982, he starred in another project based on the injustices faced by a real Mexican American, a TV movie called *The Ballad of Gregorio Cortez*. He also wrote some of the music for the film. Two years later, Olmos took a starring role in the popular TV show *Miami Vice*. In 1985, he earned an Emmy, television's top honor, for his portrayal of Lieutenant Martin Castillo.

For most of his career after *Miami Vice*, Olmos went back and forth between film and television work. His best-known movie role was as Jaime Escalante, a real-life math teacher who helped his Hispanic students excel. For his work in Escalante's story, *Stand and Deliver* (1988), Olmos was nominated for an Academy Award. He directed and starred in the 1992 film *American Me*. Other acting credits included *Mi Familia/My Family* (1995) and the television series *American Family* (2002).

Thanks to the success of his many projects, Olmos has used his star status to promote a variety of causes. He has been actively involved with community service projects and nonprofit groups. In 1999, Olmos Productions, a company he founded, created a multimedia project called "Americanos: Latino Life in the United States." It included a book of photographs, a documentary film, a CD of Hispanic music, and a traveling exhibit.

In 2001, Olmos participated in a movement to end trial bombing runs by the U.S. Navy on the inhabited island of Vicques in Puerto Rico, where he and other protesters were arrested for trespassing. Their subsequent prison sentences brought a great deal of attention to the issue and helped force the departure of the navy from the island in 2003.

Olmos, however, did not forget his acting career. In 2004, he took a lead role in the TV show *Battlestar Galactica* while continuing to work in films. Once again, he was drawn to the true challenges of Mexican Americans, directing the story of a 1968 protest by Hispanic high school students in Los Angeles. The film, *Walkout*, made its debut on HBO in 2006.

★ BILL RICHARDSON
GOVERNMENT OFFICIAL, POLITICIAN
1947–

From his seat in the U.S. Congress representing northern New Mexico, Bill Richardson made his mark as an intelligent, caring lawmaker. He also showed a flair for diplomacy, traveling overseas to win the release of Americans held captive in various places. President Bill Clinton saw Richardson's skills and in 1997 chose him to represent the United States at the United Nations. Richardson became the first Hispanic American to hold that post, and the next year he served as Clinton's secretary of energy. Later elected governor of New Mexico, Richardson set his sights even higher, suggesting he might one day run for president.

William Blaine Richardson was born in Pasadena, California. His mother was Mexican, and his father was a native of Boston who worked for Citibank as an executive in Mexico. Richardson was raised in Mexico City, but as a teenager he attended a high school near Boston, Massachusetts. He went on to Tufts University, where he majored in French and political science. He then added a master's degree from the Fletcher School of Law and Diplomacy at Tufts.

Settling in New Mexico, Richardson entered local politics there in 1978. Two years later, he ran for a seat in the U.S. House of Representatives but lost. In 1982, he ran again and won, holding the seat for the next fourteen years. In Congress, Richardson rose to leadership within the Democratic Party, eventually serving as whip. In that role, his job was to make sure his party won enough votes among its House members on key bills. In addition, Richardson tried to create new jobs in New Mexico, and he supported an amendment to the U.S. Constitution that would require the government to spend only as much money each year as it brings in.

While a congressman, Richardson was asked to serve on several international missions. Through his efforts, American servicemen, prisoners, and hostages held in North Korea, Iraq, Cuba, and Sudan won their freedom. Richardson also observed elections in several foreign countries to make sure they were run fairly. His diplomatic work while in Congress and after earned Richardson four nominations (1995, 1997, 2000, and 2001) for the Nobel Peace Prize.

In December 1996, President Clinton asked Richardson to become the U.S. ambassador to the United Nations. With that position, Richardson joined Clinton's cabinet, his circle of closest advisers. At the UN, Richardson continued to use his skills as a negotiator to good affect. He said that he saw the UN as a "venue for advancing American interests in promoting human rights, supporting democracy, dealing with refugees, and furthering the causes of women." After a little more than one year at that job, Clinton appointed Richardson to be secretary of energy. In that position, which he held until

Governor Richardson gives a speech in 2005

2001, he stressed creating more competition in the electric-power industry, cleaning up radioactive material, and safely disposing of old nuclear weapons. He also called for developing new energy sources so the United States would not have to rely so heavily on imported gas and oil.

After leaving Washington, Richardson took a job teaching at Harvard University, but soon he immersed himself again in the world of politics. In 2002, he was elected governor of New Mexico. At the time, he was the only Hispanic governor in the country. While trying to address poverty and problems with education in his home state, Richardson kept an eye on the national scene. His expertise in so many areas has made him a popular guest on new shows, and in 2004 the Democrats named him the chairman of their national convention. During the presidential campaign that year, Richardson actively worked for Democratic candidate John Kerry, who eventually lost the race.

Richardson was once asked if politicians are different from other people. He said, "Politicians have a certain amount of power-driven blood that makes them more active than normal. Politicians feel they have to be everywhere, tireless. I have a sense of there's little time to do all the things we need to do . . . so I rush myself." All politicians may have Richardson's drive, but few match his wide-ranging experience and his level of dedication to protecting the rights and improving the quality of life of people in New Mexico, the United States, and around the world.

CARLOS SANTANA
MUSICIAN
1947–

In 1969, with a distinct guitar sound and a musical style influenced by his Hispanic roots, Carlos Santana burst onto the rock music scene. Since then, he has recorded with his own group and with a wide range of musicians from diverse fields such as jazz, pop, and hip-hop. Along the way, he has become one of the most successful and beloved rock musicians in the world. Over the decades, what has always remained constant is Santana's passionate guitar playing and his love of good music, whatever its source.

Carlos Santana was born in Autlán de Navarro, Mexico, the fourth of José and Josefina Santana's seven children. His father was a violinist, and Carlos followed in his

Santana performs at the 2005 World Music Awards

footsteps, picking up that instrument for the first time when he was five. The family was immersed in mariachi, the vibrant Mexican dance music that combines violins, trumpet, and guitar.

By the time Carlos was eight, his family moved to Tijuana, and he soon had a new musical love: the guitar. Listening to U.S. radio stations with signals that reached over the border, he was inspired by blues guitarists John Lee Hooker and B. B. King. By age thirteen, Carlos was playing with a band at clubs in Tijuana. When he was fifteen, his family moved to San Francisco, but Carlos returned to Tijuana to keep performing. He was determined to follow in his father's footsteps and become a professional musician. His parents, however, were concerned for their young son, and a year later Carlos rejoined his family in northern California.

Carlos's taste in music continued to grow. He listened to Latin jazz artists Tito Puente and Mongo Santamaría, and in San Francisco he was exposed to the city's growing music scene. He spent time at local clubs, occasionally getting a chance to play. In 1966, he formed the Santana Blues Band and soon met Bill Graham, the most important concert promoter in rock music at the time. In 1968, Santana's band performed at Graham's famous concert hall the

Fillmore West. That year, Santana also made his recording debut, playing on a live album that featured blues guitarist Mike Bloomfield.

Graham was so impressed with Santana and his group, now known simply as Santana, that he gave them a slot at the Woodstock Festival, a three-day music festival held in August 1969. There, Santana's Latin rhythms, accentuated by conga drums and the timbale and mixed with blues and bold guitar solos, established his band as a new sound in rock 'n' roll. By that time, the group had already released its first album, *Santana*, and had a hit single, "Evil Ways."

In 1970, Santana released its second record, *Abraxas,* which contained two hits. The first, "Black Magic Woman," was written by Peter Green, a founder of Fleetwood Mac, but Santana's version became the one known around the world. Santana and his band also recorded "Oye Como Va," by Tito Puente, bringing the Latin jazz master's work to a new audience. Like the first album, *Abraxas* went gold in less than a year. It eventually sold more than 4 million copies.

Over the next several years, the members of Santana changed, but Carlos and his guitar playing remained the center of the band's work. At times, he did side projects with other musicians he respected. One project, with jazz-rock guitarist John McLaughlin, was *Love, Devotion, Surrender*. The title and the music reflected the two guitarists' shared interests in Eastern religion. Throughout his life, Santana has felt a strong calling to a spiritual path, which has influenced his music.

Going into the 1980s, his music made its way onto radio and video less often than in the past. Santana's desire to experiment and fuse different styles could not find a receptive audience. Still, the band continued to record and play concerts, and in 1988 the title instrumental from the album *Blues for Salvador* earned Santana his first Grammy, the highest award in music.

After staying below the pop-music radar for many years, Santana made a dazzling reemergence in 1999. That year, he released his thirty-sixth album,

Supernatural. The record featured Carlos Santana playing with a variety of performers, including Eric Clapton, Lauryn Hill, and Dave Matthews. With Rob Thomas, singer and songwriter for Matchbox 20, Santana recorded the song "Smooth," which became Santana's first number-one hit in decades. Thanks to "Smooth" and *Supernatural,* Santana took home eight more Grammys in 2000, including Record of the Year and Song of the Year. *Supernatural* went on to sell more than 25 million copies, making it one of the most popular albums of all time.

In 2002, Santana released the album *Shaman,* and then three years later came out with another collection of musical collaborations, *All That I Am.* Performers included Steve Tyler of Aerosmith, Joss Stone, and Big Boi. Like *Supernatural*, it reached number one on the record charts. In a 2005 interview, Carlos Santana reflected on his musical choices and where it has led him. "I made a conscious decision to play music not necessarily for musicians . . . I wanted to play for people, period. Grandparents, parents, teenagers and little children. That's how I see Santana. It just happens that hippies come along. Straight people come along. Guys with green mohawk hair—they're all in it now."

Santana has used his tremendous success to create the Milagro (Miracle) Foundation to promote art, education, and health among poor children. The foundation is supported by private donations as well as money Santana contributes. He also takes time to support causes close to his heart, such as world peace. Among his honors, he and the original Santana band members were inducted into the Rock and Roll Hall of Fame in 1998, and Carlos Santana has received several national awards for his work in the Hispanic community.

PART SIX

INTO THE TWENTY-FIRST CENTURY

231

RUBEN BLADES
SINGER, SONGWRITER, ACTOR, POLITICIAN
1948–

Born and raised in a gritty section of Panama's capital, Ruben Blades was surrounded by music. He soon developed his own musical talents, which helped him leave Panama City and go to the United States. There, he continued to pursue his education as well as his career. By the late 1970s, Blades was one of the most exciting figures in the world of Latino music, blending sizzling rhythms with lyrics about the poor and powerless and unlucky. After becoming an international star, Blades returned to his homeland and entered politics, hoping to bring positive change to the country he loves. At the same time, he still entertained millions with both his music and his talents as an actor.

Blades was born in Panama City, Panama, in 1948. His mother was a Cuban-born pianist and singer, and his Panamanian father was a bongo player. Blades listened to the radio and heard American rock 'n' roll, and he taught himself how to play guitar. He made his first public appearance as a singer in 1963, fronting the Saints, a rock band led by his older brother, Luis. Soon the young vocalist focused on Latin music. He also became politically aware for the first time, after student riots in 1964 led to the death of more than twenty people. At the time, the United States controlled the Canal Zone, the land surrounding the Panama Canal. The students tried to hoist a Panamanian flag in the zone, sparking the riots. Blades later said the Americans "turned friends into enemies" because of the killings, some carried out by U.S. troops.

During the late 1960s and early 1970s, Blades juggled music and education. For a time, he left school in Panama and recorded an album in New York, then he returned home to finish his studies in law. He also performed with several bands that played salsa, lively dance music found throughout Latin America. In 1974, he gave up a comfortable law practice to pursue a musical career in New York as a salsa singer and songwriter.

For a time, Blades played with Ray Barretto and the Fania All Stars, a band heavily influenced by Latin jazz. He then joined forces with the trombone-playing bandleader Willie Colón in 1977. Colón was interested in more traditional Latin music, and he let Blades record some of the songs he wrote. For the next five years, they produced some of the best-selling records in U.S. salsa history, including *Metiendo Mano* (1977) and *Siembra* (1978). Their collaborations redefined the nature of the salsa movement and contributed greatly to its growing international popularity by including socially inspired lyrics. Blades's song "Pedro Navaja" hit the top of the Spanish-language music charts and sold more than a million copies. Blades later said that his musical characters, such as Pedro, were inspired by his youth in San Felipe, the neighborhood where he grew up. Blades also wrote songs that became hits for other salsa performers.

In 1982, Blades tried something new, starring in a low-budget boxing movie called *The Last Fight*. Musically, he was also ready for something new, hoping to create a sound that went beyond traditional salsa boundaries. He became the first Latin artist to be signed by the mainstream U.S. label Elektra/Asylum, and he led his own band, called Seis del Solar, on the 1984 album *Buscando América* (*Searching for America*). Blades used jazz, rock, soul, and Latin music as the background for stories about life in Latin America. He said he "wanted to make an urban American album that can be appreciated by any American city dweller." The album sold well and won praise from critics.

In 1985, Blades took a break from performing and went back to school, earning a master's degree in international law at Harvard University. The same year, he released *Escenas*, which earned him the first of five Grammys, the awards given to honor the best recorded music. Blades also appeared in his second film, *Crossover Dreams.* He played a salsa singer who tries to cross over from Latin music to Anglo music and faces many problems along the way. Blades continued to act in more Hollywood films, winning favorable reviews for his roles in *Fatal Beauty, The Milagro Beanfield War,* and other motion pictures. At the same time, he continued to record, and in 1988, he won new Anglo fans with *Nothing But the Truth*, his first album in English.

During the late 1990s, Blades began to search for a new musical approach, recording with the versatile Costa Rican ensemble Editus. Before meeting these classically trained musicians, Blades said, "I was very bored actually with repeating the same sort of formats . . . I wanted to experiment with different instrumentation." Blades said he was tired of the label "salsa" for his art because he wanted to make the lyrics, not a danceable beat, the focus of his work.

Despite his busy schedule with music and films, Blades has taken time to explore his interest in politics and social issues. In 1994, he ran unsuccessfully for president in Panama, calling for greater equality among the country's different classes. Six years later, the United Nations asked him to be a goodwill ambassador. He went to colleges to speak against racism. In 2004, Blades returned to Panama once again and supported the presidential campaign of Martín Torrijos. After Torrijos won, Blades joined his government as its minister of tourism. He hoped to use the popularity of his music as a way to attract visitors to Panama.

★ CRISTINA SARALEGUI
TALK SHOW HOST
1948–

Nearly all Americans know Oprah Winfrey, who used her daily talk show to launch a business empire. But one of Oprah's main rivals as the queen of talk is Cristina Saralegui. Her Spanish-language talk show, based in Miami, Florida, is seen on three continents, and her own media empire—with a radio show and popular Web site—has earned her the nickname "the Hispanic Oprah." In 2005, *Time* magazine named Saralegui one of the twenty-five most influential Hispanics in the United States.

Saralegui was born in Cuba and learned to speak both English and Spanish as a child. Her grandfather, Francisco Saralegui, built a fortune by publishing magazines, and Cristina had an easy life as girl. But in 1959, Fidel Castro took power in Cuba, and the Saraleguis joined other wealthy Cubans who fled to Miami.

Saralegui before her induction into the Broadcasting and Cable Hall of Fame in 2005

Saralegui attended the University of Miami, then followed in her grandfather's footsteps by becoming a journalist. In 1979, she was named editor of the Spanish-language edition of *Cosmopolitan*, a popular magazine for young women. On the job, she traveled throughout Latin America.

Saralegui made her television debut in the mid-1980s, when she occasionally appeared on the Spanish show *Sabado Gigante* (*Giant Saturday*). The show was produced by the U.S.-based network Univision, and company officials saw that Saralegui had a flair for intelligent, entertaining comments. In 1989, the network gave her a daily talk show of her own.

El Show de Cristina (*Cristina's Show*) sometimes shocked audiences with its topics on sex and relationships. But Saralegui also tried to educate her audience about important issues, such as the dangers of AIDS and how to prevent it. Over the years, the show's popularity grew thanks to such big-name guests as Arnold Schwarzenegger, Jennifer Lopez, and Antonio Banderas. But the core of the show was Saralegui, with her ability to make audiences laugh, sometimes cry, and usually learn something new. She saw her show as a way to unite Hispanics from many different countries, especially people living in the United States. "What I try to do is play down the differences and portray us as what we are—which is that everyone is in this together."

Over the years, *El Show de Cristina* grew tremendously, eventually reaching a worldwide audience of one hundred million people every day. Soon after the show went on the air, Saralegui introduced a Spanish-language magazine, *Cristina: La Revista (Cristina: The Magazine)*, which she published for fifteen years. In 1998, she released her autobiography, *Cristina! My Life as a Blonde*, in both Spanish and English. Three years later, she opened Blue Dolphin Studios, a state-of-the-art facility with three separate television studios, where she tapes her show. By this time, she was taping a daily radio show as well.

In 2001, she ended her daily talk show to focus on an hourly prime-time show that aired once a week. That switch gave her more time to focus on new interests, which also helped introduce her to Anglo audiences. She appeared on *Hollywood Squares* and the TV sitcom *George López* and introduced a line of furniture bearing her name. Saralegui hopes to produce a film based on the life of Cuban salsa singer Celia Cruz.

By 2006, her show had won eleven Emmys, the highest honor in television, and Saralegui had become the first Hispanic TV personality to receive a star on the Hollywood Walk of Fame. In the midst of all her entertainment and business activity, she still found time to work for social causes, especially related to AIDS prevention. Yet it is her weekly TV show that keeps her connected to her core audience of Hispanics. They have watched her deal with personal changes, such as going through cosmetic surgery and other issues related to aging. She has made them confront social issues, such as inequality toward gays and lesbians. And she has entertained. "I don't want to bore people," she said, "and I especially don't want to be bored." While reaching that goal, Saralegui also created one of the first positive images of Hispanic women on television.

★ OSCAR HIJUELOS
WRITER
1951–

I consider myself a New York writer of Cuban parentage, with different influences. My background is an important element, the most important, but not the only one.

—Oscar Hijuelos

Like the majority of today's Hispanic American authors, Oscar Hijuelos writes only in English. Although Cuban culture plays a role in his work, the voice that speaks in his novels is that of a second-generation Cuban American, someone whose ties to that culture are deep but distant. Although Cuba provides Hijuelos with a subject, it does not determine his views or his audience. Hijuelos pays tribute to things Cuban even as he bids them farewell. This approach was prominently displayed in his novel *The Mambo Kings Play Songs of Love*, which earned him one of literature's top honors, the Pulitzer Prize. Hijuelos was the first Hispanic novelist to win that award.

Oscar Hijuelos was born in New York City to working-class Cuban parents. He grew up speaking Spanish, but when a childhood illness put him in a hospital for a year, he emerged speaking English. After attending public schools, Hijuelos left New York City and worked odd jobs before returning to study at the City College of New York. He earned a degree in English there in 1975. The next year, he completed a master's degree program in English.

After completing his studies, Hijuelos worked in the advertising department of a New York firm. Writing, however, was his true focus, and he spent most of his free time working on short stories. In 1978, some of his work was published in an annual collection of the best American short stories. That recognition helped Hijuelos earn scholarships and grants that gave him the opportunity to spend even more time writing. In 1983, he published his first novel, *Our House in the Last World*. It follows the fortunes of the Santinio family over several decades, as Alejo Santinio and Mercedes Sorrea marry and immigrate to the United States, where they lead a

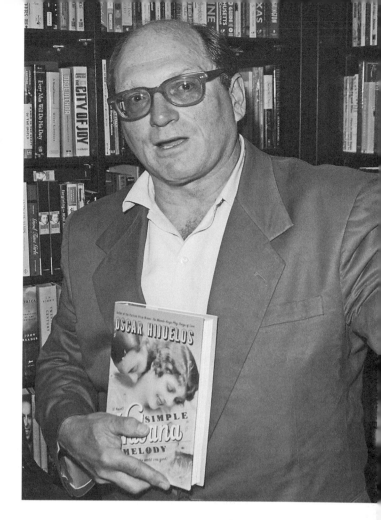

difficult life in Spanish Harlem. The central figure in the novel is Hector, the Santinios' second son, who, like the author, was born in New York in 1951. Too Cuban to be American but hardly Cuban enough to resemble his father, Hector sees himself as a freak, a "Cuban Quasimodo."

Hijuelos tackled the issue of being Cuban again in his second novel, *The Mambo Kings Play Songs of Love* (1989). The book reconstructs the lives of two brothers, Cesar and Nestor Castillo, musicians who play the Cuban music called mambo. The story was partially influenced by the stories Hijuelos heard as a boy from his uncle, who had played bass in a band led by Cuban musician Xavier Cugat. In *Mambo Kings,* the Castillo brothers achieve fleeting fame one night in 1955 when they appear on an episode of *I Love Lucy* as Ricky Ricardo's

Cuban cousins. Later, Nestor dies in a car accident on the way back from a singing engagement. Cesar blames himself for the death, and he descends into a depression from which he never recovers. Hijuelos used powerful prose to portray a man's inner torture and create a rousing picture of the New York Latin music scene of the 1940s and 1950s. *Mambo Kings* has been praised as one of the masterworks of contemporary Latino fiction, and it was made into a motion picture in 1992.

Some critics thought Hijuelos sometimes treated Hispanics in a stereotypical way. He seemed to accept the concept of machismo, or extreme manliness, which has sometimes been a part of Hispanic culture. Perhaps in response to those comments, Hijuelos chose to use girls and women as main characters in his next book, *The Fourteen Sisters of Emilio Montez O'Brien* (1993). The novel tells the story of Nelson O'Brien, an Irish photographer who travels to Cuba in 1898 to photograph the Spanish-American War. There he meets Mariela Montez, a Cuban beauty. They marry, move to Pennsylvania, and have fifteen children, only one of them a son. The story is told through the eyes of several female members of the family over many years. Although some reviewers criticized the novel for its length and lack of focus, Hijuelos paints a vivid look at life in twentieth-century America.

Hijuelos took another new approach to his work with *Mr. Ives' Christmas* (1995), as the hero is not openly identified as Hispanic. But in his two most recent works, *Empress of the Splendid Season* (1999) and *A Simple Havana Melody* (2002), Hijuelos returned to Cuban themes. Hijuelos called *A Simple Havana Melody* a "prequel" to his most popular work, the *Mambo Kings,* as it focuses on the world of Cuban music during the 1920s and 1930s. For Hijuelos, the book also deals with one of his larger concerns: "What I'm interested in, is going back in . . . time and looking at our sources and where we come from . . . because, I mean, we're products of the past. I think it's a good thing to bear that in mind as we move into the future."

SANDRA CISNEROS
WRITER
1954–

I am a woman and I am a Latina. Those are the things that make my writing distinctive. Those are the things that give my writing power. They are the things that give it sabor *[flavor], the things that give it* picante *[spice].*
—Sandra Cisneros

As a Mexican American growing up in Chicago, Sandra Cisneros saw the diversity of the United States, the "melting pot" in action. She saw many immigrants, such as her father, working hard to make a living for themselves and their children. Those struggles, and the challenges of being a woman in a "man's world" and of being a Hispanic woman in an Anglo world, shaped Cisneros as she began to write. On the strength of just one novel, *The House on Mango Street*, Cisneros became one of the most popular and widely read Hispanic authors in America.

     Sandra Cisneros was born in Chicago in 1954. Her father, Alfredo, was a Mexican immigrant who, while visiting that city, met and fell in love with a

Mexican American woman. They married and had seven children; Sandra was the only girl. Starting at an early age, Sandra expressed herself through poetry, and she studied English at Chicago's Loyola University. After graduating from there in 1976, she entered the highly regarded creative writing program at the University of Iowa, earning a master of fine arts degree in 1978. It was at Iowa that she truly developed her voice as a writer, realizing she could offer a unique view of the world as both a woman and a Mexican American.

After Iowa, Cisneros returned to Chicago and began teaching at the Latino Youth Alternative High School. Outside of class, she continued to write poetry, and her first collection of poems, *Bad Boys*, appeared in 1980. By 1983, she had moved to San Antonio, Texas, where she worked as the director of literature for a Hispanic cultural center. The next year, her big break came with the publication of her first novel, *The House on Mango Street*. The book has been called a collection of stories more than a true novel, focusing on the life of a young Latina who lives in Chicago. The book had elements of poetry, and when it was translated into English in 1991, some of the Spanish words remained. These were mostly words with no clear equivalent in English, yet which helped give the book its lyrical, powerful effect. *Mango Street* appeared at a time when teachers were looking for books that explored the experiences of young people from non-Anglo cultures. It was soon required reading in many middle school and high school classes, and it went on to sell more than 2 million copies.

The success of *Mango Street* helped Cisneros win awards and grants that let her put even more time into her writing. She also taught writing at several universities. In 1987, she published her first full-length book of poems, *My Wicked, Wicked Ways*. The title reflected her struggle to juggle the teachings of the Catholic Church, in which she was raised, with her desire for sex and other forbidden pleasures. (She later left the church and became a Buddhist.) Four years later, Cisneros published a collection of short stories, *Woman Hollering Creek and Other Stories*. In these works, she moved beyond the relatively limited space of

Mango Street to paint, on a larger canvas, life among Hispanics not only in the United States but also in Mexico City.

Cisneros branched out into a new literary field in 1994, when she published the bilingual children's book *Hairs=Pelitos*. The same year, another collection of poems appeared. In 1995, she received a MacArthur Foundation fellowship, known as the "genius grant." The fellowship came with a large cash prize, giving Cisneros time to focus on her work and tend to her father, who was dying of cancer.

During the late 1990s, Cisneros also waged a cultural and political battle in San Antonio. She wanted to paint her house a shade of purple associated with the native people of Mexico from centuries ago. The house, however, was in a historic district, so the city tightly restricted how houses could look and what colors they could be painted. Cisneros went ahead and used the purple paint, and her battle with city officials drew national attention. The purple stayed, though she later repainted the house blue.

In 2002, Cisneros published her second novel, *Caramelo*. The work grew from a short story to a book more than four hundred pages long, tracing the history of her family. The original story came from an idea she had during one of her family's annual trips to Mexico. She wanted to honor her father and other immigrants like him—the hardworking, honest, and largely unknown people who have made America great. *Caramelo* is a mix of fact and make-believe. As Cisneros told the *New York Times*, "I have invented what I do not know and exaggerated what I do, to continue the family tradition of telling healthy lies." When she went on tour and read from the book, Cisneros found that members of many immigrant groups, not just Mexican Americans, responded strongly to her work.

When not writing, Cisneros travels the country talking about her work. She has said, "Everything that I write comes when it wants to, out of its own need and it dictates its form. I don't say, 'I am going to write a novel.' . . . I never know what something is going to be until it emerges. . . . So in my life if another book wants to be born, it's not for me to choose."

★ ALBERTO GONZALES
LAWYER, JUDGE, U.S. ATTORNEY GENERAL
1955–

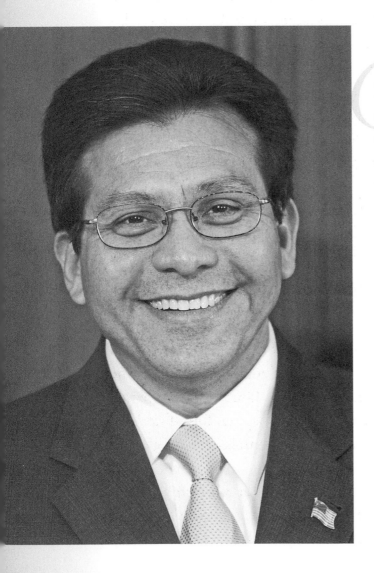

Each U.S. president draws on the advice and expertise of his cabinet, the heads of the most important government departments and agencies. Within the cabinet, several people are usually closest to the president and have the most influence in the government. The U.S. attorney general has almost always been one of those most respected and powerful cabinet members. In 2004, George W. Bush chose Alberto Gonzales as his new attorney general, making Gonzales the highest-ranking Hispanic cabinet member ever. Gonzales took that crucial job as the government's top attorney after years of loyal service to Bush in both Washington, D.C., and Texas.

Gonzales's rise to the highest level of government service is a classic rags-to-riches story. He was born in San Antonio, Texas, and grew up in Houston. His parents were poor, uneducated migrant workers who barely spoke English. Alberto lived with his family of ten in a two-bedroom house with no hot water or telephone. Although the Gonzales family lacked money, they believed in the benefits of hard work. Alberto took his first job at age twelve, selling soft drinks at Rice University during the school's football games. He would sell the drinks and wonder what life was like for the students at Rice. Through his determination and intelligence, he eventually found out for himself.

During high school, Alberto took classes designed to prepare students for college, even though his family did not have the money to send him. Along with taking classes, he played sports and made friends with students of all ethnic backgrounds, at a time when Anglo and Hispanic students in Houston rarely mixed. After high school, Gonzales joined the air force, serving two years in Alaska. In 1975, he entered the U.S. Air Force Academy near Colorado Springs, Colorado, but he soon decided the classes he was expected to take there did not match his interests. In 1977, he transferred to Rice University, where he developed an interest in law. One professor was so impressed with Gonzales's work that he used one of Gonzales's papers as a model for future students to follow.

From Rice, Gonzales went on to Harvard Law School. When he graduated in 1982, he joined a powerful Houston law firm, Vinson & Elkins. One of the firm's partners later described him as "extremely thoughtful" as he made "very careful and reasoned decisions." In 1990, Gonzales met George H. W. Bush. At the time, the elder Bush was serving as the forty-first U.S. president, and he offered Gonzales a government job. Gonzales, however, chose to stay at Vinson & Elkins.

Through professional contacts, Gonzales was later introduced to President Bush's son George W. In 1995, the younger Bush was elected governor of Texas, and he chose Gonzales as his general counsel—his personal lawyer for government affairs. Now a partner at Vinson & Elkins, Gonzales gave up a high-paying job to enter the government. He served Bush well, and the governor rewarded him by naming him the Texas secretary of state in 1997. Two years later, Governor Bush appointed Gonzales to the Texas Supreme Court.

In 2000, George W. Bush was elected president, and he once again chose Gonzales as his counsel. The job took on added significance after September 11, 2001, when terrorists killed three thousand people in New York City, Washington, D.C., and Pennsylvania. Bush soon declared a "war on terrorism," and Gonzales was called on to offer legal advice on delicate issues, such as the treatment of prisoners and the use of torture. Gonzales drew criticism after he suggested that the president could ignore parts of the Geneva Convention, an international agreement about the treatment of prisoners of war. He called certain parts of the convention "quaint." Gonzales also seemed to promote strengthening the power of the president at the expense of the other two branches of the U.S. government, Congress and the courts.

Despite some public outcry against Gonzales, he kept the confidence of President Bush, who named him attorney general in November 2004. The U.S. Senate approved the choice the following February. Gonzales saw his latest appointment as a sign of what all Hispanics can achieve, no matter how humble their roots. "Just give me a chance to prove myself," he said, summing up what others have felt. "That is a common prayer for those in my community."

GLORIA ESTEFAN
SINGER
1957–

For years, Latin recording stars focused on the Spanish-speaking market. They were either unwilling or unable to sing in English or otherwise tailor their sound for the Anglo audience. But starting in the 1970s, more recording artists tried to "cross over"—go from the world of Latin music to the English record charts and concert halls. The most popular crossover artist ever is Gloria Estefan. A singer and a songwriter, she topped both Latin and English charts in the 1980s and 1990s. Her range covered pop, salsa, and blues, from dance hits to ballads. Her recording success has continued into the twenty-first century, and she has branched out into new artistic areas as well.

Gloria María Fajardo was born in Havana, Cuba. Her family fled the island when Fidel Castro took over in 1959. Her father, José Fajardo, had been a security guard for Fulgencio Batista, the Cuban leader overthrown by Castro. In 1961, Fajardo and other Cuban exiles who opposed Castro took part in the Bay of Pigs invasion, which was sponsored by the United States. The invasion failed, and Fajardo was jailed in Havana after being turned in by a cousin. He was able to return to Miami, Florida, in 1963. He volunteered to serve in the military during the Vietnam War, and he saw action in 1967. Back in Miami, he fell ill with multiple sclerosis. Fajardo was bedridden for twelve years until he died in 1980. Given the hardships she and her family faced, Gloria said years later that "music was my escape," and she often sang as a child.

In 1975, while a student at the University of Miami, Gloria met her future husband, Emilio Estefan. He talked her into auditioning for his group, the Miami Latin Boys. She sang with the band while pursuing a degree in psychology. She graduated in 1978—the same year she married Estefan—and turned to music as her full-time career.

At first, Estefan and the band performed only in Spanish. For a time, the group was bigger in Latin America than in Miami. It would alternate between playing stadiums abroad and performing at weddings back home. But by the mid-1980s, after changing their name to the Miami Sound Machine, Estefan and the group recorded in English for the first time and saw their popularity grow. Their first major success came with *Eyes of Innocence* and *Primitive Love*. The latter record, released in 1985, included the hits "Conga," "Bad Boys," and "Words Get in the Way." By 1988, the band was called Gloria Estefan and the Miami Sound Machine, and the group sold more than 4 million copies of *Let It Loose*. In 1989, Estefan marked her solo debut with *Cuts Both Ways*. One song from the record, "Don't Wanna Lose You," hit number one on the record charts and was also nominated for a Grammy, the highest honor in the music industry.

While on tour promoting her solo album, Estefan's tour bus was struck by a semitrailer. Estefan was temporarily paralyzed—her back was broken, and she had to have two metal rods implanted. Her husband and son were also injured in the accident. After her recovery, Estefan released *Into the Light* in 1991. The next year, she used her popularity to help raise more than $4 million in aid for victims of Hurricane Andrew, which devastated South Florida. In the years that followed, Estefan expanded her humanitarian efforts through the Gloria Estefan Foundation. She also took an interest in politics, defending U.S. policies meant to weaken the Castro government in Cuba and calling for freedom for the island's citizens. Castro and his supporters, she said, "took away my country, they stole the most intimate thing a human being can have. How could I forget that Fidel Castro was the person who did me so much harm?"

In 1993, Estefan returned to her Latin roots and recorded the Spanish-language *Mi Tierra*. It won her the first of five Grammys and was followed by several other albums recorded in Spanish. In 1996, her song "Reach" was the official anthem of the Summer Olympics in Atlanta, Georgia. Expanding her range further, Estefan was featured in the 1999 film *Music of the Heart*, starring Meryl Streep. She recorded the title song for the movie with the "boy band" *NSYNC, and together they earned a Grammy nomination for their efforts.

In the fall of 2003, Estefan released her twenty-third album, *Unwrapped*, her first English-language album in five years. She paired with several well-known recording artists on the album, including rocker Chrissie Hynde of the Pretenders and Stevie Wonder. And once again showing her wide range of talents, Estefan published the children's book *The Magically Mysterious Adventures of Noelle the Bulldog* in 2005. Reflecting on her career, Estefan once said, "I set out to do something I really love and live my life. I always knew I would help people in some way. I knew that would be my calling. Fame? I never looked for that. I just wanted to leave something behind for people to enjoy."

NANCY LÓPEZ
GOLFER
1957–

Growing up in Roswell, New Mexico, Nancy López knew prejudice because she was Mexican American. She also knew prejudice on the golf course, since many men did not want to share the course with women, even if they played as well as López did. From an early age, Nancy showed tremendous skill with a club in her hands, and as an adult she went on to become one of the greatest female golfers of all time. Both her talents and her charming personality helped attract new fans to the women's game.

López was born in Torrance, California, but her family soon moved to Roswell. Her parents, Domingo and Marina López, enjoyed golf and played at the local municipal course. The family, however, could not join the private Roswell Country Club, because of discrimination.

When López was eight years old, her father handed her one of her mother's golf clubs and began teaching her the game. As she later recalled, "One time I was behind him, and I hit it right over his head. His reaction was 'Oh, my gosh, who hit that?' I think it was then that he realized I might actually become a good little golfer." At age nine, she won a pee-wee tournament. The following year, she won the state championship. And at age twelve, López won the New Mexico Women's Amateur title and successfully defended it for the next two years.

In 1970, López enrolled at Roswell Goddard High. The school did not have a girls' golf team, so she played on the boys' team and helped it win the state championship in 1971. The next year, she won the first of two United States Golf Association (USGA) Junior Girls' Championships, and in 1975 she won the Mexican Amateur. That year, she entered the U.S. Women's Open, the top event on the Ladies Professional Golf Association (LPGA) tour. As an amateur playing against professionals, some much older than she was, López finished in a tie for second. That fall, she entered the University of Tulsa, in Oklahoma, after being heavily recruited by several schools. She finished the 1976 season as the national champion in the Association of Intercollegiate Athletics for Women (AIAW) and was named an All-American and Tulsa's Female Athlete of the Year.

López left college after her sophomore year to pursue a professional golf career. She played her way onto the pro tour with a good performance on the qualifying tour. The success was marred, however, by the death of her mother. For a time, her father left his business in New Mexico so he could travel with his daughter as she began her career.

During her official rookie season as a pro golfer (1978), López had nine wins, finishing second in her first three tournaments and winning five consecutive tournaments, including the LPGA Championship—her first major tournament victory. She was named Rookie of the Year and Player of the Year, making her the first woman golfer to win both honors in the same season.

She was also the highest money winner and won the Vare Trophy, given to the player with the best scoring average on the LPGA tour. López repeated as Player of the Year and Vare Trophy winner in 1979. At age twenty-two, López was the new sensation of golf. The next year, she became the youngest female golfer to win twenty tournaments.

In 1982, López had a rewarding year both on and off the golf course. She shot her first hole in one during a professional tournament and increased her career tournament victory total to twenty-five. She also married baseball player Ray Knight, a star infielder for the Cincinnati Reds (and later the New York Mets). They became one of the most celebrated sports couples in America. They soon had a baby, and López found her golf game changed. "It was hard for me to feel as competitive, as tough. Once I became a mother, the professional athlete got pushed to the side." Still, López continued to compete and win, even as she and Knight went on to have two more children.

Motherhood did not keep López from winning the LPGA Championship again in 1985 and 1989, or from earning two more Player of the Year honors (1985, 1988). With thirty-five tour victories by age thirty, she was inducted into the LPGA Hall of Fame in 1987. Her greatest regret was not winning the U.S. Open, instead finishing second four times. In 2000, during the LPGA's fiftieth anniversary, López was recognized as one of the LPGA's top fifty players and teachers. She retired from the LPGA Tour at the end of 2002, with forty-eight career tournament wins—and as one of the most beloved players ever in the women's game.

★ ELLEN OCHOA
ENGINEER, ASTRONAUT
1958–

As a teen, Ellen Ochoa could have pursued a career in music. She played the flute well and entered college thinking of a music major. But she was also drawn to math and science, and those interests led to a career in electrical engineering. Even more appealing to the young engineer was space exploration, and in 1990 Ochoa became the first Hispanic woman chosen to become an astronaut. Three years later, flying on the space shuttle *Discovery*, she became the first Hispanic woman in space.

Ochoa was born in Los Angeles, California, but she was raised just outside of San Diego, in La Mesa. During junior high school, her parents divorced, and her mother, Rosanne, raised five children while working and also earning a college degree. Ellen's mother gave her daughter a strong belief in the importance of education.

Ellen attended Grossmont High School in La Mesa, then entered San Diego State University, where she majored in physics. In 1980, she graduated first in her class. She entered graduate school at Stanford University, earning a master of science degree in electrical engineering in 1981 and a doctorate in 1985. During Ochoa's time at Stanford, Sally Ride made history when she became the first U.S. female astronaut. Inspired by Ride's example, Ochoa applied to the National Aeronautics and Space Administration (NASA), the U.S. space agency, hoping to become an astronaut, too.

While waiting to hear from NASA, Ochoa worked at Sandia National Laboratories in Albuquerque, New Mexico, and NASA's Ames Research Center in Livemore, California. Her work focused on optics, the study of light and its properties. She investigated optical systems that could process information and developed computer programs to be used on aeronautical expeditions. As a result of her research, she shared three patents. During this time, in 1987, Ochoa learned that NASA had named her one of the top one hundred candidates to become an astronaut, out of more than two thousand applicants. Her wide-ranging interests by now included playing volleyball and flying private planes. These interests along with her musical talents and scientific skills made Ochoa an attractive candidate to NASA. "If you are motivated to excel in one area," she later said, "you are usually motivated to excel in others. NASA looks for that."

In January 1990, Ochoa finally received the news she had waited so long to hear: NASA was sending her to astronaut's school. She trained at the Johnson Space Center in Houston, Texas, studying geology, oceanography, and astronomy, as well as how to survive if stranded alone on water or land. She passed all her courses in July 1991 and officially became an astronaut. Her first duties consisted of developing and testing flight software, computer hardware, and robotics. But what Ochoa and every other astronaut trains for and truly wants is to fly into space. Almost another two years passed before she finally got her chance.

Ochoa's first space mission left Cape Canaveral, Florida, on April 8, 1993. She and the rest of the crew studied the effect of solar activity on Earth's climate and environment. She also used a robotic arm on *Discovery* to retrieve a satellite. Her next flight came the following year, on *Atlantis*. Ochoa took part in another first on her third mission, as *Discovery* became the first space shuttle to dock with the International Space Station. She and her crewmates delivered four tons of supplies to the space station, which were later used by astronauts living there. Ochoa returned to the space station on her next flight. Once again, she operated a robotic arm during the mission.

Back on Earth, Ochoa has received many awards, including the Congressional Hispanic Caucus Medallion of Excellence in 1993; NASA Space Flight Medals in 1993, 1994, 1999, and 2002; the Women in Aerospace Outstanding Achievement Award in 1997; and the Hispanic Heritage Leadership Award in 1995. In 1999, President Bill Clinton chose Ochoa— considered one of the most successful Hispanic women in the twentieth century—to serve on the Presidential Commission on the Celebration of Women in American History. Her outstanding scientific research has opened up new possibilities in optics and its application to aeronautics. And her success tested the barriers that had long hindered both women and Hispanics.

ANTONIO BANDERAS

ACTOR

1960–

After building a career as a film star in his native Spain, Antonio Banderas wanted to work at the top of his profession, which meant going to Hollywood. Even though Banderas did not speak English when he arrived in the United States, he found work in a variety of movies, sometimes drawing on his handsome looks. Over time, however, Banderas showed a range of skills and he became one of the biggest stars in the film industry.

José Antonio Dominguez Banderas was born in Málaga, Spain. Like many European boys, he grew up dreaming of playing soccer professionally, and as a teenager he played with a Spanish team until a broken foot sidetracked his career. That's when he began thinking about acting, so he signed up for classes at the School of Dramatic Arts in Málaga. At age nineteen, he moved to Madrid, and within one year he made his stage debut with the National Theater of Spain.

Banderas's big break came in 1982, when he began working with Pedro Almodóvar, a rising star in the Spanish film industry. Almodóvar was known for writing and directing dark comedies about human relationships. Banderas's first movie with the director was *Laberinto de pasiones* (*Labyrinth of Passion*), and through the 1980s they worked together on four more films. For Banderas, the most successful was *Mujeres al borde de un ataque de nervios* (*Women on the Verge of a Nervous Breakdown*, 1988), as his work earned him a Spanish film award nomination for Best Lead Actor. He also won wide recognition for his acting in the 1990 Almodóvar movie *¡Atame!* (*Tie Me Up! Tie Me Down!*).

In 1992, Banderas came to the United States to make his first English-language movie, *The Mambo Kings*. The picture was based on the best-selling novel by Oscar Hijuelos, *The Mambo Kings Play Songs of Love*. Banderas knew very little English, and he learned his lines phonetically—by the sound of the letters. The next year, he played Tom Hanks's lover in the popular film *Philadelphia,* winning praise for his work. More opportunities quickly came his way, and Banderas appeared with such major stars as Jeremy Irons and Meryl Streep (in *The House of the Spirits*) and Tom Cruise and Brad Pitt (in *Interview with the Vampire*).

In 1995, Banderas had his first leading role in an American film in the action picture *Desperado*. The film was written and directed by Robert Rodriguez, a Mexican American from Texas who had filmed his first full-length picture, *El Mariachi*, for just $7,000. *Desperado* was the sequel to that film, and it marked the beginning of a long personal and professional relationship between Banderas and Rodriguez. Banderas began another important new relationship that year when he met actress Melanie Griffith. The two worked together and their friendship quickly led to romance. They married in 1996 and had a baby daughter, Stella, that same year.

The relationship with Griffith brought Banderas to the gossip pages. Banderas, however, quickly brought comments back to his acting with his bold decision to play Communist rebel leader Che Guevara in the film version of the hit Broadway musical *Evita*. Starring alongside Madonna, Banderas showed he could sing and dance as well. Soon he established himself as one of Hollywood's top leading men.

Banderas won great reviews for his portrayal of the title character in *The Mask of Zorro*. As well as playing a sword-wielding action hero, Banderas showed a flair for comedy that he had not displayed before in his U.S. films. In 2001, Banderas teamed up again with Richard Rodriguez to make the family movie *Spy Kids*. Two sequels followed, and the films gave Banderas the chance to show more of his talents as a comic actor while poking fun of his image as a "Latin lover." Another project with Rodriguez was *Once upon a Time in Mexico* (2003), a sequel to *Desperado*.

Continuing to branch out, Banderas made his Broadway debut in 2003, returning to his roots as a stage actor. He played the lead role in the musical *Nine*. Banderas was nominated for a Tony, the highest honor in theater. He also used his voice to bring to life the character Puss in Boots in the 2004 animated film *Shrek 2*. Although he played a secondary role, some critics thought Banderas stole the show. The next year, he reprised the role of Zorro in *The Legend of Zorro*.

As he approached middle age, Banderas said he wanted to "work less—way less" but "work better." In addition to directing two films, he has talked of working with Almodóvar again, and he will always work with Rodriguez when he's asked. Reflecting on the rise of Hispanic stars in Hollywood, he observed, "For me it is beautiful that because there is a character in [a] film that speaks with a Spanish accent, the Spanish-speakers answer to that. . . . They are part of the American melting pot."

★ JENNIFER LOPEZ
SINGER AND ACTOR
1970–

From a young age, Jennifer Lopez planned to make her living in show business. But even as a determined child, she could not have imagined the fame and fortune she would one day earn. Starting out primarily as a dancer, Lopez went on to incredibly successful careers in both the film and music industries. She was the first female Hispanic movie star to earn more than $1 million for a picture, and her records soared to the top of the charts. Her popularity and financial success let Lopez branch out into new fields as she became a film producer and the owner of a fashion design company. By her midthirties, she was already one of the most successful women in show business and eager to explore new opportunities.

Lopez was born in the Bronx, part of New York City. Her parents were born in Puerto Rico and met in the Castle Hill section of the Bronx. They encouraged Jennifer and their other two children to work hard and learn English. The Lopezes also paid for Jennifer to take dance classes, which she started when she was five years old. She studied a number of styles—flamenco, ballet, jazz—and learned to sing. Her idols were the multitalented female stars who she saw in movies or heard on the radio, such as Rita Moreno, Diana Ross, and Barbra Streisand. Lopez also heard Latin music, such as salsa and meringue, thanks to her father's love of those styles.

After high school, Lopez attended college for just one semester then decided to pursue show business, taking more lessons while working part time. She appeared in some professional dance productions and had a small part in *My Little Girl* (1987), but her big break came in 1990. Lopez beat out two thousand other young women to land a spot as a "Fly Girl," one of the dancers on the comedy show *In Living Color*. From there, she appeared in a television movie and two series that quickly flopped. Still determined to make acting her career, she managed to get parts in several Hollywood films. These included *Money Train* (1995), which teamed her with stars Woody Harrelson and Wesley Snipes, and *Jack* (1996) starring Robin Williams.

In 1997, Lopez earned her first starring role when she was selected to play Selena, a popular singer of Tejana music who was murdered by a fan. The same year, she married Ojani Noa, but the marriage did not last, failing under the strains of Lopez's rising stardom. She continued to play the leading lady in a number of films, showcasing her good looks as well as her acting skills. She was eventually named in several polls as one of the sexiest women in the world.

In 1998, starring opposite George Clooney in *Out of Sight*, Lopez showed a flair for both comedy and romance, and those skills would be featured in her later work. The part she played was not written for a Hispanic actress; director Steven Soderbergh cast her because of her acting talents. "She can do just about anything," he said, "and it's not often you find someone with that kind of range."

López showed her range as an entertainer again the next year, releasing the record *On the 6*. She combined a number of musical styles—pop, rhythm and blues, hip-hop, Latin—and had a hit single, "If You Had My Love." *On the 6* sold more than 8 million copies around the world, and Lopez followed it up with *J. Lo* (2001), with the title taken from her nickname. Since then, she has continued to both sing and act.

As López's popularity grew, so did interest in her private life, which was often not so private. Her romance with rap star Sean "Puffy" Combs was often in the press—especially after the two were arrested in December 1999. Charges against Lopez were dropped and the relationship with Combs fizzled in 2000. Soon after that, Lopez married Cris Judd, a dancer, but like her first marriage, this one did not last. Lopez supposedly paid Judd millions of dollars not to write a book about their life together. Then, in 2003, Lopez became engaged to actor Ben Affleck, but that romance died before the two stars reached the altar.

Despite her stormy love life, Lopez continued to earn millions in Hollywood. In 2001, she made *The Wedding Planner* with Matthew McConaughey, and the romantic comedy opened as the number one film in America. At the same time, Lopez's *J. Lo* hit the top of the record charts. This marked the first time one star was at the top of both the film and record charts at the same time. Not all her later films were hits, however. In 2003, she starred with Affleck in *Gigli*, one of the biggest flops in her career. She bounced back in 2004 with *Shall We Dance*, which gave her the chance to perfect her ballroom dancing skills.

Lopez returned to comedy the next year in *Monster-in-Law*, and in 2006 she starred in *Bordertown*, with Antonio Banderas. The film was the first one made by her own production company, Nuyorican. The company also produced the television show *South Beach*. In 2006, López appeared in the film *El Cantante* with Marc Anthony, a salsa and pop singer who became her third husband in 2004.

SELENA
SINGER
1971–1995

Playing Tejano music, a lively combination of Mexican and American musical styles, Selena became a hit in her native Texas and Mexico. Onstage, she charmed audiences with her playfulness and sweet smile, and her talents and personality seemed poised to help her attain even greater success. Then on March 31, 1995, a fan shot Selena at a Texas motel, ending her life and a promising music career.

Selena Quintanilla-Pérez was born near Houston, Texas. Her father, Abraham, had played in a Tejano band for many years, so she grew up with music all around. He taught his children to play instruments and taught Selena how to sing in Spanish. The Quintanilla family played together at the restaurant they owned and at local weddings. When the restaurant was forced to close in the early 1980s and Selena and her family moved to Corpus Christi, her career started to take shape. She attended junior high school there, but did not go to high school so she could focus on her musical career. (She later earned a high school diploma through the mail, at a special school for artists.) With her older sister Suzette and her brother Abraham (A.B.), Selena formed the group Selena y los Dinos. A.B. played bass and composed; Suzette played the drums; Chris Pérez joined later as lead guitarist.

The group started focusing on Tejano music, and, in 1987, at age fifteen, Selena was named Female Vocalist of the Year at the annual Tejano Music Awards. Selena and her band recorded their first albums on a series of independent labels, with little chart success. But on the strength of her awards and her live performance, Selena signed a contract with a major label in 1989. Soon she was known as *La Reina de la Onda Tejana* (The Queen of Tejano Music).

Selena and her band spiced their Tejano with pop and rhythm and blues (R&B). Selena's voice was a soulful soprano, and onstage she was in constant motion. She sometimes wore revealing clothes, earning her comparisons to Madonna. The R&B sound in her vocals owed something to disco queen Donna Summer, and Selena sometimes sang Summer's hit "On the Radio" in concert.

Selena's 1990 album *Ven Conmigo* became the first Tejano recording to sell more than three hundred thousand copies, and by the mid-1990s she was at the top of the Tejano market. With her catchy tunes and party spirit, Selena's influence spread far beyond Tejano fans, winning followers in Mexico, Latin America, and eventually in the U.S. Top 40 scene. In 1994, she and the band won a Grammy Award, the highest honor in the music industry. Her music, she told one newspaper, has "got a little polka in it, a little bit of country, a little bit of jazz." The next year, *Texas Monthly* magazine named her one of the state's most influential residents. Along the way, she became an idol for a generation of young women pursuing their artistic dreams.

Selena holds her Grammy Award in 1994

Many fans and critics consider *Amor Prohibido* (1994) both Selena's best album and one of the best Tejano albums of the 1990s. It produced several hit singles: the title track, the reggae-flavored "Bidi Bidi Bom Bom;" a mariachi bolero called "No Me Queda Mas;" and the hip-hop fusion "Techno Cumbia." Often the lyrics in Tejano songs are simple, but Selena and her songwriting team worked hard to write words that painted vivid, poetic portraits of barrio life and relationships gone wrong. *Amor Prohibido* sold four hundred thousand copies in the United States and even more in Mexico.

Early in 1995, two years after signing with SBK Records to an English pop deal, Selena began making what she hoped would be her crossover breakthrough, a record that would bring her more attention on Anglo radio stations. Before she finished working on the album, Selena went to the Tejano Music Awards in San Antonio, where she was once again named Female Entertainer and Female Vocalist of the year.

Soon after that, however, Selena's rise to stardom came to an abrupt and heart-wrenching end. On March 31, 1995, a former fan club president, Yolanda

Saldivar, shot and killed Selena at a Corpus Christi hotel. The family suspected that Saldivar had been taking fan club money for personal use. Saldivar was convicted of murder and sentenced to life in prison. The news of Selena's death stunned Tejano fans. A receptionist at one Texas radio station reported that fans were calling "in awe . . . they cannot believe that it happened."

Selena's crossover album, *Dreaming of You,* came out that summer, and it fulfilled her dream for wider success. It sold more than three hundred thousand copies in just one week and was at that time the fastest-selling release by a female artist. Selena had not finished recording *Dreaming of You* before her death, so the record included a song she had recorded for the film *Don Juan DeMarco* (in which she also appeared) and several of her older Spanish-language hits. The album produced the Top 40 hits "I Could Fall in Love" and the title track.

In 1997, Selena was the subject of a film biography. She was played by Jennifer Lopez, who won acclaim for her portrayal of the singer. Selena's influence remained strong as young female artists entered the Tejano and regional Mexican music scene, formerly a male-dominated market. Scores of them openly admitted their admiration of her pioneering efforts in bringing new pop sounds to Tejano. Selena's albums and greatest hits collections continue to sell well years after her departure. In 2004, her husband and former bandmate Chris Pérez released "Puede Ser," a song Selena had recorded just before her death.

★ OSCAR DE LA HOYA
BOXER

1973–

As a six-year-old, Oscar de La Hoya found himself the target of neighborhood bullies. When his father heard this, he marched Oscar off to a local gym so his son could learn how to box and defend himself. Oscar favored baseball over boxing, but as he grew, he showed impressive skills in the ring. By age fifteen, he was among the best in the nation in his weight class, and he went on to win a gold medal at the 1992 Olympics. When he turned pro, de La Hoya became one of the greatest champions of all time and a hero to both Hispanic and Anglo sports fans.

De La Hoya was born in East Los Angeles, California, a mostly Mexican American community. His parents, Joel and Cecilia de La Hoya, were Mexican immigrants. In Mexico, Joel had boxed for a living, and he continued to fight professionally for a time in the United States. With his father's encouragement, Oscar began the rigorous training that would lead to his own success in the ring.

In 1988, de La Hoya won the national junior 119-pound boxing championship, and he won the 125-pound title in 1990. That same year, at age seventeen, he was the youngest boxer at the Goodwill Games. His youth, however, did not keep him from going home with a gold medal. The triumph of that year, however, was marred by his mother's death from breast cancer at age thirty-eight. In the months that followed, de La Hoya trained for the 1992 Olympic Games in Barcelona, Spain, vowing to win the gold in his mother's honor. But before going to Barcelona, he competed in the 1991 World Championship, fighting at 132 pounds. He won the silver, losing his final match to Marco Rudolph of Germany.

The next year in Barcelona, de La Hoya easily beat his first three opponents, then barely scraped by in his semifinal match. In the gold medal round, he once again faced Rudolph. This time, de La Hoya knocked him out in the third round, making him the only U.S. boxer to win gold at the 1992 games. Afterward, he said, "The most important thing I've done in my life was winning the Olympic gold medal for my mother." After his Barcelona victory, sportswriters and fans began to call de La Hoya "The Golden Boy." With his amateur career at an end, he had amassed a record of 223 wins and just 5 losses.

Winning an Olympic gold medal has boosted the careers of many American boxers, including Muhammad Ali and Sugar Ray Leonard. Like them, de La Hoya had the skills, good looks, and charming personality to become a superstar. In 1994, he won his first world title, as a junior lightweight (130 pounds), defeating the previously undefeated Jimmi Bredahl. Later in the year, he moved up to lightweight and won his second title. During the next three years, he won two more titles, with most of his bouts coming as a welterweight (147 pounds). In 1999, he took a perfect record of 31–0 into his title fight with Puerto Rico's Felix Trinidad, who was also undefeated. The match captured the interest of boxing fans like few others in recent history. De La Hoya lost a twelve-round majority decision, and his World Boxing Council (WBC) welterweight title went to Trinidad. The decision upset de La Hoya, who said afterward, "I thought I won the fight easily. Felix never hurt me, but I know there were several times I hurt him."

In 2000, de La Hoya suffered the second loss of his professional career, to Shane Mosley, and then decided to take a break from boxing. He pursued his lifelong interest in singing to record a bilingual album, *Oscar de la Hoya*. The record was nominated for a Latin Grammy Award, the highest honor in the Latin music industry.

De La Hoya returned to the ring in 2001 determined to become a champion again. In June, he won the 154-pound WBC super welterweight title, defeating Francisco Castillejo by decision after bloodying his opponent's nose during the eighth round. Later that year, he married Millie Corretjer, a singer from Puerto Rico. During 2001, he also founded Golden Boy Promotions, to promote other boxers' fights. De La Hoya became the first Hispanic to become a national boxing promoter, saying, "It was time for a Hispanic to enter . . . the business in a meaningful way."

In his next fight, in 2002, de La Hoya won the World Boxing Association (WBA) super welterweight title when he knocked out Fernando Vargas in the eleventh round. The fight was one of the toughest of his career, as Vargas gave him a bloody nose and stunned him with hard punches. The next year, de La Hoya lost his WBC and WBA titles to Shane Mosley in a twelve-round unanimous decision. In 2004, de La Hoya moved up in weight to fight at 160 pounds (middleweight) and won another championship. The title did not last long, however, as he lost it to Bernard Hopkins a few months later. In that fight, the former champ suffered the first knockout of his career. Still, de La Hoya was not ready to retire. Boxing "is in my blood," he said. "I sometimes say I hate the sport, but deep down inside I love it." De La Hoya fought again in 2005, earning millions of dollars for each fight, but announced he would leave the ring for good at the end of 2006. He planned to remain active as a promoter in the sport he loves so much and that has made him one of the most recognized athletes in the world.

THE GROWING HISPANIC AMERICAN POPULATION

With their early explorations of Florida and the Southwest, the Spanish were the first Europeans in what would become the United States. As the centuries unfolded, the Spanish lost their grasp on North America, even as they spread their language and culture across huge portions of the New World. By the twenty-first century, however, the Spanish influence was once again strong in the United States. In 2002, the U.S. government reported that Hispanics had passed African Americans as the largest minority (non-Anglo) group in the country. Three years later, just over 41 million Hispanics lived in the United States, and the rate of their population growth was three times the rate of growth for the country as a whole. Sometime in the middle of the twenty-first century, one out of every four Americans will be Hispanic, with political and economic power that Hispanics could only dream about centuries before.

As the Hispanic population increases, there is heightened concern about undocumented immigrants. Although they come to the United States from all over the world, those from Mexico are receiving the most attention. For many years, that country's 2,000-mile (3,219 km) border with the United States was lightly patrolled by law-enforcement agencies and easy to cross.

In 1986, the U.S. Congress passed a law that placed tougher penalties on businesses that hire undocumented workers. At the same time, the law offered amnesty to people already in the country illegally. By 1989, almost 3 million had applied for amnesty, which let them remain in the United States legally. If they wanted, they could also begin the process for obtaining citizenship. About 70 percent of the workers who applied for amnesty were from Mexico.

In 2006, President George W. Bush saw border security and undocumented workers as two important issues. Stopping the flow of undocumented immigrants into America had taken on new urgency after September 11, 2001, when terrorists had virtually declared war on the United States, killing three thousand people. Yet the president also knew that about 7 million immigrants were already in the country illegally, and most were not terrorists. They simply wanted jobs and the opportunity for success that the United States had long offered immigrants.

The rising Hispanic population shows a blend of the old and the new. As of 2000, most Hispanics still lived in states that historically had high Hispanic populations: Texas, California, Florida, and New York. But more were moving into what population experts call "new settlement states." These included Massachusetts, Virginia, North Carolina, Georgia, and Washington. Wherever they lived, just over half of Hispanic Americans settled in neighborhoods where Hispanics were not the majority of residents. About two-thirds of Hispanic Americans, whether newcomers or descendants of earlier immigrants, trace their roots to Mexico. Central and South Americans make up another 13 percent, followed by Puerto Ricans at 9 percent and Cubans at 4 percent. The rest came from other Hispanic nations.

Speaking Spanish as a native language was once a major distinction between Hispanics and other Americans. Figures from 2000, however, show that 21 percent of Hispanics speak only English. Just 9 percent said they could not speak any English. More Hispanics were also speaking "Spanglish," a combination of English and Spanish with variations within different Hispanic communities.

The ability to speak fluent English has given more Hispanics the chance to excel in school and in their chosen professions. A 1998 study reported that "a substantial and prosperous middle class has emerged in the United States." Yet the same report also said that Hispanic households, on average, were not keeping pace with all U.S. households in terms of their family income. The large number of Hispanic immigrants was part of the problem, as many of them have found it hard to escape poverty.

Beyond the numbers, the Hispanic presence is seen across America on a daily basis. Mexican food can be found at almost any mall or on any suburban "restaurant row" of fast-food chains. In larger cities, diners can also find the specialties of other Hispanic cuisines. Hispanic music has been popular in the United States for decades, and new generations of stars continue to blend their culture's sounds with African American influences and more traditional pop stylings. Singers such as Christina Aguilera, Marc Anthony, and Jon Secada are examples of current standouts. Hispanic actors appear more frequently on TV and in film: Salma Hayek, Penélope Cruz, Andy Garcia, and Jimmy Smits are just a few examples. And Americans from coast to coast marvel at baseball greats Alex Rodriguez, Nomar Garciaparra, and Roberto Alomar, among many others. The number of Hispanics who serve in government is also on the rise. As more Hispanics become voters, they have a growing power to influence the outcome of important political races, especially for the presidency.

Growing power and numbers have not ended discrimination against Hispanics or cured all their ills. In some cities, Hispanics still struggle to improve or escape bad neighborhoods, where weak schools, crimes, and gangs are common. New immigrants, especially, grapple with the language barrier and social ills. But the Hispanic influence will only get stronger, creating new opportunities for a people who have shaped America since 1492. Ilan Stavans, a college professor originally from Mexico, sums up the relationship between Hispanics and the United States: "We have a lot to offer to this country and we have a lot to learn from this country as well. . . . We're white, we're black, we're upper class, we're middle class, we're lower class. There is a new nation that is beginning to shape itself." Hispanics of different backgrounds and cultures are building that Hispanic nation and, in turn, shaping the United States.

GLOSSARY

amnesty—a promise to pardon a crime

ancestors—members of one's family who lived long ago

anthropologist—a person who studies the ways of life of different peoples around the world

architect—a person who designs and oversees the construction of buildings

artisan—a person who uses his or her hands while working in a particular craft

autobiography—a book in which the author writes about his or her own life

avenge—to take action against an insult or crime

barbarism—a condition or act that is cruel or uncivilized

bilingual—able to speak in two languages; available in two languages

cabinet—a group of advisors for a government leader

colonize—to establish a new colony, which is a territory in one country controlled by people of another country

Communist Party—a political party that practices communism, a government system in which all property is owned by everyone and all profits are shared

conquest—the act of defeating or controlling an enemy or an enemy's territory

convert—to cause someone to change his or her religious beliefs

culture—the beliefs, ideas, traditions, and customs of a group of people

curator—someone in charge of a museum or gallery

discrimination—unfair behavior based on differences in race, age, or other personal characteristics

distinction—something that makes a person unusual or different

diversity—variety; the inclusion of people from a number of backgrounds

economy—a country's system of trade, industry, and use of money

entrepreneur—someone skillful in making money and starting new businesses

epic—a long story, often involving historic battles and heroic adventures

epidemics—the rapid spread of an infectious disease throughout a group of people

ethnic—relating to a group of people with a common racial, national, or religious background

exile—the condition of being sent away from one's country and told not to return

expedition—a long journey, usually to explore a new place

hybrid—something that has been bred from two different varieties

immigrant—someone who comes from one country to live permanently in another

immunity—the condition of being protected from disease or physical harm

inhabitants—people who live in a particular place

legacy—a memory, accomplishment, or gift that a person leaves behind after he or she has died

mainstream—the common direction or trend of a movement

memoir—the story of one's personal life experience

migrant worker—a laborer who moves around doing seasonal work, often farming

missionaries—people who are sent by a religious organization to teach their beliefs to others, often in a foreign country

negotiator—a person who helps others bargain and discuss an issue so they can come to an agreement

nomads—people who travel around instead of living in one place

perseverance—the act of trying over and over again and not giving up, even when faced with difficulties

prejudice—an unfair opinion based on race, religion, age, or other personal characteristics

rebellion—an armed fight against a government or other powerful group

reform—to improve or correct something

revolt—to fight against a government or other authority

smuggling—the act of transporting materials secretly or illegally

squadron—a group of military ships or troops

stereotypes—overly simplified opinions of people or groups

stucco—a material made of sand, cement, and lime that is used for exterior walls

union—an organized group of workers who try to improve their wages, conditions, and benefits

vast—huge in area or range

★ BIBLIOGRAPHY

Acuña, Rodolfo. *Occupied America: A History of Chicanos*, 4th ed. New York: Longman, 2000.

Bohlander, Richard E., ed. *World Explorers and Discoverers*. New York: Macmillan, 1992.

Clare, John D., ed. *The Voyages of Christopher Columbus*. New York: Random House, 1992.

Daniels, Roger. *Coming to America*, second edition. New York: Perennial, 2002.

Dor-Ner, Ziv. *Columbus and the Age of Discovery*. New York: William Morrow, 1991.

Dyson, John. *Columbus: For Gold, God, and Glory*. New York: Simon & Schuster, 1991.

Fowler, William F., Jr. *Under Two Flags: The American Navy in the Civil War*. Annapolis: Naval Institute Press, 1990.

Genet, Donna. *Father Junipero Serra: Founder of California Missions*. Enslow, 1996.

Hofstadter, Richard, and Michael Wallace, eds. *American Violence: A Documentary History*. New York: Vintage Books, 1970.

Josephy, Alvin M., Jr. *500 Nations: An Illustrated History of North American Indians*. New York: Alfred A. Knopf, 1994.

Katz, Ephraim. *The Film Encyclopedia*, fourth edition. Revised by Fred Klein and Ronald Dean Nolen. New York: HarperResource, 2001.

Meyer, Nicholas E. *Biographical Dictionary of Hispanic Americans*, second edition. New York: Checkmark Books, 2001.

Notable Hispanic American Women. Detroit: Gale, 1993.

The Oxford Encyclopedia of Latinos and Latinas in the United States. New York: Oxford, 2005.

Roberts, David. *The Pueblo Revolt; The Secret Rebellion That Drove the Spaniards Out of the Southwest*. New York: Simon & Schuster, 2004.

Simmons, Marc. *New Mexico: An Interpretative History*. Albuquerque: University of New Mexico Press, 1977.

Sinette, Elinor Des Verney. *Arthur Alfonso Schomburg: Black Bibliophile and Collector*. New York Public Library, 1989.

Waldman, Carl. *Atlas of the North American Indian*, revised edition. New York: Checkmark Books, 2000.

★ FOR FURTHER INFORMATION

Books

Amdur, Melissa. *Linda Ronstadt.* Broomall, Pa.: Chelsea House, 2001.

Bachrach, Deborah. *The Spanish-American War.* Minneapolis: Lucent, 1991.

Benson, Michael. *Gloria Estefan.* Minneapolis: Lerner, 2000.

Byers, Ann. *Jaime Escalante: Sensational Teacher.* Berkeley Heights, N.J.: Enslow, 1996.

Carter, David. *George Santayana.* Broomall, Pa.: Chelsea House, 1992.

Chrisman, Abbott. *Hernando de Soto.* Austin, Texas: Steck-Vaughn, 1991.

Cruz, Barbara C. *Ruben Blades: Salsa Singer and Social Activist.* Berkeley Heights, N.J.: Enslow, 1997.

Garza, Hedda. *Joan Baez.* Broomall, Pa.: Chelsea House, 1991.

Jones, Veda Boyd. *They Died Too Young: Selena.* Broomall, Pa.: Chelsea House, 2000.

Paige, Joy. *Ellen Ochoa: The First Hispanic Woman in Space.* New York: Rosen, 2004.

Soto, Gary. *Cesar Chavez: A Hero for Everyone.* New York: Aladdin, 2003.

Stein, R. Conrad. *Hernando Cortes: Conquistador and Empire Builder.* Chanhassen, Minn.: Child's World, 1992.

Suntree, Susan. *Rita Moreno.* Broomall, Pa.: Chelsea House, 1993.

Internet Sites

CELEBRATE HISPANIC HERITAGE!

http://teacher.scholastic.com/activities/hispanic/

Activities, games, and information about famous Hispanic Americans

HISPANIC AMERICANS IN CONGRESS

http://www.loc.gov/rr/hispanic/congress/

For information about Hispanic Americans in national government

HISPANICS ACROSS AMERICA

http://www.haamerica.org

A nonprofit organization that serves as an advocate for Hispanic Americans

NATIONAL ASSOCIATION OF LATINO ELECTED AND APPOINTED OFFICIALS

http://www.naleo.org

Encourages Hispanics to participate in the U.S. political process

NATIONAL COUNCIL OF LA RAZA

http://www.nclr.org/

Home page for a national Latino civil rights and advocacy group

SMITHSONIAN: LATINO HISTORY AND CULTURE

http://www.si.edu/history_and_culture/latino/

Articles about agriculture, history, migration, identity, and much more

DVDs

Bronze Screen: 100 Years of Latino Image. Questar, 2003.

La Bamba. Sony Pictures, 1987.

Selena. Warner Home Video, 1997.

Stand and Deliver. Warner Home Video, 1998.

★ INDEX

★ PHOTO CREDITS

Photographs © 2007: American Jewish Historical Society, New York/Newton Centre, MA: 44; AP/Wide World Photos: 127, 259 (Lionel Cironneau), 178 (Coca-Cola), 191 (Ricardo Figueroa), 241 (Eric Gay), 262 (George Gongora/Corpus Christi Caller-Times), 257 (Jennifer Graylock), 217 (Bebeto Matthews), 226 (Andrew Poertner/Roswell Daily Record); Archives of the Puerto Rican Diaspora, Centro de Estudios Puertorriquenos, Hunter College, CUNY: 145 (The Antonia Pantoja Papers), 96, 115 (The Jesus Colon Papers); Arizona Historical Society, Tucson: 71 (AHS 1929); Art Resource, NY/Smithsonian American Art Museum, Washington, DC, Teodoro Vidal Collection: 51; Bancroft Library, University of California, Berkeley: 60 (Unit 1D:1c.2); Bridgeman Art Library International Ltd., London/New York: 47 (Agnew's, London, UK/ Private Collection), 62 (Library of Congress, Washington DC, USA), 32 (Peter Newark American Pictures/ Private Collection); Brown Brothers: 143, 181; Claude Moore Health Sciences Library, University of Virginia, Historical Collections & Services: 83, 84; Corbis Images: 209 (Sophie Bassouls/Sygma), 15, 23, 30, 89, 94, 126, 137, 167, 168, 183 (Bettmann), 173 (David Butow/SABA), 232 (Stephane Cardinale, Eric Robert/Sygma), 221 (Ning Chiu/ZUMA), 155 (Najlah Feanny), 264 (Mitchell Gerber), 187 (Hulton-Deutsch Collection), cover top right, 1 right, 212 (Brooks Kraft), 40 (Lake Country Museum), 236 (Justin Lane/epa), 102, 135 (National Archives), 107 (Fabio Nosotti), 219 (Roger Ressmeyer), back cover center right (Reuters), back cover bottom left, 227 (Eric Robert/Sygma), 244 (Ron Sachs/CNP), back cover center left, cover top left, 1 left (John Springer Collection), 151 (Manuel Zambrana), 148; Getty Images: 266 (Evan Agostini/ImageDirect), 18 (Archive Photos/Hulton Archive), 224 (Abdel Aziz/AFP), 196 (Michael Buckner), 201, 203 (Ralph Crane/ Time Life Pictures), 195 (Evening Standard/Hulton Archive), cover top center, 1 center (Tim Graham/Evening Standard), 215, 247 (Scott Gries), back cover top right (Scott Halleran), 80 (Hulton Archive), 120 (John Kobal Foundation/Hulton Archive), 197 (Frederic Lewis/Hulton Archive), 251 (Andy Lyons), 239 (Robert Mora), 11, 29, 57 (MPI/Hulton Archive), 231, 253 (NASA/Liaison), back cover bottom right, 124 (Pictorial Parade), 90 (Sylvia Plachy/Three Lions/Hulton Archive), cover bottom center, 184 (Louis Requena/MBL Photos), 175, 176 (Walter Sanders/Time Life Pictures), 86 (George Silk/Time Life Pictures), 204 (Matthew Stockman), cover bottom right (Time Life Pictures/DMI), 159 (Diana Walker/Time Life Pictures), 228 (Kevin Winter), 235; Kobal Collection/Picture Desk: 118; Library of Congress: 26, 55, 68, 99, 104; Magnum Photos/Eve Arnold: 64, 93; Mary Evans Picture Library: back cover top left, 131; North Wind Picture Archives: 20, 38; Palace of the Governors (MNM/DCA): 52 (010308), 112 (019576), 34 (152680); Sonoma State University Library: 161; State Archives of Florida: 65; Superstock, Inc./Cummer Museum of Art & Gardens: 16; Texas A&M University-Corpus Christi: 139 (Special Collections and Archives, Dr. Hector P. Garcia Papers, Bell Library); The Art Archive/Picture Desk: 13 (Dagli Orti/Army Museum Madrid); The Image Works: 7, 9 (David M. Grossman), 138, 157 (Jason Lauré), 193, 207 (Topham); University of Miami Libraries, Coral Gables, FL, Cuban Heritage Collection: cover bottom left, 109; University of Southern California, Specialized Libraries and Archival Collections: 77; University of Texas at Austin: 169.

Copyright extends to corresponding image on Contents page.

ABOUT THE AUTHOR

César Alegre earned his PhD in Hispanic Linguistics from the University of Massachusetts at Amherst in 1999. He is a popular lecturer in the Spanish Department at Amherst College in Amherst, Massachusetts.